*Somerset
in the Civil War
and Interregnum*

David Underdown

Professor of History
Brown University Providence Rhode Island

Somerset in the Civil War and Interregnum

DAVID & CHARLES   *Newton Abbot*
ARCHON BOOKS   *Hamden, Connecticut*
1973

To Harold, Peter and Philip

This edition first published in 1973 in Great Britain by
David & Charles (Holdings) Limited, Newton Abbot, Devon,
and in the United States by Archon Books, Hamden,
Connecticut, 06514

ISBN 0 7153 5805 7 (Great Britain)
ISBN 0 208 01385 7 (United States)

Set in 10/12 point Baskerville
and printed in Great Britain
by W J Holman Limited Dawlish

Contents

		page
	List of plates	6
	List of maps	7
1	A County Divides *1640-2*	11
2	Roundhead Somerset *August 1642 - May 1643*	31
3	The Royalists Triumphant *June - July 1643*	49
4	Royalist Somerset *July 1643 - March 1645*	67
5	The Battleground *March - July 1645*	86
6	The War's End *July - September 1645*	105
7	The Committee and the County *1645-6*	121
8	Conflict and Revolution *1646-9*	138
9	The County and the Commonwealth *1649-53*	155
10	A County Reunites *1654-60*	175
	List of abbreviations	196
	Notes to the text	197
	Bibliography	216
	Acknowledgements	220
	Index	223

List of Plates

	page
Ralph, Lord Hopton	65
(National Portrait Gallery)	
Edward Popham	66
(present ownership unknown)	
William Strode of Barrington	83
(Viscount Cowdray)	
Robert Blake	84
(National Maritime Museum)	
Monument to John Somerset	165
(Brent Knoll church)	
Sir John Horner	166
(The Earl of Oxford and Asquith)	
William Prynne	183
(Lincoln's Inn)	
Francis Wyndham	184
(Mrs S. W. Bates Harbin)	

These plates are reproduced by kind permission of the owners listed above. Photographs supplied by

National Portrait Gallery (1 and 2);

Courtauld Institute of Art (3 and 7);

National Maritime Museum (4);

and Eric Purchase (5, 6 and 8).

List of Maps

page

Somerset   8

Operations near Wells, 1-6 August 1642   33

The Lansdown Campaign, 2-5 July 1643   58

The Langport Campaign, 5-10 July 1645   101

In the Text

A roundhead propaganda tract   88
     (British Museum)

Humphrey Willis denounces Colonel Pyne   134
     (British Museum)

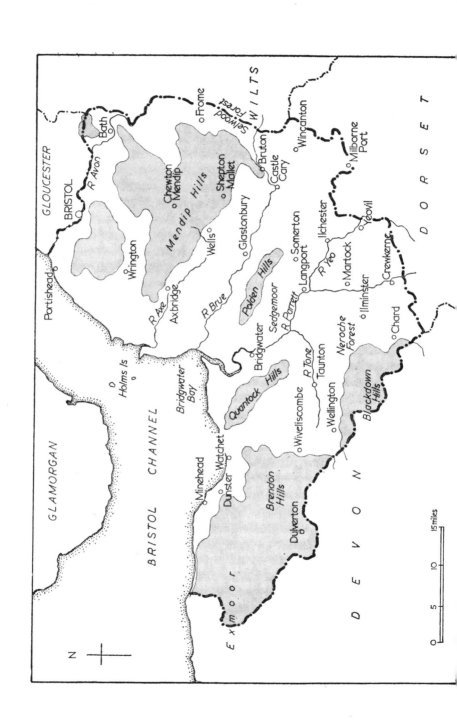

Introductory Note

Throughout this book quotations have been modernised in both spelling and punctuation; abbreviations have normally been extended or made to conform with current usage. Dates are given in the old-style calendar, except that the year is regarded as beginning on 1 January, not 25 March.

I

A County Divides
1640-2

In the last days of July 1642 the Marquis of Hertford, accompanied by Lord Poulett, Sir John Stawell, Sir Ralph Hopton, and other prominent gentlemen, rode into Wells to raise the county of Somerset for Charles I. It was the first step on a long road that was to lead to Lansdown and Langport, to heroic siege for Taunton and brutal storm for Bridgwater; to the burning of mansions and the ravaging of farms, the agonising division of friends and families, the awakening of wild dreams and the frustration of noble hopes, the stimulation of fierce avarice and the release of pent-up ambition. It was the opening move in a civil war. Hertford found himself not in a friendly county turning out loyally in defence of church and king, but in a hornet's nest of hostility. There soon gathered above him on the open Mendips not the deferential tenants of the Rodneys and the Berkeleys, but aroused clothiers and farmers, preparing to defend 'Liberty and Property' under the menacing leadership of Alexander Popham and Sir John Horner. The 'county community', the 'Country' as men called it in those days, was dividing as never before. Not until 1660 would its unity be fully restored.

What kind of county was this in which civil war was so unthinkably yet so inevitably brewing? Geographically it was very much the Somerset that we know today, bounded by the same Bristol Channel, rimmed by the same hills—by Quantock, Brendon, and Exmoor, by Blackdown and Mendip—the watery central plain broken by Glastonbury Tor and the gentler slopes of the Poldens. It was a green and fertile land, the local antiquary Thomas Gerard never tired of noting, adorned by 'fair houses and parks', by Dunster, Brympton, and Montacute, by Barrington,

Cothelstone, and Hinton St George. There were handsome towns:
at Taunton, as at Wells, the streets were kept clean, unusual in
an insanitary age, by 'springs of most sweet water continually
running through them'. There were great stone churches, famous
for their stately towers. It was a fair county, unending in its
variety. Near Brompton Regis Gerard found the whole countryside 'encrusted with broom'; he admired the 'rich red earth' of
Taunton Dene, 'which produceth all fruits . . . in great plenty';
around Orchard Portman 'the hedgerows and pasture grounds are
full fraught with fruit trees of all sorts fitting to eat and make
cider of'.[1]

It was the same county, but not quite the same. Along the
shores of Bridgwater Bay the untamed sea could still break in
disastrously. In January 1607 the villages from Huntspill to Brean
had been almost swept away. Such catastrophes were exceptional;
the winter floods in the undrained levels through which the Axe,
Brue, and Parrett meandered to the sea were not. It was a time of
great interest in fen drainage, but Somerset shared surprisingly
little in the wave of engineering by such men as Sir Cornelius
Vermuyden, which was transforming the landscape of East Anglia.
The Stuart kings, whose crown lands included large areas of the
moors, had promoted ambitious schemes, but the only recent
success had been the draining of Alder Moor, between Glastonbury and Street. Even this minor project was vociferously opposed
by the poorer inhabitants, who saw their rights of common vanish
in the name of agricultural efficiency and profit for the few. In
the much larger King's Sedgemoor, however, the greater number
of commoners gave them more leverage, and so the drainage
schemes of the 1630s remained unfulfilled promises—or threats,
according to one's point of view.[2]

The levels were impassable in winter, but communications in
other parts of Somerset were little better. Minehead, Bridgwater,
and the smaller ports, to be sure, had some coastwise contact with
their giant neighbour, Bristol. Barges travelled the Parrett and
Tone as far as Langport and Taunton. On the northern border
of the county the Avon had always been a busy waterway. But
most of Somerset's rivers were too small and unimproved for use-
fulness. As for the roads, they were no worse and no better than
those in other parts of England, which is not saying much. Those
over the Mendips were particularly bad, reinforcing the natural

tendency of the northern villages to be more closely related to
Bristol's economy than to the rest of the county. Second only to
the hills as barriers to travel were the half-cleared forests along
the county's borders: Neroche to the south, Selwood to the east.
Both were disafforested early in Charles I's reign. There was some
minor resistance in Neroche, but nowhere in Somerset did hostility to the king's enclosure policy reach anything like the level that
brought neighbouring counties, especially Wiltshire, to a state of
near-rebellion in the years 1629-31. Still, the foresters, like the
Mendip miners, were a turbulent lot; not until after 1700 was
Selwood really brought under control.

Somerset's economy was notably diversified. There were several
small but busy ports. Minehead and Bridgwater, the two biggest,
depended on the Irish trade, exporting cloth and importing
cattle; Minehead also had a considerable passenger traffic. Even
the little harbours of Dunster and Watchet shared in the trade,
as well as engaging in various kinds of fishing. There were thriving market towns, showing in the new buildings which Gerard so
much admired the prosperity that attended their local speciality.
At Yeovil's Friday market it was cheese, 'weekly transported
hence both unto Wilts and Hampshire'; at Langport waterfowl
and other products of the moors, such as pecked eels ('but I cannot commend the goodness of them', Gerard remarks).[3] Even a
run-down place like Somerton had its Monday market and its
great cattle fair running from Palm Sunday to the middle of
June. Decaying Ilchester was saved by its importance as an
administrative centre, for both the County Court and Quarter
Sessions met there, and it was the site of the county gaol. Chard
was an occasional assize town, sparing Exeter-bound judges a
tiresome detour through Bath or Taunton. Wells attracted not
only the clergy and ecclesiastical lawyers, but also a quasi-gentry
population forming the polite society of the cathedral Liberty.
At all these places there were inns, good, bad, and indifferent,
but at none were they as central to the life of the town as at
Bath. Although not yet the fashionable spa of a century later,
Bath already depended on 'the resort of strangers' come to take
the waters, and contained a more cosmopolitan population than
any other Somerset town.[4]

But Somerset was not an urbanised county. Even many of its
industries were largely rural. Prominent among them were the

extractive ones. There were famous quarries at Ham and Doulting; alabaster was produced near Minehead. More spectacular was Mendip lead-mining, which was enjoying a boom in the first half of the seventeenth century. The robust miners had always resisted large-scale capitalist development, and they still preserved a brawling, riotous independence. Profits, to be sure, were often small, a good part being creamed off as royalties by the four lords, of whom the Bishop of Bath and Wells was one. On the northern Mendip slopes coal was beginning to be exploited. It too was mined chiefly by small producers, though there were some larger enterprises, like those of William Long at Stratton-on-the-Fosse.[5]

More important than lead or coal was the cloth industry. The county was not a great producer of raw wool, though what there was was of good quality. But throughout Somerset the manufacture of cloth was a vital source of employment, impressing travellers from Leland's time to Gerard's. Both of the West of England cloth industry's two main divisions extended into Somerset. The north and east, from Bath to Frome and Shepton Mallet, lay within the great broadcloth region stretching into Gloucestershire and Wiltshire. In the south and west—at Chard, Wellington, Taunton, and Bridgwater—were outposts of the Devon kersey-broadcloth industry. Both regions had been badly hit by the failure of James I's Cokayne project and by the depression which followed the outbreak of the Thirty Years War, and both were experimenting with new fabrics.[6] The depression, coming on the heels of earlier over-expansion, brought severe unemployment and discontent.

Cloth might be crucial to Somerset's prosperity; agriculture was even more so. Then as always, most Somerset men were engaged in farming or its related trades. The county's varied soil and topography gave rise to equal variety of production. The north supplied corn and dairy products for the Bristol market. On the hills to the west and south the grazing of sheep and cattle was the rule. The moors and the coastal plain also supported both fatstock and dairy cattle, with elaborate arrangements for inter-commoning of pasture. Most of the county had long since been enclosed, but there were still common pastures and even open strip fields in both the moors and the eastern parishes. Around Somerton, Gerard noted, the farmers were

'much given to feeding and grazing of cattle'. Its orchards and
cornfields made the Vale of Taunton one of the richest areas
of the kingdom: 'the paradise of England', John Norden had
called it. And there were parishes almost as rich. Martock, Gerard
thought, was 'seated in the fattest place of the earth of this
county, especially for arable, which makes the inhabitants so fat
in their purses'.[7]

We need not romanticise the lot of the pre-industrial Englishman, wresting his living from the soil with primitive implements,
confronting regular visitations by plague and tempest, drought
and flood. But on the eve of the Civil War there were many who
could contemplate their county with gratitude for God's mercies.
A local saying attests their pride: 'Where should I be born else
than in Taunton Dene?'[8]

*   *   *   *

Many and complex were the ties which united the people of
this county. The bonds of kinship and acquaintance, habit
and custom, common assumptions about God and man: space
permits only the briefest reminder of them. But a few preliminaries cannot be omitted. To begin with, this was a deference
society; secondly, it had been subjected to increasing strain
during the previous century by population growth and monetary
inflation; thirdly, its chief industry, cloth-making, had been in
a severe depression for most of the past twenty-five years; and
finally, it was united by a variety of grievances against the king's
government ('the Court', to use the period's shorthand term),
though not yet the king himself.

A deference society: in theory at least everyone knew his place
and accepted it. In practice there was a good deal of social mobility, but it was within an accepted hierarchy of the orders and
degrees of men. Somerset's hierarchy followed the normal pattern,
from the peers at the summit—Hertford, Poulett—down through
the gentry and yeomen to the humblest artisans and paupers.
Inevitably we know little about the outlook and aspirations of
the really poor—the landless cottagers, the day labourers, the
vagrants—in Somerset or elsewhere. Their lot was probably so
miserable as to destroy all but the last spark of conscious reflec-
tion about their lives, though this did not stop them enjoying

themselves at wakes and revels when opportunity arose. At worst their fate was likely to be an early death in one of the recurrent epidemics. Plague was a regular visitor, and returned with great intensity after 1636. It was still raging at Taunton in 1640, and in the following year the justices of assize noted that Langport 'now and for a long space hath been infected'.[9] At best they might expect to survive their short working life to end as recipients of poor relief. Their function, in a famous phrase, was 'only to be ruled', and whether they liked it or not, perforce they accepted it.

We know all too little about the poor. But above this level, among the 'middling sort' of people, we know or can deduce a good deal. The traders and craftsmen of the small towns, the husbandmen or small farmers, the freeholders and wealthy yeomen of the countryside have left little in the way of personal records. But at least the general character of the most successful of this middle category, the yeomen, can be delineated. In times of reasonable prosperity they seem to have been content enough. Certainly they shared in the growing resistance to Charles I's government in the 1630s, disliked heavy taxes arbitrarily imposed, resented the impressment and quartering of soldiers and the general drift towards centralisation. But this did not mean that they wanted a radical reconstruction of society. They wanted, most of all, to be left alone. Thomas Gerard's description of the men of Martock might serve for the rest of Somerset, though the absence of gentry in the parish may here have produced an unusual degree of independence. They were, says Gerard, 'wealthy and substantial men though none of the best bred, which is the cause their neighbours about them are apt enough to slander them with the title of clowns; but they care not much for that, knowing they have money in their purses to make them gentlemen when they are fit for the degree'. Such men, Gerard adds, were rated highly in the subsidy rolls, and served the state well.[10]

Service to the community was a regular part of the lives of these men of the 'middling sort'. In manor courts and parish vestries the habit of participation was deeply ingrained; even the poorer husbandmen were involved in minor posts. As petty constables, sub-collectors and churchwardens the richer yeomen naturally took the lead. If they were qualified as forty-shilling freeholders they also voted in parliamentary elections, and served on juries at Quarter Sessions. In public matters they usually deferred to their superiors. But they were not slavishly obedient, and the gentry knew well enough that they could not govern without their co-operation. Their resistance had obstructed the drainage of King's Sedgemoor, delayed the disafforestation of Neroche and Selwood, and assured the gentry of support against ship money and other unpopular features of royal government. The great educational revolution of the previous century meant that they were quite likely to be literate and well informed. Grammar schools had been founded at Ilminster, Bath, Frome, Taunton, and many other places. There were more than twenty in the county, and a recent authority concludes that outside the sparsely populated Brendon–Exmoor region, 'no family in Somerset lived more than twelve miles from a school'.[11] Even smaller places like Mells and Martock had endowed schools, and the number of 'petty' elementary schools which had a brief, irregular existence must have been legion. Men who had received the rudiments of education and were accustomed to the responsibilities of local government might normally accept the authority of their betters. But if anything should happen to that authority, it may not be surprising to find the Somerset yeomen quite capable of acting alone.

Hierarchy might be unquestioned, but Somerset, no less than other counties, had suffered badly in the previous century. Excessive population growth, inflation, and depression in the cloth industry combined to reduce the region around Frome and Shepton Mallet to a state of marked insecurity in the twenty years before the Civil War. Over-population was a convenient, often exaggerated scapegoat for all kinds of economic woes. But there is no doubt that it existed in many parts of England, with recurrent danger of famine when harvests failed. The population explosion was particularly noticeable among the landless poor. In 1624 Richard Eburne, vicar of Henstridge, recommended colonising Newfoundland (he had never been there) in order to reduce 'the excessive multitude of people'. The recent increase, he pointed out, had been among the cottagers and paupers, with no corresponding growth in the number of 'subsidy men'. Not far removed from the worst centres of distress in the clothing villages, Eburne noted that this region was no longer self-sufficient in foodstuffs, 'unless it be in an extraordinary fruitful year'.[12]

Eburne's words were repeatedly echoed by the JPs of Frome

and the neighbouring hundreds. 'The country,' they reported in 1623, 'a great part of it being forest and woodlands, and the rest very barren for corn,' had to rely on grain supplies from Wiltshire and west Somerset. The cloth trade had produced 'many cottages erected' for people 'which have no means of living but the said trade'. However unstable the industry, poor people often preferred to bring up their children to 'some of these mechanical trades' rather than as farm labourers. Meanwhile inflation depreciated the earnings of those who could find work. Wages were rising, but not as fast as prices: during the sixteenth century real wages had fallen by about half. Eburne argued that 'the meaner sort of people . . . do live, in respect of that they did for thirty or forty years past, in great neediness and extremity'; the poor might well 'raise tumults and fall to uproars for their bellies' sake'.[13] This prediction was fulfilled in 1630, and although conditions improved with better harvests and more efficient administration of the poor law, starvation and disorder were never far from the surface in east Somerset.

Rising prices did not of course impose equal hardship on everybody. Wage-earners suffered the most, but many fewer people depended on wages than in modern times. The farmers, whether substantial yeomen or poorer copyholders, were often self-sufficient, and if they produced for the market, selling corn, cheese, and butter in Bristol and other towns, they might in fact profit from the inflation. Not all the clothworkers were unemployed, and the wealthy clothiers who marketed the cloth at Blackwell Hall in London often did well enough. Some of these fortunate capitalists were to be prominent in the Civil War on the side of parliament. William Strode, son of a Shepton Mallet clothier, bought Sir Thomas Phillips's great house at Barrington and other vast properties in south and central Somerset. John Ashe of Freshford was described as the 'greatest clothier in England' in 1637, employing over 1,000 workpeople; by the time he died in 1659 he was worth over £60,000. There were still profits in the cloth trade.[14]

*   *   *   *

Although the yeomen were far from politically impotent, the men who governed Somerset were the gentry. The heads of nearly 1,000 families could legitimately use the title 'gentleman'. But the leadership came from a much smaller group, perhaps two dozen, who were the county's real governors. The line separating them from the lesser or parochial gentry was indefinite and often crossed; but everyone could recognise the distance between Sir William Portman or Sir John Stawell at one extreme and the minor gentleman with only one or two manors at the other. There were many families on the margin between gentry and yeomanry, moving up or down. The Trevillians of Midelney, for example, indifferently describe themselves as 'Gent.' and 'yeoman' in wills of successive generations.[15] But common opinion knew pretty well who was a gentleman and who was not, and there were occasional visitations by the heralds to placard as *ignobiles* those who presumed to the title without cause.

The Somerset gentry of the years 1625-40 have recently been the subject of a brilliant historical study.[16] We can therefore content ourselves with only a brief survey of their social origins and their politics. Somerset had its ancient families: there had been Luttrells at Dunster and Stawells at Cothelstone for centuries. But most of the county families were of Tudor origin. Ancestors of the Berkeleys of Bruton and Yarlington, the Horners of Mells, and the Hoptons of Witham Friary had all served Henry VIII and been rewarded with monastic lands. The fortunes of the Pophams of Wellington and Hunstrete and the Phelipses of Montacute had been established by successful Elizabethan lawyers and civil servants. Secure in their great houses, their descendants dominated the political life of the shire. And it was the gentry who governed, for there was in Somerset no resident nobility to exert a sway comparable with that of the Herberts in nearby Wiltshire. Of the two local peers, Lord Poulett of Hinton St George was ambitious enough to lead one of the county's political factions. But his peerage was a recent creation, and even with it he had less influence than Sir Robert Phelips had without one. Henry Ley, second Earl of Marlborough, was *custos rotulorum* until 1636, but took little interest in county affairs; his son, the third earl, took even less. The Earl of Pembroke (lord lieutenant in the 1630s) and the Marquis of Hertford were bigger men and each had broad acres in the county. But they were not residents, and they were not Somerset's real governors.

The gentry might divide into factions, as in the great struggle of the 1630s between Poulett and Phelips, but these were family quarrels. More important were the things that united them. Through a common education at the universities and the Inns of Court—Oxford and Middle Temple usually, for Somerset men— and through occasional service in parliament, they were developing a national perspective. But in normal times the county was their horizon, and service to their 'Country' meant service to their local community, Somerset, as much as to their national community, the kingdom. Marriage, acquaintance, and social life were largely confined within the borders of their shire. And politics meant struggles for local pre-eminence far more than the pursuit of national objectives.

In their own eyes the gentry *were* the 'Country': public-spirited, independent, suspicious of the corrupt, expensive Court. Through the parliaments of the 1620s the 'Country' became an embryonic opposition, attacking extravagance and misgovernment (personified by the Duke of Buckingham), and asserting the claims of a virtuous, protestant, public interest. In that opposition Sir Robert Phelips played a leading part. 'It concerns us to preserve the Country in freedom': so Sir Robert defined the issue.[17] At home in Somerset, too, Phelips led a widespread opposition to the king's arbitrary measures. He was not the only one to express it, and there were some who went much further than he. Hugh Pyne, deputy *custos* (chairman of Quarter Sessions), was removed from the bench and narrowly escaped a charge of treason for intemperate language against Buckingham, and by inference the king, at Ilchester in 1626. But even if it had been possible to silence men like Phelips and Pyne, it would not have been enough. As a political entity the Country was more than the leading gentry. It encompassed the whole of county society: all free men of property, including certainly the yeomen, and perhaps even the poorer farmers and clothworkers. Phelips led and articulated their opposition; he did not create it.[18]

Inexorably the first fifteen years of Charles I's reign confirmed the alienation of the Country from the Court. The milestones are familiar: the Petition of Right, the 1629 dissolution, Hampden's case, the Bishops' Wars. And in Somerset as elsewhere the Country became steadily more united. There was the free gift and forced loan of 1626. There were the complaints about impressment and quartering of soldiers at the time of the Isle de Ré expedition. There were the fiscal exactions of the 1630s, beginning with composition for knighthood and ending, overwhelmingly, with ship money. Until 1638, with infinite grumbling, Somerset paid most of its assigned quota. But therein lay the trouble, for in both magnitude and regularity ship money was unprecedented. For the first time the county had to deal with a modern government demanding annual taxation on a large scale. The gentry and freeholders were not prepared for it, were indeed convinced that it was for the support of arbitrary and 'popish' policies. Any seventeenth-century government which imposed such burdens was bound to encounter massive local resistance. The lesson was to be repeated in the 1640s, when king and parliament in turn met precisely the same kind of Country opposition.

Well-intentioned and often reformist, Charles I and Archbishop Laud nevertheless demanded an unacceptable degree of centralisation. Although in some respects Lord Poulett's faction were agents of the Court, they too disliked government from Whitehall. Future royalists like Sir Henry Berkeley and Sir Francis Dodington were as unhappy about ship money as Phelips himself, though it was a future parliamentarian, the clothier William Strode, who actually refused to pay. Loyal gentlemen like Sir William Portman who had the misfortune to serve as sheriffs learnt the full meaning of conciliar rule. The Book of Orders of 1631 led to a marked improvement in the administration of the poor law, the regulation of wages, and the rest of the JPs' multifarious functions. But the new system involved the justices in a far heavier burden of work—divisional meetings in Petty Sessions, regular reports to the Council—which severely strained their loyalty. They and the deputy lieutenants who organised the reformed militia were working harder than ever before, often at unpopular tasks that divided them from friends and neighbours. By 1640 there were occasional resignations from the magisterial bench, and it became more difficult than usual to find replacements.

Meanwhile the county was becoming dangerously alienated from the crown's ecclesiastical policy. Somerset was not as puritan as the counties of East Anglia. There were few in the 1630s who shared the fanaticism of one Somerset man, the lawyer William Prynne, notorious for his heated invective against Court immorality and episcopal tyranny, and for the savage punishment inflicted on him in the Star Chamber. But if by puritanism is meant bitter hatred of popery, a general attachment to the Calvinist protestant-

ism of the Elizabethan church, and a dislike of Laudian cere-
monial innovations, then Somerset was puritan. A typical outlook
was that of Sir Ralph Hopton, who fought for the protestant
cause in the Thirty Years War, and who as a JP showed the hatred
of disorderly alehouses and sabbath-breaking so common among
his kind. A few were more obviously committed. Hugh Pyne's
successor as deputy *custos* was John Harington of Kelston, one of
the best and least factious of the county's governors, whose charges
to his fellow-JPs constantly reiterated the puritan ideal of the
godly magistrate. Puritanism and opposition politics did not
always coincide, as was evident in the uproar over churchales in
1633. Most of the Somerset JPs endorsed the puritan demand for
an end to these unruly festivities. Sir Robert Phelips, however,
took the Laudian side, in order to strike down his old enemy
Poulett and Chief Justice Richardson. Gentry puritanism was
thus complicated by politics. The movement's real strength was in
the 'middling sort', especially the clothworkers. Taunton, Wellington, Bridgwater, the villages of the Bath–Frome–Shepton
Mallet triangle: here were the puritan parishes.[19]

Hard on the heels of the churchales controversy came the first
attempt to impose Laudian conformity. There were few puritan
lectureships in the county, but to Laud even a few 'factious and
disorderly sermons' were too many. They were systematically sup-
pressed by the new bishop, William Piers. Samuel Crooke, rector
of Wrington since 1602, no longer gave the Tuesday lectures there,
and the equally venerable John Devenish was suspended at Bridgwater; his churchwarden, Humphrey Blake, brother of the more
famous Robert, had to do penance for not having informed
against him. Laud's victory in the churchales affair encouraged
him to take the offensive and compel the clergy to read the Book
of Sports, so hated by sabbatarians for its definition of permissible
Sunday amusements. There were resentful mutterings in puritan
villages like Batcombe. Most of the ministers complied, but there
were a few suspensions. Some of the victims, like William Thomas
at Ubley, were later to be prominent in the presbyterian movement in the county.[20]

After 1635 puritan opposition became more vocal. Central to
the whole Laudian programme was the removal of the 'protestant'
communion table to the east end of the church: to be railed in
as a popish altar, the puritans complained. For the most part the

Somerset churchwardens grumbled but obeyed. By January 1638 Piers had convinced Laud that the diocese was 'in marvellous good order for all things'. But Laud was living in a fool's paradise. There was opposition even in the cathedral church at Wells, where a quarrelsome archdeacon accused the Laudians of obscuring the gospel with their 'mist of ceremonies'. Compliance everywhere was grudging, and at Beckington, with the encouragement of the clothing magnate, John Ashe, the churchwardens refused to comply at all. There was a minor riot, and they were excommunicated and imprisoned, eventually having to make humiliating submission. One of them died soon after his release of an illness contracted in prison, adding one more to the number of puritan martyrs.[21]

A wide variety of grievances thus inflamed the men of Somerset against the Court. At Bath Assizes in 1638 a representative grand jury listed the most pressing ones, with ship money ('the great and heavy taxations by new invented ways upon the county') at the head.[22] This did not mean that Country sentiment was necessarily revolutionary: several of this outspoken grand jury were soon to risk lives and estates in Charles I's service. Phelips shows the limited degree to which the Country was a consistent opposition. He might use strong language in the House of Commons, might resist the Court's more offensive measures in the county, but he was also a loyal subject. King, parliament, and county were all essential parts of the mixed government which Phelips and hundreds like him regarded as the time-honoured constitution of England. If opposition could be combined with a shrewd blow at local rivals like Poulett, so much the better; still, the king's government had to be carried on. Sir Robert died in 1638, and we can only speculate which side he would have taken in the impending conflict. He always sought, he said, 'the good opinion of the Country'.[23] But soon the lines were redrawn, and the Country was divided.

*   *   *   *

By 1640 the king's attempt to govern from Whitehall and Lambeth had collapsed. It had failed because it had antagonised the kingdom's natural rulers, the country gentry—and no monarch could rule England for long without their co-operation. A tax-

payers' strike brought collection of ship money to a halt. When
in the spring the militia mustered to fight the Scots there was
widespread refusal to pay the coat-and-conduct money needed to
pay and equip them; the constables reported that in some hundreds 'the names of every man' would have to be listed among
the delinquents. The soldiers assembled at Bruton, but 'all things
were full of tumult' when they were ordered to march, and they
deserted in droves. At Wellington a mutinous Devon regiment
lynched an officer while the townspeople watched approvingly.
At Brislington there were heretical sermons against the bishops.
All over the county there were mutterings, alarming signs of a
breakdown of law and order.[24]

Somerset was united against the Court, united as never before.
Only a parliament, it seemed, could heal the nation's sickness.
When, late in 1639, Charles decided to call one, there had been,
Edward Phelips declared, 'much joy amongst all country people'.
The elections produced 'great factions' in the county, but not
because there was any support for the Court. These were personal
struggles, the old politics of local precedence, though none the
less intense for that. Edward was soon regretting the decline in his
family's influence since Sir Robert's death: 'the old man is gone
and all friendship with him'.[25] The Short Parliament met in April
1640 but fell into total deadlock; not until the autumn, after one
last feeble effort to revive the 'Thorough' system, was the triumph
of the Country assured. Whether the organised opposition campaign that was observed in other counties during the summer
affected Somerset is unknown. But John Pym had already emerged
as the great spokesman for the Commons; he was involved in the
summer's electioneering; and for all his absorption in national
affairs, he was a Somerset man.

Whatever the truth about Pym's campaign, the Long Parliament
elections in Somerset were eventually of the old kind, with personalities looming larger than policies. In the end Lord Poulett's
son, Sir John, and his principal ally Sir John Stawell, defeated
John Coventry and Thomas Smyth of Long Ashton. Edward
Phelips had not aspired to fill his father's shoes, and he even ran
into difficulty at the family borough of Ilchester, which returned
Sir Henry Berkeley and Robert Hunt of Speckington. A petition
unseated Berkeley, however, and Phelips got the seat. Only one
courtier was elected: Edmund Wyndham at Bridgwater. He was

soon expelled as a monopolist to make room for Thomas Smyth.
William Basset of Claverton (Bath); Sir Ralph Hopton and Sir
Edward Rodney (Wells); Sir William Portman (Taunton); John
Digby and Hertford's steward Edward Kirton (Milborne Port):
all were later to become royalists, but in 1640 were as 'Country'
in their outlook as anyone else. There were only a few future
parliamentarians: Alexander Popham (the other Bath member);
his father, old Sir Francis (Minehead); and the townsman George
Serle (Taunton). But several others sat for places outside the
county, including Pym, John Pyne (Hugh's equally turbulent
nephew), and the lawyer Roger Hill of Poundisford. The Country
had made a clean sweep.[26]

On 3 November 1640 the Long Parliament assembled in an
atmosphere of high expectation: the day of 'godly reformation'
was at hand. Petitions protesting at oppression 'during the long
intermission of parliament' were soon flooding in. Among them
was one from Somerset, and a second was presented by Hopton in
February 1641, complaining about ship money and abuses by the
deputy lieutenants. Denunciations of Bishop Piers's Arminian
innovations were backed up by accusations from the people of
Beckington, Mells, and Hemington against their Laudian parsons.
The Commons were told that Piers had attempted 'the corruption
and subversion of the religion in that diocese', and before 1641
was out he was in the Tower. Another victim was the bishop's
son, William Piers, archdeacon of Bath. He was alleged to have
said of the Short Parliament: 'A pox of God take them all for a
company of puritanical factious fellows. . . . The king would never
be at quiet till he had taken off twenty or more of their heads.'[27]
The archdeacon was duly sent for, and with several of the lesser
clergy remained in custody for months. Thus were the Laudians
dealt with, and there were few to lament their passing.

The Somerset members remained impressively united well into
1641. Hopton took a leading part in the proceedings against the
hated Earl of Strafford. He and his countrymen regularly supported the reform measures that Pym was piloting through the
Commons. Coventry (by now MP for Evesham), Kirton, and
Portman, to be sure, voted against Strafford's attainder, but they
were the only Somerset men to do so.[28] On the abolition of ship
money, Star Chamber, and High Commission, and the punishment of 'evil counsellors' the Somerset MPs, like their constitu-

ents, were at one. So far the Long Parliament was doing no more than fulfil Country expectations: to assert the rights and liberties of parliament, reform the church, and restore to the counties the freedom from Court interference which the gentry regarded as their right. A moderate, peaceful revolution was being achieved, under the conservative banner of an appeal to ancient tradition.

But revolutions have a way of outrunning the intentions of their initiators, and when that happens underlying inconsistencies are revealed. All too soon the unity of 1640 disintegrated, the Country interest divided, and the result was civil war. Three great issues emerged on which compromise seemed impossible, and passionate invective replaced reasoned argument: the future settlement of the church; the Long Parliament's appeal to the people at a time of growing disorder; and the control of the sword when the Irish rebellion made it necessary to raise an army.

The church question was essentially the question of the bishops. Should episcopacy be reformed or, as a vocal puritan minority demanded, taken away 'root and branch'? Somerset, where root-and-branch puritans were few in number, would probably have been content with the reduction of the bishops' excessive powers, and the recovery of the church's protestant purity by prohibiting 'popish' ceremonies and returning the communion table to the nave. Hopton, as usual, reflected the consensus position. He accepted the reformation but not the abolition of episcopacy, and opposed the bill excluding the bishops from the House of Lords. In common with almost the entire population of the county, he took the Protestation against the vaguely sensed Catholic danger, but only after unsuccessfully trying to write into it a specific endorsement of the church 'as it is now established'.[29]

As the summer of 1641 wore on a violent puritan campaign, in sermons and pamphlets no longer restrained by censorship, alarmed the moderates. There were disorderly outbreaks in churches, attacks on clergy, the destruction of altar rails and 'popish images'. The moderates retaliated with a campaign of their own, which in December produced several petitions in defence of episcopacy. One from Somerset was presented by the Marquis of Hertford. It carried an impressive array of signatures —some 14,000, its supporters claimed, over 200 of them knights and gentlemen. The petition accepted the punishment of evil-doers, bishops included, and gave no credence to the Laudian argument that episcopacy existed *jure divino*. But episcopacy should be reformed, not taken away. The petitioners complained that use of the prayer book had been 'interrupted and despised by some misled people', and demanded the silencing of all 'who, under a veil of religion, publish pamphlets conducing to confusion and rebellion'.[30]

'Confusion and rebellion': puritan enthusiasm was beginning to shake the ordered fabric of society. Even John Harington felt obliged to warn the JPs against radical separatists as well as against the conventional Catholic menace. Those who 'seditiously and wickedly presume of themselves to alter anything in the service of God or the decent order lawfully used in the church' should be severely punished. The warning had no effect. In April 1642 there was even a disturbance in Wells Cathedral. A visiting Londoner, attending the induction of the puritan Richard Allen to the living of Batcombe, smashed a 'very fair' crucifix with a well-aimed stone. Allen and his father, the rector of Ditcheat, watched approvingly.[31] Such behaviour seemed threatening to many who had hitherto welcomed measures for reform. Church, magistracy, and property were parts of a single whole. Men who took the law into their own hands in church matters might one day do the same in state matters. The next step to defying the authority of the clergy was to defy that of the JPs and the gentry.

Nor was the attack on law and order confined to the extreme puritan zealots. The cloth trade still suffered from chronic depression; the villages were angry and discontented. All over the country pent-up bitterness over loss of rights of common exploded as the hand of authority weakened. 'Violent breaking into possessions and enclosures, in riotous and tumultuous manner', the House of Lords declared, had been 'more frequently done since this parliament began than formerly'. Hertford's pastures in Godney Moor were invaded by rioters who threw down fences and gave out 'threatening speeches' against his bailiffs.[32] Meanwhile Pym was using the London mob to terrorise the Lords into voting Strafford's attainder and the exclusion of the bishops, and in the Grand Remonstrance parliament took the unprecedented step of adopting a manifesto aimed more at public opinion than at the king. Moderates like Hopton decided that Pym was going too far. Sir Ralph did his duty when chosen to present the Remonstrance to the king, but a few weeks later he openly parted company from the 'popular party', even going so far as to defend the king's actions in the attempted arrest of the Five Members. In March 1642 he spent a fortnight in the Tower for indiscretions in debate, and soon withdrew from the Commons altogether.[33]

The Long Parliament's appeal to the people, coupled with the threat of disorder from the puritans and the under-privileged, created an imposing dilemma for the country gentlemen. Many, like Hopton, concluded that it was time to consolidate and trust the king to observe the reformed constitution. But others feared that to draw back now and leave Charles, still surrounded by malignant advisers, in possession of uncontrolled armed force, would endanger all that had been won. Vague fears of a vast Catholic conspiracy against English liberties seemed to be dramatically confirmed in November 1641, when Ireland exploded in rebellion. Minehead and the other Somerset ports were soon swarming with refugees, full of lurid atrocity stories. The crisis atmosphere persisted into 1642, with soldiers and supplies for Ireland thronging the little harbours. Somerset's small recusant population was no threat to anybody, but the county was already on guard, commissioners having been appointed in the previous August to disarm the Catholics. In the hysteria that followed the news from Ireland all kinds of wild stories were believed. One Somerset recusant was said to have a veritable arsenal in his house, including three brass cannon. The sheriff, Martin Sanford, was sent to investigate. He found a few popish books, but the arms turned out to be only a few ancient pieces collected generations earlier. Anti-papist prejudice, however, did not need facts to sustain it. Fear of an Irish army supported by a rising of English Catholics confirmed the attachment of many Somerset men to the parliament.[34]

The country, like the kingdom, was dividing. The December petitions in defence of episcopacy were answered by a wave of declarations supporting the liberties of parliament. Sir Thomas Wroth, the puritan recorder of Bridgwater, delivered a Somerset one to the Commons on 25 February. It denounced the attempt on the Five Members as part of a plot by 'a malignant party of popish lords and bishops' to subvert English liberties, and its subscribers declared their willingness to defend parliament, with the sword if necessary. For the first time, men began to speak of 'the king's side and the parliament's'. Sir John Stawell and John

Coventry were summoned before the House for divisive language of this kind.[35]

By now king and parliament had reached an impasse over the militia, the immediate, precipitating cause of civil war. Pym had moved from reform to revolution by asserting parliament's right to the militia power, and when that was refused, by claiming that parliamentary ordinances had the force of law even without the royal assent. In February parliament nominated Hertford as lord lieutenant of Somerset. The marquis politely declined the honour and went off with the king to York. The young Earl of Bedford, whose chief connection with Somerset was his deceased father's patronage of John Pym, was appointed in his place. On 31 March the Commons approved the list of deputy lieutenants who were to organise the parliamentary militia: Sir John Horner, Alexander Popham, William Strode, John Ashe, and John Pyne were at the head. 'Gentlemen of worth and quality' were directed to assist.[36]

Tension was rising. Men feared to travel or to drive their cattle to market. As early as Whitsun week the great Saint White Down fair, near Chard, was seriously affected, with sales down to about half the normal volume.[37] While men looked to their weapons, royalist opinion was mobilised by yet another petition. Episcopalian and monarchist, it proposed an accommodation on Charles I's terms. It also appealed to Country sentiment, protesting against the behaviour of the parliamentary deputy lieutenants and the burdensome taxation imposed from Westminster. Behind it stood some of the most powerful of the county magnates: Pouletts, Dodingtons, Berkeleys, Phelipses. Alexander Popham headed it off at Bath with a speech which warned the corporation not to endorse the 'great aspersions laid upon the parliament in it'. Strongly partisan on the other side, Popham could not admit that most of the leading gentry were emerging as royalists, but he recognised how deeply Somerset was divided: 'there are many earnestly for it, but as many violently against it'.[38] The spectre of civil war, the ultimate and unthinkable calamity, brooded heavily over the county.

The last negotiations dwindled into empty propaganda salvoes, and both sides prepared for war. On 11 July Charles ordered Hertford to Somerset to raise forces by commission of array; letters were sent to gentlemen of known loyalty asking them to join in executing the commission. On the 19th the Commons retaliated by sending Alexander Popham back to Somerset to put the Militia Ordinance into operation. Associated with him were the other leaders of the emergent parliamentarian cause: Horner, Wroth, Harington, Pyne, Strode, Ashe, and a few of lesser eminence. They were to aid the deputy lieutenants and to receive money lent on the 'Propositions' of 10 June, parliament's initial scheme for financing its forces.[39] Civil war was at hand.

Notes to this chapter are on pages 197-9.

2

Roundhead Somerset
August 1642-May 1643

Hertford set out from Yorkshire with a light heart. He was getting old and had no serious military experience, but neither had many other people for that matter. A handful of tedious puritans might cause a little trouble, but it would soon be over, and 'hey then! down go they!'[1] The marquis's reception during his journey south may have led him to revise this comforting prediction. At Marlborough, in the heart of their territorial power, Hertford and his brother Lord Seymour were unable to arouse their dependants' loyalty. Parliamentarians seized the local magazine and defied them.

By the time Hertford reached Somerset a turbulent session of the Assizes was in progress at Bath. The calendar contained the usual routine business, but the great political crisis smouldered dangerously behind it. There must have been angry arguments in the inns and taverns. The Militia Ordinance or the Commission of Array: which of the rival authorities, parliament or king, should the county obey? Sheriff Sanford had empanelled a safely parliamentarian grand jury, which petitioned the king to recall the commission. The constables of the neighbouring hundreds demanded that the judge, Sir Robert Foster, read parliament's declaration against it in open court; he may have done so, though he steadfastly refused to rule on its validity.[2] A judicial opinion might have been useful to one side or the other to swing the waverers. But a good many minds were already made up.

For the parliamentarians were winning the argument. They had convinced the Country—all but its magnate leaders—that the commission was an even more sinister threat to 'Liberty and Property' than ship money itself. The commission was in Latin, and the Earl of Clarendon recalls that the roundheads translated it 'into what English they pleased', persuading yeomen that it contained provisions for extorting crippling taxation, and poorer people that it would make them pay the equivalent of a day's work a week to the king. As he progressed through the circuit Foster found all the western counties 'much possessed with the illegality of the Commissions of Array, and the unlimited power, as is alleged, in the commissioners'. A stream of royalist denials showed how effective the charges had been. On 12 August Hertford repudiated 'false and scandalous suggestions' that the commission was intended to 'enthral the people'. On the 25th he again denied that the commissioners had power 'to take what they please of any man's estate'.[3]

On Thursday 28 July Hertford moved on to Wells. The city was chosen for the cavalier rendezvous—unwisely, Hopton later thought—because of its central location, its magazine, and its supposedly royalist sympathies. Wells was not a good choice, strategically or even politically. It was defenceless against any force controlling the Mendips, looming above it; and although the cathedral population was royalist, this was no guarantee that the rest of the citizens were. Most of the governing corporation were men of narrow, intensely parochial views, seeing their first duty as protecting the immediate interest of the city, anxious to avoid committing themselves to either side. And Wells was on the edge of strongly parliamentarian country.[4]

With the Assizes over, the royalist gentry were already drifting into Wells. Among them was an impressive collection of county magnates: Poulett, Stawell, Hopton, Dodington, Rodney, several of the Berkeleys. Three troops of horse under Hopton, John Digby, and Sir Francis Hawley were hurriedly assembled. An officer of the king's army, Lt-Col Henry Lunsford, had accompanied Hertford with a commission to remuster the foot regiment that had been so mutinous in 1640. Lunsford was unable to raise any men, but he did recover a cache of arms stored at Wincanton. The parliamentarian leaders quickly responded. A committee of MPs and deputy lieutenants had been formed; it was to be parliament's chief administrative body in the county. On Saturday the 30th some of the members met at Shepton Mallet, and invited their supporters to join them there on the following Monday. A feast of venison was promised as an added inducement. William

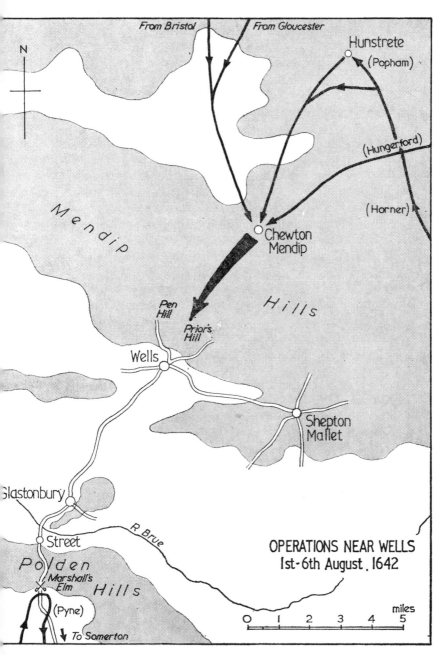

From Bristol From Gloucester

Hunstrete
(Popham)

N

(Hungerford)

(Horner)

M e n d i p

Chewton
Mendip

Pen
Hill

Prior's
Hill

H i l l s

Wells

Shepton
Mallet

Glastonbury

Street

R Brue

P o l d e n

Marshall's
Elm

H i l l s

(Pyne)

To Somerton

OPERATIONS NEAR WELLS
1st-6th August, 1642

miles
0 1 2 3 4 5

c

Strode, who had strong family connections at Shepton, organised the collection of arms and ammunition. Royalists were threatened by 'divers low persons' (so Hertford described them), told that their houses would be burnt, 'and that the streets should run with blood'.[5] On Sunday the rector, John Cooth, appealed to Hertford for protection. The marquis promptly ordered Rodney's regiment of trained bands, the 'Wells regiment', to assemble.

On Monday morning Hertford sent Sir Ralph Hopton with his troop and about 100 gentlemen volunteers to confront the parliamentarians. They were soon overtaken by Thomas Smyth with a message from Hertford's council: Hopton was to 'forbear any hostile act' or he would be disowned. Sir Ralph left his troop in the fields outside Shepton and, escorted only by the gentry and their servants, went on to the market place. He was talking to some royalists at the cross when Strode arrived with his son and a couple of armed men. When Hopton invited him to listen to the inhabitants' petition to Hertford, Strode replied that 'he came not to hear petitions, but to suppress insurrections and tumults', and in parliament's name called on the people to disperse.[6] There was an altercation. Hopton and Smyth tried to pull Strode off his horse, Sir Ferdinando Gorges struck at him with a halberd, other cavaliers drew their swords, and eventually Strode had to dismount. Hopton took away his pistols and committed him to the constable, George Milward; but Milward was Strode's chief ally and released him as soon as Hopton's back was turned.

By this time great crowds were gathering outside the town. Hopton and his gentlemen withdrew and joined their soldiers (reinforced by two more troops of horse from Wells) in a field to the south-west. The countrymen, an 'unruly rabble' as they seemed to Hopton, straggled through the town over 1,000 strong, and were eventually enlisted as a *posse comitatus* by the sheriff's son, Henry Sanford. For several hours the hostile forces glared at each other. Then the parliamentarian committee sent two of their members, William Long and William Bull of Shapwick, to negotiate; they rode back to Wells with the royalists.[7] The day ended with further angry exchanges, each side accusing the other of illegality and breach of the peace.

No one had been anxious to fire the first shot. But the county was at the brink of war. Hertford's commission as lieutenant-general of the western counties became effective on 2 August. He could now take all necessary military steps for the king's service. He had the authority, but did he have the men? The younger Pouletts and Stawells were sent galloping back to Hinton St George, to Ham and Cothelstone. They returned in three days with forty horse, twenty dragoons, and a waggon-load of arms. It was not enough. In all the time at Wells, Hertford never had more than 1,000 men, most of them horse: the few hundred men of the trained bands who obeyed his summons were unreliable and disaffected. Among the clothworkers and yeomen of the villages to the north and east his enemies were having much more success. Sir John Horner, Alexander Popham, and John Ashe made plans for a great rendezvous at Chewton Mendip on Friday, 5 August.

Hertford made a feeble attempt to take the initiative. On Wednesday he sent Hopton and Stawell to make a reconnaissance in force. The royalist cavalry clattered through Shepton Mallet to the summit of the Mendips. Messengers were soon on the way to Popham and Horner; there was great 'stir and combustion... every man armed and made ready'.[8] However, Hopton soon returned to Shepton. After suitable refreshment in the taverns his men wandered about the town, threatening the leading puritans (most of them went into hiding), and confiscating arms and ammunition. Having billeted 100 of his men at Shepton, Hopton returned to Mells. Little had been achieved by the raid, apart from a further spur to parliamentarian preparations. That same day, or the next, Horner assembled his neighbours and tenants at Wells and marched them away to join Popham at Hunstrete. Already 1,000 armed men had collected.

By Thursday the 4th Hertford was in danger of being surrounded. In the western part of the county John Pyne was at work. Although there was less enthusiasm for parliament here than in the clothing districts of the north-east, Pyne got together 600 men, some from Taunton, others 'good yeomen' as Ashe described them. Joined by a handful of gentry—John Fraunceis of Combe Florey, Hugh Rogers of Cannington, and John Preston of Cricket St Thomas—Pyne was now on his way through Somerton, to block Hertford's line of retreat to the south. Strode awaited him in his house at Street. But though short of numbers, the cavaliers had the advantages of mobility and high spirits. Stawell, with three troops of horse and a few dragoons, rode quickly through Glastonbury to intercept. Some of Hertford's gentlemen went too: Sir John Poulett, Hawley, John Digby, Edmund Wyndham. More important, Stawell took with him the experienced professional, Henry Lunsford.

At Marshall's Elm, where the road to Somerton dips down off the Poldens, the cavaliers sighted Pyne's force below them in the cornfields. While the gentry parleyed ineffectively, Lunsford made his dispositions. The horse were drawn up behind the brow of the hill, the dragoons dismounted and hidden in quarry pits by the road, lower down. Pyne hesitated and lost control. His first order was to continue the advance, then he thought better of it. There were jeers from his men: the cavaliers 'were but a few horse and would run away'. Blindly, instinctively, the roundheads moved up the slope, halting occasionally to fire their muskets. They were met by a volley from the dragoons, and one of their leaders fell. As they wavered, Stawell led the cavalier horse in a charge down the hill. The countrymen broke and fled; seven were killed, another score later died of wounds, and sixty prisoners were taken as the jubilant royalists pursued them as far as Somerton. John Preston was among the captives, but Pyne escaped by what Hopton scornfully describes as 'good horsemanship'. It was first blood to the royalists.[9]

Marshall's Elm showed that the cavaliers, even if outnumbered, were strong in cavalry and led by resolute men, accustomed to command and confident of their ability to defeat larger forces of poorly officered farmers. Even Ashe admitted that it 'very much daunted the honest countryman'. Strategically it was important in that it kept open Hertford's escape route. But as Popham and Horner gathered their men beyond the Mendips it became clear that Hertford would soon have to face much larger numbers, under better officers than Pyne. Furthermore, it was unlikely that the citizens of Wells regarded the prospect of fighting in their streets with enthusiasm. Under the watchful eyes of Sir Edward Rodney and John Coventry, the corporation voted to buy an ox at Lydford fair as a gift for the marquis; they responded to Rodney's demand for powder, bullets, and match, for which Coventry deposited £30 in part payment; and they handed over the key of the magazine to Sir Francis Dodington. They did as they were told, but the ammunition was sold, not given.[10]

On Friday morning the roundhead host assembled near Chewton Mendip. Alexander Popham's 'Bath' regiment of trained bands was there, 'doubled twice over, by means of volunteers', Ashe gleefully reported. So was part of the Wells regiment (the rest were unhappily awaiting Hertford's orders). Sir Edward Hungerford of Farleigh brought 300 horse from the Wiltshire border, another 300 came from Bristol, and a company of foot from south Gloucestershire. Popham also managed to acquire two waggon-loads of arms from Bristol, in spite of obstruction by the royalist mayor and sheriffs. These organised forces were joined by a great crowd of countrymen, some armed and on horseback, others with only 'pitchforks, dungpicks, and suchlike weapons'.[11] Besides Ashe, Horner, and the Pophams, the presence of John Hippisley of Ston Easton, Richard Cole of Nailsea, and Robert Harbin of Newton Surmaville gave the parliamentarian leadership a respectable appearance. But there was a serious shortage of officers, and hours passed before they could get their men in order.

Early in the afternoon the huge throng, some 12,000 it was said, moved slowly across the open Mendips to the escarpment overlooking Wells. Hertford was reviewing Rodney's reluctant regiment when the advance guard, colours flying, was sighted on either Pen or Prior's Hill. The roads were immediately barricaded and the royalist horse moved out to 'a little hill at the foot of the great hill' to face the enemy.[12] Hertford decided to negotiate. He sent three moderate JPs to tell the committee that he was ready to 'find a way to preserve the peace of the county'. Stonewalling while they awaited the arrival of more forces, the committee agreed to abstain from hostilities at least until the next day. The great host, without food or shelter, settled down among the gorse bushes. There was much puritan enthusiasm among the campfires, prayers and pious psalm-singing. Hertford, by contrast, spent an uneasy night. The gentry held firm, but many of the trained band soldiers deserted, some to join the roundheads on the hill.

If there were any doubts about the sympathies of the countrymen they were soon dispelled. By daybreak on Saturday the Mendip plateau swarmed with horses and waggons bringing supplies to the parliamentarians. According to Ashe, the country folk 'would not take one penny for it'. And the noose was tightening. Roundhead volunteers were still arriving: 120 horse from

Taunton under John Pym's son Alexander, for example. Horner moved off the hill with one force to try to cut the Glastonbury road; others occupied Knapp and Tor Hills to the east. The Bristol cannon fired a few futile rounds towards Hertford's headquarters in the bishop's palace. Further negotiations were academic. However, at ten o'clock the committee sent four gentlemen into Wells with an ultimatum. Hertford was to disband his forces and hand over the leaders to parliament. In a conciliatory reply the marquis offered to suspend the Commission of Array if the committee would do the same with the Militia Ordinance. But by the time his messengers rode up the hill, carriages were streaming down the Glastonbury road, and an emissary from the mayor soon reported that the whole force was leaving. An attempt to cut off the rearguard, Hopton's troop, just failed; a parliamentarian soldier describes how the royalists' superior horsemanship enabled them to gallop 'with their utmost speed at a passage between the wood and us'.[13]

Hertford had escaped, but he had been driven out. The elated committeemen watched the royalist cavalcade dwindling across the levels towards Glastonbury. The retreat continued to Somerton, where the cavaliers spent the next two nights. They then established themselves in Sherborne Castle, over the Dorset border and thus legally out of the power of their enemies. Most of the parliamentarians went home in relief. Some, however, descended the hill into Wells, and the committeemen could not restrain them from some vengeful outbursts. Stained glass in the cathedral was smashed and the bishop's palace looted; a painting of the Virgin was derisively paraded about on a pike.[14] In spite of Marshall's Elm, the committee had won the first round.

*   *   *   *

The events of early August 1642 are interesting not only as the initial episode of the Civil War in Somerset, but also for the light they throw on local opinion. So far it had been largely a propaganda war. Popham, Horner, and their friends had convinced the freeholders that the Commission of Array implied a resumption of the arbitrary taxation of the 1630s by a corrupt, popishly-inclined Court, bent on reducing them to slavery. Stories of cavalier malevolence to the lower orders were skilfully disseminated. Lord Poulett was alleged to have said at Wells that 'it was not fit for any yeoman to have allowed him from his own labours any more than the poor moiety of ten pounds a year, and ... when the power should be totally on their side, they shall be compelled to live at that low allowance'.[15] Poulett's contempt for lesser men was well known, but he can hardly have been as stupid as this. Still, even if the story was an invention, it did the royalists no good. The roundheads had won over the Country.

At the upper levels of society it was, of course, a different matter. Most of the greater gentry—Pouletts, Stawells, Berkeleys —had responded to the king's appeal. Only the puritan Horners and Pophams stood on the other side, supported by a few of slightly lesser stature such as Pyne, Rogers, and Fraunceis. Confronted with the agonising prospect of civil war, many people naturally tried to avoid taking sides, or emerged as conciliators. Anthony Stocker of Chilcompton and William Basset went to Wells on summons from Hertford, and played a useful peace-keeping role. Before it ended, Stocker found himself taking the examination of his own brother-in-law, John Preston, a prisoner after Marshall's Elm. Basset and William Bull both acted as parliamentary committeemen in August 1642, but continued to serve as magistrates when the royalists took over in the following summer. We might think of them as having changed sides, but they had not: they were Somerset men first, partisans second. In the western part of the county, remote from these events, it was easier to avoid commitment. Pyne had induced only a few hundred farmers of this region to march with him to Marshall's Elm; and apart from Sir John Stawell, who came to Wells well attended, the royalist gentry had done even worse.

In the clothing districts to the north and east, the turnout for parliament by the yeomen and clothworkers had been more impressive. It is true that in this area the influence of the Horners and Pophams was considerable. But, as John Ashe pointed out, so was that of Hopton, Dodington, and Thomas Smyth. Many of Hopton's tenants, 'unto his very gates', came to Chewton, as did forty of Smyth's. There is no doubt that the overwhelming majority of the great host on Mendip came of their own free will, and that they genuinely regarded themselves as the Country and Hertford's men as intruders, 'incendiaries, ... desperate cavaliers'.[16]

Distortion of the Commission of Array may have helped to arouse the people, yet even the royalist Clarendon could see that in some respects this was a conflict between two different kinds of society. On one side stood most of the richer gentry and such of their tenants as they could persuade to follow them. Apart from the Pophams and Horners, the other was led by 'people of an inferior degree, who by good husbandry, clothing, and other thriving arts, had gotten very great fortunes'. Clarendon omits the driving force of puritan idealism, but otherwise this is not an inaccurate description of such men as Ashe and Strode. As for their supporters, John Corbet's analysis of parliamentarian strength in neighbouring Gloucestershire will serve: 'Yeomen, farmers, petty freeholders, and such as use manufactures that enrich the country . . . a generation of men truly laborious, jealous of their properties, whose principal aim is liberty and plenty'.[17] Such men remembered only too well the Court's earlier violations of 'Liberty and Property'. If the king was victorious they would face them again, and worse. In the past there had been the gentry to lead them; now, if the gentry were more afraid of popular disorder than royal centralisation, they would act alone. Not all of them were puritans. But these were neighbours of the Beckington men who had defied Bishop Piers, and it was easy for the zealous minority to play on the general dislike of interfering bishops, the pathological hatred of popery, and the common revulsion at the flamboyant life-style of the younger cavaliers. Long hair can be a symbol of much that offends sober citizens.

Later events were to show that the parliamentarians' popularity was precarious. The issue in August 1642 was the Commission of Array. Once that threat was removed, the normal apathy of the freeholders was likely to return. But for the time being the roundheads could consolidate. Soon they were touring the county remodelling the trained bands and conducting thorough searches for arms, of which they made a rich haul. At Taunton, in the house of the bishop of Winchester's receiver, they found arms for 100 men and two barrels of gunpowder. At Bath they uncovered more arms and a hoard of £10,000; in a farmhouse near Glastonbury arms for another 100, hidden there by Sir John Stawell six weeks earlier. While arms were being carried out of a recusant's house in a village near Bridgwater, a little boy among the bystanders innocently remarked that his father 'had a great company of such 'uns too', leading to the discovery of yet more. Altogether arms for 1,800 men were seized in less than a week, showing how busily the royalists had been preparing.[18]

Even cavalier sympathisers co-operated. At Taunton, the committee reported, Sir William Portman was among those 'who immediately came and assisted us with horse and foot'. Portman was prudent: the men of Taunton, soon famous for their puritan zeal, had formed a volunteer company which was arming and drilling. When the committee turned up at Rodney's house at Pilton they were admitted without demur, and Sir Edward helpfully mustered his militia regiment to assist them the next day— yet Rodney had been with Hertford at Wells a fortnight before. Only at Lord Poulett's house was there resistance. Hinton was held by about fifty men, who told the approaching trained bands to 'begone otherwise they would let bullets fly amongst them'. The soldiers forced the gate and seized arms and horses, but a man was killed in the struggle.[19]

*   *   *   *

The next step was to deal with Hertford. We have the men, ran the repeated refrain of John Ashe's reports to parliament, but not the leaders: 'we are lost and spoiled if we have not commanders'. The royalists had the cavalry, the gentlemen's sons: it would be Marshall's Elm over again if good officers were not sent from London. Anxiously the committee awaited the arrival of the Earl of Bedford, who was on his way with Col Charles Essex, a seasoned Low Countries veteran, and eight troops of horse. When he sat down before Sherborne on 2 September, Bedford commanded an army of about 7,000 men; levies from Dorset and Devon joined the Somerset men under Alexander Popham, Pyne, and Strode. Hertford had been reinforced by the courtier Sir John Berkeley and a few officers from outside the county; Hopton raised forty dragoons 'armed with good fowling pieces', and Poulett brought two small cannon from Hinton. But the royalists still had less than 1,500 men, only 400 of them foot.[20]

The operations near Sherborne soon exposed the limitations of parliament's local forces. Even the officers were 'astonished', Bedford complained, 'when they heard the bullets whistle about their ears'; their men ran 'as if the devil had been in them' as soon as the royalist cannon opened up.[21] In two days of skirmishing, desertions reduced Bedford to less than half the 3,000 foot he had brought to Sherborne. On 6 September he raised the siege and retreated five miles westward, to Yeovil, billeting smaller detachments at Ilchester and Somerton.

The next day there was more serious fighting. During the morning royalist reinforcements making for Sherborne were sighted: some Dorset men collected by Richard Rogers of Bryanston. Bedford sent some of his horse to cut them off; there was a running fight but most of Rogers's party got into Sherborne. Seeing the enemy divided, Hertford made a sortie. Early in the afternoon he sent Hopton with a strong force to occupy Babylon Hill, two miles east of Yeovil. Placing musketeers to guard the two deep lanes leading up the hill, Sir Ralph stationed his horse at the summit, while the rest of his musketeers opened a brisk fire on the parliamentarians guarding the bridge over the Yeo beneath them. Bedford's men barricaded the roads into Yeovil; at last Hopton decided that they could not be dislodged and ordered a retreat to Sherborne. His foot were marching off the hill when the parliamentarians attacked. Facing about, the royalists greeted them with shouts of 'rogues and roundheads'. But the London horse were made of sterner stuff than the trained bands. They charged up the lane on the royalist left, braving fierce fire from the musketeers. At the top they encountered a troop of horse under young Edward Stawell. They exchanged 'two or three brace of bullets together, with a little slashing' but the roundheads were being forced back until they were rescued by a second wave of horse. A third group of parliamentarians came up the lane on the other flank. Their leader was shot dead, but their charge drove the cavaliers from the hill. Fortunately for Hopton, at this point darkness fell, and he was able to get his disordered forces back to Sherborne. Five parliamentarians had been killed, perhaps a score of royalists. More important, Babylon Hill was a welcome fillip for roundhead morale, showing that the cavalier horse were not invincible.[22]

After the battle Bedford resumed a desultory blockade of Sherborne—as he moved his main force to Dorchester, it would be an exaggeration to call it a siege. The cavaliers settled down for a long stay. They needed money and tried to get it from the tenants of loyal landowners. A Mendip miner named William Bushell was sent secretly to the Court at Derby. He brought back a letter from Lord Capell ordering his stewards at Wrington to deliver all rents collected 'unto such persons as the Marquis Hertford shall send unto you', but was arrested during his return journey.[23] Soon more bad news arrived: the nearest friendly garrison, under George Goring at Portsmouth, had surrendered. Hertford decided to retreat into Wales by way of Minehead and the Welsh cattle-boats which put in there every Thursday. Hopton was not optimistic—it meant a fifty-mile march through hostile country, and there was no certainty about the ships—but complied.

On 19 September Hertford's dispirited garrison evacuated Sherborne and marched west to Poulett's mansion at Hinton. The next day was full of tension. With the Blackdowns to their left and hostile Taunton only a few miles to their right, the cavaliers picked their way apprehensively to Bradford, midway between Taunton and equally puritan Wellington. The area, Hopton recalls, was 'in continual alarm, ringing their bells backward, and making fires to draw people into an uproar'. Turning north-west, the fugitives at last reached the coast on the 22nd, with Bedford in laborious pursuit a few miles behind. To the end they were treated as outsiders. At Dunster Thomas Luttrell refused to open his gates. Much worse, instead of being full of Welsh boats, Minehead harbour contained only two, the rest having been mysteriously diverted by 'the malicious activity of the Country'.[24] After some recrimination, Hertford and Hopton divided their dwindling forces. The marquis, with Poulett, Smyth, and a few others, took the cannon and what was left of the foot in the two crowded boats across to Wales; Smyth died at Cardiff a few weeks later. Hopton and the rest of the horse rode over Exmoor, across Devon, and into Cornwall. There were stirring days ahead for them.

For more than eight months after Hertford's departure the parliamentarians governed Somerset. Trade was badly affected, for the clothiers depended on unhindered access to their London market, and the western carriers were repeatedly plundered by forces of both sides near Reading: John Ashe was one to suffer. In the general breakdown of law and order that followed the outbreak of war, people with special grievances saw their opportunity. The simmering discontent among the foresters of Selwood again boiled over in the spring of 1643. Armed rioters destroyed enclosures and invaded the lands of royalists and roundheads alike; near Bruton, Sir Charles Berkeley's fences were among those to go down, and the disorders continued into the summer.[25]

Enclosure riots were routine matters. More directly political outbreaks showed that the parliamentary committee was not all-powerful. When news of Charles I's victory at Edgehill arrived, royalist rejoicing could be restrained only when there were troops or officials at hand. Hugh Collins, rector of Compton Pauncefoot, made a bonfire on a hilltop to celebrate the rebels' defeat. In December parliament was alarmed by reports of cavaliers raising volunteers in the county at beat of drum. In February 1643 one of the younger Berkeleys was involved in a plot to seize Ilchester and Bruton. Several hundred men were recruited and there was a pitched battle with the puritan villagers of Batcombe, quaintly recorded in the Bruton parish register:

> All praise and thanks to God still give
> For our deliverance Matthias' Eve.
> By his great power we put to flight
> Our foes the raging Batcombites,
> Who came to plunder, burn, and slay,
> And quite consume our town this day.

Strode came hurrying back from Devon to restore order, and Sir Charles Berkeley (in prison in London) was ordered to tell his tenants 'not to bear arms' against the parliament.[26]

The committee's own troops, too, were liable to get out of hand. In October 1642 Wells was thrown into panic by reports that soldiers bent on pillage were on the march from Glastonbury; a delegation was hastily sent to the committee 'touching the safety of the town'. The danger was averted, but in 1643 Wells was twice the target of puritan violence. On 15 April soldiers again plundered the palace, destroyed crucifixes in the cathedral, confiscated and sold linens and vestments, and menaced royalist citizens. On 10 May they came back. After dinner Alexander Popham's men 'rushed into the church, broke down the windows, organs, font, seats in the choir...besides many other villainies'. Images and vestments were fast disappearing from village churches as well. At Tintinhull troopers took surplices from the vestry 'and cut them in pieces, and the poor of the parish had the pieces'.[27]

By this time the leading cavaliers, such as had not left with Hertford or Hopton, had been arrested. Rodney and Sir Edward

Berkeley were taken early in October 1642; they were soon joined in prison in London by Dodington and Sir Charles Berkeley. Lesser men, including some of the more outspoken clergy, were also rounded up: Dr James Dugdale of Evercreech, for example, and Thomas Holt, vicar of Weston Zoyland. Holt had accused the parliamentarians of having plotted to 'take away the king's crown from his head', and even 'his head from his body'. In 1643 the king's worst enemies shuddered at such appalling ideas.[28]

In fact moderation had not been extinguished in this first year of war. John Preston's life had been saved at Marshall's Elm by Sir John Poulett, who told men standing over the prisoners with drawn swords not 'to spill the blood of the poor fellows'. Early in 1643 the royalist prisoners in London were granted more comfortable conditions of house arrest instead of their disagreeable gaols. When Ladies Poulett and Stawell complained about the plundering of their houses, they were immediately granted protection orders by parliament. And a sick child of Sir Charles Berkeley was given a pass to go to Oxford to be touched for the King's Evil.[29]

Generosity to defeated enemies might be possible, but the war came first. Three urgent tasks confronted the roundhead leaders: to co-ordinate Somerset's defences with those of the surrounding counties; to raise and train the necessary forces; and to collect the money to pay and equip them.

Some co-ordination with the counties to the north and east was achieved in October 1642 by an association of Somerset, Wiltshire, and Gloucestershire, for which a joint committee was set up. But the association affected only north Somerset, and although it was reorganised under Sir William Waller's command in February 1643, it never achieved very much. Still, money was borrowed for the defence of Bristol; Sir Edward Hungerford got parliament to make the reluctant mayor admit Col Thomas Essex with 2,000 men in December; and when the Earl of Stamford passed through on his way to command the parliamentarian forces in Devon, he thought it worth stopping to meet the leaders of the three counties concerned. Early in 1643 Somerset forces joined in defending Cirencester against Prince Rupert.[30]

Over the rest of the county the committee of MPs and deputy lieutenants held sway without much reference to the association. In January parliament redefined the committee's responsibilities.

It was to see that arrears of past assessments were collected, punish tax evaders and 'malignants', and supervise the rating of parishes to raise 8d a day for each man in arms for parliament. Of the various sources of money, the 'loans' raised on the Propositions of June 1642 were probably the most important; large sums were raised in spite of the system's deceptively voluntary appearance. In the northern parishes the money was paid to Alexander Popham's client, John Locke of Pensford; Popham was later to reward him by getting Locke's promising son admitted to Westminster School. The other military leader in the eastern division, William Strode, also appointed agents to receive money from the constables and collectors; among them was George Milward of Shepton Mallet. Parliamentarian gentry subscribed generously: £210 by the Hippisleys of Cameley was one of the larger sums. But even men who were to defect to Charles I after the royalist victories of 1643 often made no difficulty about subscribing: the parson John Morley of Wootton Courtney, the lawyers William Morgan of Wells and Thomas Warre of Dillington were among many others contributing.[31]

Money raised on the Propositions was spent entirely for local military needs. There were in theory two treasurers—John Ashe for the eastern division and Roger Hill of Taunton, uncle of the MP, for the western—but according to Ashe the money went directly to the military commanders, 'who disbursed the same as they themselves pleased'. In January 1643 a committee was appointed to levy a tax of one-twentieth of the estates of 'malignants' who had contributed less than they could afford on the Propositions. Its records perished in the parliamentarian disaster of the following summer, but a few royalists are known to have been assessed: Sir Thomas Bridges of Keynsham, for instance, paid £161. Gradually these amateurish arrangements were replaced by a more efficient, centralised financial system. In February a weekly assessment of all landed property was introduced: Somerset's share was £1,050. A month later a committee to sequester the estates of royalists in the county was nominated. Troops were sometimes used to enforce these ordinances. In April men of Popham's regiment were sent from Bristol to collect Lord Poulett's and other cavaliers' rents.[32]

Parliament's new administrative system had little time to take root. But the largely identical membership of the various committees gives a useful indication of the quality of parliamentarian leadership during the early part of the war. Only a minority of gentry families supported parliament, but they dominated the committees. At their head stood the Pophams and Sir John Horner. Less energetic, though of equal status, was John Harington of Kelston. Not far behind were Sir Thomas Wroth, Pyne, Hugh Rogers, and John Fraunceis. Other solid county families were represented by Henry Henley of Leigh, near Winsham, John Preston and his son-in-law John Hippisley, William Bull, and old John Hunt of Speckington, father of the Ilchester MP. Among a number of lesser gentry were the sheriff's son, Henry Sanford of Nynehead, William Samborne of Paulton, and Roger Hill of Taunton. But parliament could not rely on landed wealth alone: there were the clothiers Ashe and Strode, the coalowner William Long, and two merchants' sons, Richard Cole and Robert Harbin. Clement Walker was an Exchequer official, recently established at Charterhouse-on-Mendip. Finally there were three townsmen: George Serle and Jasper Chaplain of Taunton, and Robert Blake of Bridgwater.[33] This was a far less eminent group than the Pouletts, Stawells, and Berkeleys who had joined Hertford at Wells. Nevertheless, most of them were men of substance: the parliamentarian committees were manned largely by the gentry. Months of war would be needed to weed out the hangers-on from the activists, to distinguish between the ideologically committed and those who put friendship to neighbours and kinsmen above military victory.

The committeemen strove busily to organise the county for war. Popham and Strode in the eastern division, Pyne and Wroth in the western, raised and drilled their forces. Towns were told to improve their soldiers' equipment, and to keep their trained band units up to strength. Recruits were levied for the unruly and undermanned companies intended for Ireland, still languishing at Bath and Bristol in October 1642. In December parliament ordered the committees of Somerset, Devon, and Cornwall to raise three regiments of volunteers and 1,000 dragoons; half the dragoons were to be financed by the officers on the security of Irish lands, the rest by a levy on 'papists, commissioners of array, not-contributors [on the Propositions], and delinquents'. These forces were quickly marched off into Devon under parliament's new commander, the Earl of Stamford, in whose army Pyne,

Strode, and Wroth were all serving in January 1643. At the end of February there was a local truce in Devon and Cornwall, but efforts to extend it broke down. Representatives from Somerset were expected at Exeter for a meeting to arrange this, but none arrived.[34]

While parliament was in control there would be no talk of truce. Taunton was given renewed authority over its militia forces, the town's security being regarded as 'of great concernment to the western parts'. Bristol, too, was strengthened. In March the untrustworthy governor, Thomas Essex, was replaced by Col Nathaniel Fiennes, son of the puritan Lord Saye and Sele. Almost immediately Fiennes frustrated a plot to seize the city for the king. Rupert, whose forces were to have been admitted by the conspirators, advanced threateningly from Oxford but had to make a quick withdrawal; two citizens were court-martialled and executed. So firm was parliament's hold that Somerset forces were repeatedly sent outside the county to help their neighbours. In late April 1643 Strode took several hundred men into Wiltshire to the siege of Wardour Castle. The southern border was also secured, after rumours spread that Hertford and Lord Digby were about to make another attempt on Sherborne Castle. Alexander Popham marched quickly from Wells; his brother, Capt Hugh Popham, was killed and part of Sherborne went up in flames, but the roundheads occupied both town and castle. Popham then moved further into Dorset and took part in the capture of Portland. His men returned to Bristol loaded with booty, which they refused to hand over to Governor Fiennes. The profits of local actions, they felt, should go to local men.[35]

In the early months of 1643 the king's cause in Somerset was at the lowest possible ebb. But help was at hand. Sir Ralph Hopton had ignited the loyalty of the Cornishmen into a blazing cavalier flame. In a series of hard-fought winter actions he had forged a formidable army, and on 16 May he destroyed Stamford's forces at Stratton. The royalist counter-offensive had begun.

Notes to this chapter are on pages 199-201.

3
The Royalists Triumphant
June-July 1643

Hopton's success in Cornwall had been built on a strict regard for legality, his tactful co-operation with the Cornish gentry, his own tenacious courage, and on the other side the Earl of Stamford's feebleness. Sir Ralph's military experience in the Palatinate and Bohemia were of less value than his native intelligence and integrity. Even his enemies conceded his nobility of character, and he was as much of a puritan as many of them.[1] He had been a consistent spokesman for the Country ever since the 1620s, but was not betraying his principles when in 1642 he decided that the truly constitutional cause was the king's. Aided by such local men as Sir Bevil Grenville and Sir Nicholas Slanning, Hopton had made the Cornishmen a brilliant fighting force. Even before Stratton the possibility of using them as the nucleus of an army to complete the conquest of the West was obvious to Charles I.

But the Cornish pikemen and musketeers needed cavalry. While Hopton was accounting for Stamford, therefore, new forces were raised at Oxford to support them. They were commanded by Hertford, who was still commissioned as general of the West, but was now accompanied by a whole array of cavalry officers, including Prince Maurice, younger brother of the great Rupert, and the dashing Earl of Carnarvon. Hertford's force left Oxford in mid May and proceeded by slow stages through Wiltshire and Dorset. On Sunday 4 June the Cornish army entered Somerset and linked up with Hertford at Chard. The combined force now amounted to 4,000 foot (mostly Cornish), 1,500 horse (mostly from Oxford), 300 dragoons, and about fifteen cannon. The proliferation of generals created some problems, but in the end Hertford was content with a merely nominal command, Hopton acted as chief

D

of staff, and Maurice took charge of the cavalry. It was, one of Maurice's captains observed, 'a pretty marching army'.[2]

What could the parliamentarians put against this powerful enemy? First there were the local levies raised by Pyne and Wroth in the western division, Strode and Alexander Popham in the eastern. Although better trained and equipped than the country lads who had gathered against Hertford in the previous summer, they were still an uncertain quantity, particularly those from the west, who were prone to desert at the first opportunity. But there were also more professional troops in the county. A few months earlier, command of the Western Association had been taken over by Sir William Waller, one of Hopton's old friends from Palatinate days. With some minor victories in Gloucestershire behind him, Waller had a somewhat inflated reputation as one of parliament's few commanders who had won any battles at all: 'William the Conqueror', the London propagandists were calling him. In fact his talents were mainly confined to a propensity for surprising night marches, and a good eye for choosing his ground. While the royalists concentrated at Chard, Waller was at Bath collecting a force at least equal in number to theirs, larger if the Bristol garrison is included. Waller's infantry could not rival the Cornishmen, but he was well provided with cavalry from London, among them the bombastic Sir Arthur Haselrig's heavily armoured 'Lobsters'. So well protected were these that reports of how Sir Arthur survived at Roundway a few weeks later actually provoked a witticism from Charles I: 'Had he been victualled as well as fortified, he might have endured a siege of seven years.'[3]

While Waller made ready at Bath, the Somerset forces hastily mustered. Alexander Popham and Strode took the field at Shepton Mallet; Edward Popham (Alexander's brother), Pyne, and Wroth assembled 5,000 men of the western trained bands at Taunton. Plans were laid for the same kind of general rising of the Country as had driven Hertford out in 1642. All able-bodied men of the western parts were summoned to a rendezvous at Taunton at the end of May, those of the east to one at Wells on 12 June. But unsympathetic as they might be towards the cavaliers, the ill-armed countrymen of west Somerset had no better fighting spirit than in the previous year. By the evening of 4 June the royalists had advanced rapidly from Chard to within two miles of Taunton. The countrymen melted away and even the puritan townsmen showed no stomach for a fight. Edward Popham quickly decided that the only sensible move was to abandon Taunton and fall back across the levels, to join forces with his brother, Strode, and Waller. Half the garrison had already been evacuated to Bridgwater before the enemy appeared. Popham now ordered the remainder to withdraw, first sinking their ordnance and carriages in the castle moat. They were prevented from doing this by local royalists, who were assisted by a mutiny of prisoners in the castle. On the morning of the 5th Taunton surrendered.

Bridgwater was no better defended. When the news from Taunton reached there panic spread in the garrison and the place was immediately abandoned. Forces quartered in outlying villages fled towards Somerton, with cavalier patrols in hot pursuit. Meanwhile at Dunster Thomas Luttrell, more impressed by Hertford's army than he had been by the handful of men at Minehead in the previous September, promptly handed over the castle to Col Francis Wyndham. With scarcely the firing of a shot, the whole of west Somerset was in royalist hands.

Gentlemen secretly sympathetic to the king who had perforce kept quiet in 1642 were now coming into the open on Hertford's side. Even so, the feeling of the Country, especially in north and east Somerset, was still generally favourable to parliament. And the failure of the royalist commanders to restrain their troops from plunder destroyed whatever chance they might have had of winning over the prosperous farmers of the Vale of Taunton. When they entered Somerset, Hopton observed, there were plentiful supplies of food, and people did not object to free quarter 'soberly taken'. The Cornishmen were reasonably well disciplined, and their pious commander saw to it that they attended regularly to their devotions. Sometimes, though, they got out of hand. Richard Atkyns, one of Maurice's officers, accuses them of occasionally opening fire on their own cavalry, and of being 'so mutinous withal, that nothing but an alarm could keep them from falling foul upon their officers'. But it was the Oxford horse, accustomed, Clarendon says, to 'a looser discipline', who caused most of the trouble. Taunton submitted to free quarter and agreed to provide a week's pay for the army, but this was not enough to prevent 'extravagant disorder' by Maurice's men.[4]

One reason for the restiveness of the Cornishmen may have been their reluctance to leave their own county while it was still menaced by enemy garrisons at Plymouth and Exeter. The royalist officers in Devon were uneasy about the advance, and Hopton had to assure them that his sole purpose was to protect Devon and Cornwall, 'which is and shall be our special care'.[5] With west Somerset cleared, on 9 June the Cornishmen began to march back towards Exeter. Then intelligence of Waller's preparations at Bath reached them, and they returned to Taunton. Edward Popham and Strode were now at Glastonbury with 3,000 men of the east Somerset trained bands, some of the remnants of Stamford's horse from Devon, and a few survivors of the Taunton and Bridgwater garrisons. On the 11th Hertford's army marched over the levels to Somerton to face them.

The long summer day of Monday the 12th was crowded with incident. Hopton, 'according to his custom in times of necessity', began his round of inspection an hour before dawn.[6] While he was doing so a raiding party of enemy horse fell on the quarters of some royalist dragoons a mile beyond Somerton. It showed that the parliamentarians were going to make a fight of it, but did not delay the advance. Soon the royalists were on their way towards Glastonbury, with the Somerset forces slowly retreating before them. Throughout the day they skirmished with the royalist advance guard, successfully conducting that most difficult of military operations, an orderly withdrawal in the face of an enemy of superior strength. On both sides these were forces of very different calibre from the disorganised rabbles of 1642. Between Glastonbury and Wells Popham and Strode made a stand, lining the hedges with musketeers who, says Hopton, 'held our forlorn hope in play one hour and more'.[7] At Wells there was another brief stand to cover the retreat up the steep Mendip escarpment. On the open plain at the summit the parliamentarian horse deployed in a wide arc to protect their infantry and waggons, who proceeded, still in good order, to Chewton Mendip. The royalists occupied Wells and their foot, tired after the long day's advance, took up quarters in the town. Maurice, however, continued the pursuit, and got his horse on to the Mendips without opposition.

By now it was evening. In the waning hours of daylight, the Mendips, splendid open country for horse, became the scene of a confused, exhilarating cavalry encounter. It began about a mile from Chewton Mendip. While the main roundhead force passed through the village, their rearguard of foot halted to cover the retreat, 'at the entry out of the heath'; their horse, still in a broad crescent, were drawn up about a mile ahead of them, presumably on Nedge Hill.[8] Carnarvon, the very type of impetuous cavalier, charged immediately. The roundheads were routed, and the earl gaily pursued the shattered remnants through the village, making a rich haul of their guns, ammunition, and transport. But as so often happened in civil war cavalry charges, Carnarvon was carried away by the excitement of the chase. Some of his men did not draw rein until they were within five miles of Bath. They then encountered horse and dragoons from Waller's fresh forces, who promptly pursued them back to Chewton. Maurice, who had been quartering his men in the neighbouring farms, hastily assembled them again.

Confronted by Maurice's men, Waller's cavalry halted as they came out of Chewton. They quickly deployed: a regiment of horse in two divisions, flanked by dragoons lining the hedges, and with more dragoons a few hundred yards in advance. The smaller royalist force moved towards them. 'At this punctilio of time', says Capt Atkyns, 'from as clear a sunshine day as could be seen, there fell a sudden mist, that we could not see ten yards off.'[9] A change of wind, or the evening cooling, had produced a typical Mendip fog, a cloud scudding over the hilltop. Confused by the mist, the roundhead dragoons blindly opened fire; then, uncertain of the advancing royalists' whereabouts, they mounted their horses and fled. Emerging from the mist, the cavaliers routed one wing of the parliamentarian horse, but the other closed in and charged the royalist rear, and for a time all was confusion. Maurice was wounded in the head and taken prisoner; fortunately for him he was not recognised. Atkyns found himself in a field with only thirty men, the rest having galloped off in pursuit of the dragoons, and menaced by three troops of enemy horse. However, the roundheads had to come through a farmyard, and before they could form up again, Atkyns attacked and dispersed them. Meanwhile Carnarvon had rallied parts of his scattered regiment and joined in with yet another charge, again taking the parliamentarians in the rear and driving them from the field. The prince was recognised by Atkyns's groom and rescued.

Waller's men fled back to Bath; Maurice and Carnarvon got their regiments into order and returned to Wells in the gathering darkness. In all the confused fighting the royalists had lost thirty or forty men, the parliamentarians rather more. Once again the élan of the cavalier horse had been demonstrated, but also their dangerous habit of letting their enthusiasm run away with them. And they had encountered only a small part of Waller's army.

*   *   *   *

For more than a fortnight after the fight at Chewton there was a lull. The royalists, with their headquarters at Wells, were not in an altogether comfortable position. They controlled the Mendips, but Waller was collecting large forces beyond the hills, and behind them lay a sullen, restive population. West Somerset was less parliamentarian than the region Hertford was about to enter, but it had displayed no enthusiasm for the king either, especially after experiencing the predatory indiscipline of his cavalry. Taunton, Wellington, and the other 'clothing parts' were certainly hostile: 'subdued, not converted', as Clarendon put it.[10] The parliamentarians, admittedly, had not aroused the same response that they had gained against the commissioners of array the year before: it was a different kind of war. The speed of Hopton's advance after Stratton, leaving enemy strongholds in Devon behind him, had in any case thrown the roundhead leaders off balance. The committee's attempt to raise the Country at Taunton had been a total failure. And Hopton's march from Somerton frustrated the similar gathering of the eastern division planned for 12 June at Wells: 'all from 16 to 60' had been summoned to appear in arms for parliament.[11]

The burden of war was beginning to be felt more severely. For the first time Somerset was having to support large armies from outside the county, with local resources already strained by the interruption of trade and by recurrent outbreaks of plague. Billeted at Glastonbury after the battle at Chewton, Richard Atkyns found himself in 'a handsome case of a house, but totally plundered'. The only food there was a mouldy Cheddar cheese, which Atkyns's footboy fed to his employer's greyhounds. Even disciplined soldiers were an imposition, and all too often, particularly when they were on the move, civil war armies were utterly without discipline. Maurice's horse were bad enough; later arrivals were worse. Sir James Hamilton's men, Clarendon thought, did the king more harm than good in Devon 'by the licence they took'.[12]

Their conduct in Somerset is not likely to have been any more endearing.

While the royalists alienated the Country, the parliamentarians had their own problems: London's failure to send money, and the Bristol garrison's reluctance to supply reinforcements. Waller was strong in horse, especially after the Lobsters' arrival, but the infantry at his disposal were clearly insufficient to fight the Cornish. Sir William justified his inability to take the offensive by pointing out that the country around Wells was 'altogether unfit for horse'. This was palpably untrue as far as the Mendips were concerned, but it was true that Waller lacked infantry. Appeals to the ultra-cautious Fiennes at Bristol brought the release of Alexander Popham's regiment, but even this was sent to Bath only on the eve of Lansdown. 'What good will this regiment do Bristol if we perish?' Waller and Haselrig asked prophetically. Even the puritan northern villages were becoming discontented: the inhabitants of Keynsham complained of being 'eaten up and charged more than comes to their share by the Bristol troopers.'[13] Short of money, with even his cavalry threatening to desert if they were not speedily paid, Sir William was scarcely in an impregnable position at Bath.

It was an interesting situation. Two rival armies occupied the two episcopal cities of Somerset, separated by twenty miles and the Mendip Hills, the commander of one the close friend of the chief of staff of the other. We can only guess how much Hopton knew of Waller's difficulties. But Waller was a gentleman like himself, and such men had come over to the king before after initially supporting parliament: James Chudleigh, for example, who changed sides after being taken prisoner at Stratton. After the battle at Chewton, therefore, Hopton wrote to Waller proposing a conference between them, possibly to discuss an exchange of prisoners, but more likely in the simple hope of averting bloodshed. Hopton, after all, was now in his native countryside; among the forces commanded by Popham and Strode were some of his own neighbours and tenants.

Waller replied from Bath in a letter that is justly famous. Indeed, nothing better illustrates the agonising dilemmas the Civil War created for high-principled men within a close-knit governing class. 'Certainly', he told Hopton,

> my affections to you are so unchangeable, that hostility itself cannot

violate my friendship to your person. But I must be true to the cause wherein I serve. The old limitation, *usque ad aras,* holds still, and where my conscience is interested all other obligations are swallowed up. I should most gladly wait upon you, according to your desire, but that I look upon you as engaged in that party beyond the possibility of a retreat, and consequently uncapable of being wrought upon by any persuasions. And I know the conference could never be so close between us but that it would take wind, and receive a construction to my dishonour. That great God who is the searcher of my heart knows with what a sad sense I go upon this service, and with what a perfect hatred I detest this war without an enemy. . . . We are both upon the stage, and must act such parts as are assigned us in this tragedy. Let us do it in a way of honour and without personal animosities.[14]

Honour, conscience, a sense of tragedy, an awareness of their public roles: for men like Waller and Hopton, sharing the common values of an educated élite, this was indeed a 'war without an enemy'. When their constitutional differences had been honourably settled, it was unthinkable that such men would proceed to extreme courses, either of revolution on one side, or royal absolutism on the other. Some of their inferiors, however, were soon to view the matter differently.

So there was still a war to be fought. On the day after Chewton Hopton was still talking about a march back to the west, to reduce Exeter. By the 19th, however, Hertford's council had concluded that 'it was fit to follow Waller which way soever he went'.[15] Towards the end of the month, refreshed and regrouped, the Cornish army advanced from Wells to Frome. Skirmishing was soon resumed. Sir James Hamilton unwisely quartered some of his men in villages too far from the royalists' main force. Waller sent a raiding party of 250 men under Major Francis Duet to beat up the quarters of a unit at Leigh-on-Mendip. After a night march, Duet's men charged into the village through the morning mist, hurling grenades and rounding up the startled royalists as they stumbled sleepily into the street.[16] But it took more than a raid to stop the cavalier advance. On Sunday 2 July the Cornish army marched north from Frome and secured the important bridge at Bradford-on-Avon, eight miles above Bath. The city was protected by the river on the south-eastern side; obviously the royalists were about to circle around and attack Waller from the north. Reinforced by Popham's Somerset regiment, belatedly sent from Bristol, the roundhead general therefore emerged from Bath and drew up his army on Claverton Down, overlooking the deep, narrow Avon valley.

On Sunday night Waller detached a strong force under Col Burghill, and sent them across the Avon near Claverton, where he had built a temporary bridge by the ford. Burghill occupied Monkton Farleigh Hill, and placed his infantry in an ambush in the woods towards Bradford-on-Avon. The next morning there was some skirmishing between Burghill's patrols and royalist outposts, and the whole Cornish army was soon on the move. They showed their usual quality, forcing the parliamentarians from the wood and off the hill, and capturing a couple of light cannon. Soon they advanced to the river, where they encountered stronger resistance. Maurice, however, took charge, and when darkness fell he sent the Cornishmen across the river to threaten the main roundhead force; Waller promptly abandoned Claverton Down and retreated into Bath. Meanwhile some of Burghill's horse had fled north-west from Monkton Farleigh. They were pursued by royalist cavalry under Hopton and Carnarvon, who during the night found themselves under the great dark Lansdown ridge, looming over Bath to the north. The advantages of seizing the hill were obvious, but the cavaliers were tired and divided and the opportunity was missed. Instead they withdrew to Batheaston.

Sensing the danger, and never one to neglect a superior defensive position, Waller occupied Lansdown himself in the early morning of 4 July. After regrouping, the Cornish army moved from Batheaston towards the south-eastern face of Lansdown. They were too late: Waller's men were already looking down on them from the summit. Harassed by cannon fire, and judging the position unassailable, the royalist commanders decided to retire. Soon the army was in orderly retreat to Marshfield, four miles to the north, with Hopton's rearguard holding off light roundhead attacks. By Tuesday night the royalists were quartered at Marshfield, Waller still ensconced on Lansdown.[17]

On Wednesday 5 July 1643 was fought the battle of Lansdown, the bloodiest encounter of the entire war in Somerset. For a time it seemed that the armies might glare at each other and not fight at all. Strongly entrenched on a steep hill, musketeers manning the breastworks, cannon commanding the valley below, Waller was in an apparently impregnable position. He opened with the customary dawn raid on the royalist outposts. Quickly the cavalier

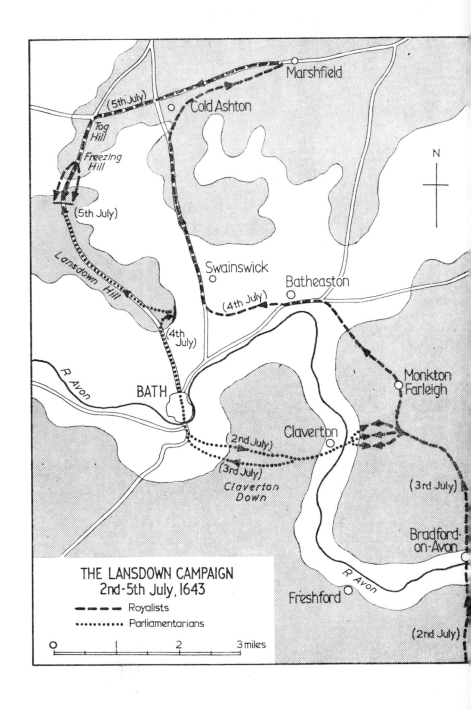

THE LANSDOWN CAMPAIGN
2nd-5th July, 1643

- - - Royalists
.... Parliamentarians

0   1   2   3 miles

army mustered and advanced west from Marshfield to Tog Hill, just over a mile from the northern slope of Lansdown. For several hours dragoons skirmished among the hedges in the intervening valley while the main armies remained quiet. By early afternoon it was clear that Waller was not going to be lured off the hill. Reason prevailed. Instead of attempting a suicidal frontal attack, the royalist generals decided once again to retreat to Marshfield. Then, suddenly, the battle began.[18]

There were two phases to Lansdown: the first in the valley to the north, the second on the hill itself. Seeing the enemy face about, Waller saw his chance to turn retreat into rout. In a rare display of boldness he launched a force of cavalry, less than 1,000 strong, in a charge down the hill as the royalists marched away. Sheltered by hedges in the valley, roundhead dragoons opened fire on the royalist rearguard of horse, which began to break up in disorder. A well timed charge by Duet's horse completed their rout: some of them galloped all the way to Oxford bearing tidings of disaster. Two things turned the tide: the steadiness of the Cornish foot, and a superb counter-attack by Carnarvon's cavalry. At Maurice's suggestion, Hopton had placed groups of Cornish musketeers to support the cavalry, and these held their ground even when the horse deserted them. Most important, they won precious time for the rest of the army to turn about and enter the battle. First Carnarvon charged and drove the roundhead horse back across Tog Hill; then Slanning and other Cornishmen began to clear the dragoons out of the lanes below. Eventually Maurice joined in with more cavalry and fought the enemy back through the valley between Freezing Hill and Lansdown. It was hot work, charge and counter-charge, and both Burghill and Carnarvon were wounded. At last the parliamentarians retired up the hill to their main force, which tried to lure the advancing enemy into an improvised assault by pretending to be retreating in panic.

It was now late afternoon, and the second phase of the battle was about to begin. Although the royalists had not been deceived by Waller's ruse, the blood of the Cornishmen was up; under fire on Freezing Hill from Waller's artillery on Lansdown, they shouted for an order to 'fetch those cannon'. Seeing that he could not restrain them, Hopton obliged. Usually in civil war battles the foot occupied the centre, with pikemen and musketeers interspersed, the cavalry the wings. In this case the terrain dictated a different arrangement. Hopton sent his musketeers through the woods on each wing, the pikes and the cavalry advancing up the open, steeply sloping ground in the centre through which the road wound up the hill towards Bath. The musketeers made good progress in the woods, and so did the pikes and horse as long as they were protected from Waller's artillery by the stone walls near the road and by the slope of the hill. But when they neared the top the Cornishmen ran into murderous fire from both cannon and muskets, and only their incomparable fighting spirit carried them through. Richard Atkyns gives an awesome description of the scene as he came up with the reserve of horse:

> When I came to the top of the hill, I saw Sir Bevil Grenville's stand of pikes, which certainly preserved our army from a total rout: . . . they stood as upon the eaves of an house for steepness, but as unmovable as a rock. On which side of this stand of pikes our horse were, I could not discover; for the air was so darkened by the smoke of the powder, that for a quarter of an hour together . . . there was no light seen, but what the fire of the volleys of shot gave.[19]

Throwing in everything he had, Waller tried vainly to dislodge the Cornishmen from their dangerously exposed position. Sir William himself led several charges, Haselrig's Lobsters hurled themselves at the pikes, but without avail. Grenville, another of Waller's old friends on the other side, fell amid the carnage. Soon Waller fell back to a new line, a stone wall some 400 yards to the rear of his original one at the brow of the hill: 'a large sheep-cote', so Atkyns describes the new position. In the fading light the two sides exchanged desultory fire, but effectively the battle was over. Waller's usual caution got the upper hand. The cavaliers were like 'a heavy stone upon the very brow of the hill, which with one lusty charge might well have been rolled to the bottom', a royalist officer, Walter Slingsby, put it.[20] They had suffered dreadful casualties, were short of ammunition, tired and dispirited by the loss of the popular Grenville. But instead of inspiring his men to a last desperate counter-attack, Waller waited until night fell. Then, leaving match burning on the walls to pretend that his army was still on the hill, he withdrew into Bath, covering the retreat with one last volley from his musketeers.

*   *   *   *

Tactically Lansdown was a royalist victory. But in spite of his inferiority in infantry Waller had been defeated, not destroyed, as he might well have been on less favourable ground. His army was intact, Bath and Bristol still in his hands, reinforcements still arriving. The royalists had sustained daunting losses. Grenville was dead, the Cornishmen seriously weakened, and many of their horse had run away. Only Cornish courage and Hopton's stout nerves had seen them through. And on the morning after the battle Hopton was effectively removed from his command. While he was interrogating some prisoners a nearby ammunition cart exploded, killing several bystanders; the burnt men made 'lamentable screeches', Atkyns recalls.[21] Hopton was badly burned and temporarily blinded: it was a miracle that he survived. His dejected army withdrew again to Marshfield and thence to Chippenham.

Waller was far from finished. As long as they were not discouraged by overwhelming royalist power, the country people were on his side. Where the three counties of Wiltshire, Gloucestershire, and Somerset come together near Bath, says Clarendon, lay 'the most absolute disaffected parts of all three'. Even Hopton admitted that the 'present general inclinations of the Country' favoured Waller, who could thus the more easily raise fresh troops and supplies.[22] Waller was still claiming victory, and there were enough fugitives from the shattered royalist cavalry to give credence to this: sixty cavalier horse turned up at Freshford, for example, on the night after the battle. Waller's warrants were soon circulating through the countryside, ordering the apprehension of the allegedly beaten cavaliers. Aided by further reinforcements from Bristol, the roundheads reoccupied Lansdown and began to pursue the royalists towards Chippenham. Exuding the same confidence as her husband, Lady Waller told the crowds outside her house in Bath to go home, 'for the work was done already'. The royalists, in hostile territory, could get neither food nor intelligence; as for Waller, 'men flocked to him as the master of the field'.[23]

Waller's march led him to Devizes and disaster. Eight days after Lansdown his army was destroyed at Roundway Down, in the most brilliant and comprehensive cavalier victory of the war. Strode and Alexander Popham were present with their Somerset regiments; the foot fought on stubbornly after the defection of the cavalry, and Popham valiantly held them together until they too were overwhelmed. The weary survivors straggled back towards

Bristol. On 16 July Sir William, no longer the conqueror, reviewed what remnants of cavalry he could muster on Durdham Down, before marching away and leaving Nathaniel Fiennes to his fate. A week later Waller was in London, receiving, rather curiously, a hero's reception.[24]

Inexorably the royalists closed in. Bristol's capture would complete the conquest of Somerset, give them the greatest port in the West and the essential link between their armies in Wales, the West, and at Oxford. While Hopton recovered from his wounds at Devizes the Cornish army marched westward again to occupy Bath and Keynsham. Royalist soldiers were soon venting their feelings against Waller by defacing his statue in the abbey, part of the noble monument to his first wife, who died at Bath in 1633. Not all the iconoclastic excesses of the Civil War were the fault of the puritans. Meanwhile Rupert left Oxford with a strong force of cavalry, fourteen regiments of foot, and a train of artillery. On the 23rd the prince arrived outside Bristol to the north; the Cornishmen were moving west from Keynsham along the Somerset bank of the Avon.[25]

Against this formidable army Fiennes had to defend Bristol with only 1,500 foot and 300 horse, plus whatever volunteers he could raise in the city. He had reluctantly weakened his garrison by sending Popham's regiment to Waller before Lansdown; few of the men returned from Roundway, and those without arms and with shattered morale. Some of the Somerset officers, among them the resolute Strode and Robert Blake, came back to take part in the defence. Most of the country gentry had left with Waller, but Sir John Horner and Clement Walker had refused to flee. New forces were frantically raised by local stalwarts: Robert Bagenall of Keynsham, for example, somehow got together a company of foot.

Bristol's defences were not to be taken lightly. The north-western suburbs were protected by a chain of forts across Brandon and St Michael's Hills, with a connecting ditch and earthwork. The castle, recently repaired, covered the eastern approaches. To the south flowed the Avon. Past Redcliffe and Temple Gates the old walls were still serviceable, with a deep graff or ditch outside them. Fiennes had plentiful supplies and was well provided with cannon. Besieged, he could probably have held out for weeks. But against a determined enemy willing to accept casualties his force, according to the best modern experts, 'was inadequate to hold a line over three miles long'.[26]

The assault began before dawn on 26 July. On the Somerset side the Cornishmen, with typical impetuosity, attacked before the agreed signal. They pressed forward ardently, but the ditch near Temple Gate was too deep to be bridged with carts or filled with faggots, and they were driven back with heavy losses. Outside the graff, says Atkyns, 'as gallant men as ever drew sword . . . lay upon the ground like rotten sheep'.[27] Slanning and several other officers were killed or mortally wounded. Maurice kept the survivors steadily in formation, but for once the Cornishmen had been worsted. Meanwhile on the other side Rupert's army was also encountering fierce resistance. Attacks on the Prior's Hill and Windmill Hill forts were repelled, again with many royalist dead. But the pressure began to tell. North-east of Brandon Hill Col Henry Washington made the crucial breach and Rupert's men were soon streaming through, advancing downhill between the houses, under fire from windows and rooftops. Among the slain was Henry Lunsford, the organiser of victory at Marshall's Elm, who fell on Christmas Steps. Roundhead horse under Major Hercules Langrish failed to charge the royalists exploiting Washington's breach, and although Fiennes himself eventually led a counter-attack, it was too late and he was beaten back.

With Rupert brilliantly co-ordinating the assault, the cavaliers moved in for the kill. Col Henry Wentworth worked his way down the hill to College Green and the quay, while Belasyse's brigade pushed on to Frome Gate. The defenders, still resisting manfully, fell back into the inner city behind the Frome, which was a formidable second line of defence. Rupert called for reinforcements from the Somerset side, and 1,000 Cornishmen were brought over the Avon and marched to the breach. Compared with Rupert's professionalism, Fiennes's generalship was irresolute. Three of the Somerset officers—Bagenall, Richard Hippisley of Cameley, and Latimer Sampson of Freshford—wanted to counter-attack and seal the breach, but instead were told to withdraw. Their men were left in Wine Street for two hours without orders, then their discipline collapsed and they dispersed into nearby taverns.

Suddenly Fiennes asked for a parley. Strode was vehemently against it, and Sir John Horner abstained when it came to a vote at a council of war. But the defenders were discouraged, powder was running short (Fiennes later admitted that supplies were not as low as he thought), and the citizens were not anxious to see Bristol go up in flames around them. Hostages were quickly exchanged, and by ten that night Fiennes had accepted Rupert's terms. The garrison would march out in the morning; they were promised three days' safe conduct on their journey towards London. Eager to be gone, Fiennes left before the agreed hour, giving the royalists a pretext for violating some of the articles of surrender. 'One whole street upon the bridge', Clarendon admits, '. . . was almost totally plundered.'[28]

Bristol had fallen, Somerset and the West were firmly in the king's hands. The cost had been heavy: over 500 royalist dead, including such good officers as Slanning, Lunsford, and many more. But to the local royalists it seemed that the war was as good as over. Richard Atkyns was one who thought so, and his duty done, he went home to Gloucestershire. Somerset was a conquered county. The cavaliers settled down to govern it, if they could, in peace.

Notes to this chapter are on pages 201-2.

Ralph Lord Hopton

Edward Popham

4
Royalist Somerset
July 1643-March 1645

Bristol's fall was dutifully celebrated with bells and bonfires. Laudian ceremonies and loyal sermons reappeared in the parish churches. In the autumn of 1643 Wells Cathedral was disturbed by nothing worse than the usual quarrels between the contentious wives of vicars-choral; Popham's soldiers were a fading memory. For almost a year—until the Earl of Essex's arrival in June 1644—Somerset was at peace, troubled only by minor incidents on its borders, and by the distant reverberations of greater events elsewhere. Money and men had to be raised for the king's forces, but the burdens were not impossibly heavy, and there were no invading armies. If the cavaliers were going to win over the Country, this was the time to do it.

At first the royalists behaved with moderation. Their leaders were local men, anxious to regain the trust of their countrymen. Hopton at Bristol, Stawell at Taunton, Edmund Wyndham at Bridgwater: all the most important garrisons were commanded by men well attuned to Somerset opinion. In September 1643 Hopton recommended the appointment of Sir Francis Hawley as his deputy-governor, largely because of the 'many assistances which cannot be so well effected by any that were not this country man'. A month later Hopton again proclaimed his belief that the king could only prosper if he entrusted his affairs to local 'gentlemen of worth'.[1] This, for several months after the capture of Bristol, is precisely what the king did, and the county remained quiet.

Men like Stawell and Hopton might strive to protect the interests of the county, but this did not make them any more tender towards their enemies. Most of the roundhead leaders had fled

E

with Waller or marched away with Fiennes. Those who remained
had their estates sequestered for the king's use and were sometimes themselves imprisoned. The puritan clergy were marked
men, and many of them quickly disappeared. George Newton, the
eminent Taunton minister, fled to his wife's old home at St
Albans and officiated there until the end of the war. Several
acquired London parishes; Timothy Batt of Ilminster became
an army chaplain. Those who stayed had to subscribe articles
upholding the prayer book, declaring resistance to the king unlawful, and condemning the defacing of church ornaments.
William Thomas of Ubley was among those suspended for refusing, though he too had a London parish by the end of the war.
Age made old Samuel Crooke less defiant. Soldiers were billeted
on him at Wrington; they abused and threatened him in his
study until he submitted.[2]

Most of the parliamentarian leaders continued the fight as
exiles from the county. Some, like John Ashe, threw themselves
energetically into their duties at Westminster, where the Somerset
MPs lost their most distinguished colleague when John Pym died
in December 1643. Others took up the sword in neighbouring
counties: Strode in Dorset, the Popham brothers in Wiltshire,
where their family had extensive estates. Edward Popham's former
lieutenant-colonel, Robert Blake of Bridgwater, played a notable
part in the defence of Lyme Regis against Prince Maurice's forces.
But the disasters of July 1643 had left deep scars, and the exiles
quarrelled bitterly over the responsibility for the loss of Bristol.
It was all Fiennes's fault, declared Clement Walker and the even
more vitriolic William Prynne. The defeated governor's father,
Lord Saye, Walker announced, was 'a base beggarly lord; . . . his
sons were cowards, and he would maintain it with his blood, and
he would bastinado them if he could find them'. The Lords sentenced Walker to fine, damages, and imprisonment, provoking
him into making the remarkable claim that they had no right to
try a commoner. Released on bail, Walker joined Prynne in
presenting charges against Fiennes for his conduct at Bristol.
Fiennes was tried by court martial at St Albans and sentenced to
death; the Earl of Essex's pardon saved his life but not his military
reputation. Other Somerset leaders took sides: John Ashe and the
Horners for Fiennes, Strode bitterly against him. A duel between
Strode and one of the younger Horners was prevented only by

intervention from the House of Commons.[3]

The exiles might fight and argue, but most Somerset men submitted. Several parliamentary committeemen went over to the king. Richard Cole, Robert Harbin, and Henry Sanford all got pardons from Oxford early in 1644, while William Basset and William Bull became more active royalists, as did Harbin's son. Prominent men like Sir Thomas Bridges and John Symes of Poundisford, lesser men such as John Bourne and Thomas Warre, all of whom had paid contributions to parliament, also cooperated. They had not really changed sides. They were men who put the unity of their county above partisan considerations, who would take part in its government under any reasonable regime, if they could, rather than see it destroyed.

Below them the hitherto vaguely parliamentarian yeomen lapsed into apathetic neutrality. The royalists were in control, and all but their most determined enemies could see good reasons for acquiescing. Sometimes they wisely put on a show of enthusiasm. George Smith of Ilchester supported parliament at first, but then as constable took orders from the royalists, enlisted under the town's new governor, Edward Phelips, and denounced those who crossed him as 'roundheaded rogues'. Local officials could usually be brought to heel by the threat of military retaliation, and even Hopton was not above this sort of thing. When the mayor and constables of Wells arrested the postmaster (a client of Hopton's) for disorderly behaviour, they received word the very next day that a regiment of foot was on the way to be quartered in the city. Four Chard men were told to collect a rate for the king, Hopton and Hertford warning them that they would be imprisoned and tied 'head and heels together' if they refused. The county's acceptance of royalist rule was not won without effort.[4]

But for the most part the cavaliers were careful to observe legal forms. Although the king, like parliament, set up an emergency wartime administration, he also worked through the traditional local government system, by sheriffs and JPs. Edmund Wyndham was high sheriff in 1643, Sir Thomas Bridges in the following year. A new commission of the peace was sent from Oxford, addressed to forty loyal gentlemen: Pouletts, Berkeleys, Wyndhams, the accustomed leaders of the county. There are no surviving records of royalist Quarter Sessions, but it is likely that they were held much as usual. Among the JPs conducting routine business in 1644 were Sir Edward and Sir Henry Berkeley, Edward Phelips, Francis Wyndham, John Baber of Newton St Loe, and George Trevelyan of Nettlecombe: men from almost every quarter of the county. And the matters before them were of the familiar kind. Somerset men were spawning bastards, engaging in petty theft, and cheating each other at Axbridge fair as they had always done. In only one of the recorded cases is there an echo of the war: a soldier in Sir Francis Dodington's regiment was accused of wounding a Wincanton man for refusing to repair his carbine.[5]

When the Assizes were held at Wells in February 1644, however, the war dominated the public business. In the previous October a commission of oyer and terminer (the traditional form of commission for assizes) had been issued at Oxford, naming most of the royalist county magnates as members of the court. Lesser men were summoned as grand jurymen, 'under great penalty' if they refused, some of them later complained. A long list of parliamentarian leaders duly suffered indictment and conviction for treason, but all the accused had of course long since left the county.[6]

Such legal measures were mere formalities. The royalists' real problem was to extract the necessary requirements of men and money without confirming old suspicions that they were simply the obedient agents of a tyrannical king, interested only in bleeding the county white for his own purposes. A new administrative structure was foreshadowed on 10 July 1643, even before Waller's defeat, when Sheriff Wyndham, Lord Poulett, Stawell, Edward Phelips, and other leading gentlemen were appointed to seize and dispose of rebels' estates for the king's service. These became the king's county commissioners, the royalist equivalent of the committeemen who had governed the county for parliament. In October, before leaving for his new campaign against Waller in Hampshire and Sussex, Hopton gave the commissioners more specific instructions, including a general supervision over military and financial administration.[7] Gradually the commissioners acquired a corporate identity and eventually a clerk, the diocesan registrar Alexander Jett. There is, however, little surviving evidence to tell us much about either their system of administration or their efficiency.

As agents of the Court, the commissioners were bound to run into local opposition in both their financial and military capacities. A weekly contribution of £1,500 was imposed on Somerset after the fall of Bristol, its proceeds divided between the Bristol garrison and the king's forces in Devon; the sum was increased to £2,000 a week at the end of September. There were the inevitable complaints. 'We are squeezed like wax in our weekly payments, still mounting', a Bridgwater man grumbled.[8] Deductions were made for quartering royalist troops, but even with this allowance it is doubtful if Somerset ever paid anything like its full quota. Some of the money was raised in the form of forced loans payable to the sheriff, and the sequestration of roundhead estates also helped to swell the county's contribution. Sir John Horner was one of those who suffered, but the subsequent destruction of royalist records makes it impossible to guess how many others were involved. There must have been a rudimentary bureaucracy to administer the system, something like that afterwards established by the parliamentarians: a few traces survive of sequestrators, the paid agents who administered the estates.[9]

The military burden on the county was of two kinds: the regular forces in the garrisons, and the militia regiments officered by the local gentry. After Bristol was taken the Cornish army marched off under Maurice to clear Dorset for the king. Hopton was left with what he described as 'some ragged regiments to begin a garrison'. Recruiting from the countryside was fairly easy at first, 'men coming in freely to the new government'. But Hopton was constantly having to send reinforcements to the besiegers of Gloucester, and in October 1643 he began an extensive programme of impressment to recruit the army which he was to lead against Waller in Hampshire. Among the Somerset officers who went with him were Sir Edward Stawell (Sir John's son, newly knighted), and Sir John Poulett. Sporadic impressment continued throughout the winter. Like the parliamentarians before them, the royalists had troops to spare to help their neighbours. Robert Phelips took part in operations against Wardour Castle in the autumn of 1643, and in the following spring Hopton sent Sir Francis Dodington with a stronger force to press the siege. Aided by Mendip miners who blew up part of the defences, Dodington regained Wardour on 18 March.[10]

The militia regiments, composed of local men usually serving part-time, were obviously less expensive. Still, there was often no great enthusiasm on the part of gentlemen compelled to provide for them. Charles Steynings of Holnicote apologised to George Trevelyan because the man he sent him was not 'so well accommodated with military necessaries as 'tis fit he should be'. While amateur officers gravely discussed the most 'soldierlike' choice of colours for their troops, or argued with each other over the scope of their commissions, there was an undercurrent of reluctance to be overcome, even among the gentry.[11]

Even in this period of relative peace some parts of Somerset suffered from military incursions. Chard certainly did so, caught between the king's garrison at Taunton and parliament's at Lyme Regis. One Chard man complained that between them he was 'so plundered that he had scarce a bed left to lie upon'. Not all the trouble at Chard could be blamed on outsiders. Two young blades named Bragg and Bancroft raised a troop of horse which terrorised the roundheads of the neighbourhood, and provoked several visits by the forces from Lyme.[12] But the problems of the southern tip of the county were exceptional, as were those of the eastern border, exposed to occasional raids from Wiltshire by Edmund Ludlow and the Pophams. Most of Somerset was at peace until June 1644, and the financial and military burdens were not intolerable. As long as the county was governed by its own men without too much interference from outside, royalist rule was bearable.

But times were changing. Hertford, who for all his aristocratic indolence still had close territorial ties with the region, was superseded as lieutenant-general of the West in February 1644 by Prince Maurice, who was a professional soldier without local influence. And on 1 May the county commissioners lost much of their independence when they were brought more firmly under Maurice's control as part of a new Western Association, which also covered Dorset, Devon, and Cornwall. All men over sixteen were to take a protestation of loyalty to church and king; an army, of which Somerset's share was 9,000 men, was to be raised by impressment; Maurice himself was to appoint commissioners for musters; and the county commissioners' powers over contributions and sequestrations were carefully defined. The association was in some ways integrated with the old system of magistracy— orders were to be given by 'the general Sessions of the Peace, or other general meeting of the commissioners'—but the reorganisation was in every other respect a step towards centralisation and military rule. By mid-June the association's central committee was at work at Exeter, sending out orders and demands for money. The royalists, the roundhead Earl of Warwick warned from Weymouth, were compelling 'many of the country people' to enlist.[13]

The association thus threatened large-scale impressment of men and heavy increases of taxation: violations of 'Liberty and Property' of just the kind the freeholders had resisted in the 1630s and fought in 1642. Since Hopton's victories the Somerset yeomen had sensibly acquiesced in moderate government by their own gentry, men they knew. But roundheads or neutrals, few of them had been converted.

*   *   *   *

In June 1644 the Earl of Essex began his fatal march into the West. His initial objective—to raise the siege of Lyme—seems an absurdly insignificant reason for diverting parliament's main southern army so far west while Charles I was still strong at Oxford. But in fact Essex was not acting merely out of capricious folly, and there were more solid arguments for his strategy than have sometimes been supposed. Chief among them was the fear that if left to themselves Maurice and Hopton would use the Western Association to recruit a great new army for the king, and thus transform the military balance of the war. The western exiles urgently pressed for a quick riposte; they were seconded from Lyme by parliament's man on the spot, their naval commander Warwick. Beyond Lyme, therefore, lay Essex's real objective: to smash the Western Association before it became dangerous.

Essex's advance ended Somerset's period of tranquillity. The county became for the remainder of the war the scene of repeated invasions, and eventually a desperate, protracted battleground, with disastrous consequences for its inhabitants. Throughout these months of privation and bloodshed, royalists and parliamentarians eagerly competed for the allegiance of the Country.

Essex had the first chance. By 14 June Maurice had raised the siege of Lyme and was retreating by way of Chard to join Sir John Berkeley's forces at Exeter. Essex occupied Weymouth and Bridport and then also marched to Chard, where his army spent the last week of June. Both the general and his officers tried to remove parliament's doubts about the purpose of the operation. They had succeeded, they claimed, in stopping cavalier recruiting in Somerset and Dorset, and they had also aroused the old zeal for parliament. But loyalty to parliament, they accepted, was combined with strong localist feeling. Volunteers flocked into Chard in hundreds, but they wanted, Essex conceded, 'to serve under their own countrymen, and not be listed in my army'. There were 'multitudes of men', but they were unusable until 'the gentlemen who have the power over them' were sent to take command. Well-affected gentry and godly ministers should be sent down immediately. The trouble, as in 1642, was that there were not enough roundhead gentry who combined local prestige with military experience. The Pophams were busy in Wiltshire, and although Blake and Strode returned to Somerset during the summer, their influence could not compare with that of the royalist magnates. Essex's care in restraining his troops from plundering was popular with the common people, the royalist Sir Edward Walker noted, but did not win over the gentry.[14]

Essex's letters convinced parliament that it was essential to counter the royalists' Western Association by setting up a similar organisation of their own. The powers of the county committees were redefined, and on 19 August an ordinance created an association of the western counties from Wiltshire to Cornwall.[15] The disasters that befell Essex after he marched west from Chard made this for the present only a paper tiger. Indeed, the earl's incursion achieved only one real success: the capture of Taunton. After his retreat from Lyme Maurice had concentrated the Somerset garrisons at Bridgwater, leaving only eighty men in Taunton Castle. Essex sent Blake with a party of foot from Lyme, supported by some of his own horse under Sir Robert Pye, to besiege the castle, which was held by Stawell's deputy governor, Sergeant-Major Reeve. For a week the little garrison held out, but on 10 July Reeve marched away to Bridgwater. He was court-martialled and sentenced to death, but escaped and joined the enemy.[16]

By now the king himself was in hot pursuit of Essex. Charles left Evesham on 12 July and on the 15th he entered Bath in state. Two days later he moved on to Sir John Horner's manor house at Mells, enjoying the enforced hospitality of a sequestered enemy.[17] The only activity when he arrived was on the Wiltshire border. Ludlow and the Pophams had established several round-head garrisons there, including a small one at Woodhouse, a mile or so from Longleat. Hopton had responded by garrisoning his house at Witham and recruiting forces in the district towards Evercreech. Early in July he sent Sir Francis Dodington against Woodhouse with a strong force from Bristol. Ludlow and the Pophams approached with a smaller relieving party, but were badly beaten by Dodington near Warminster and fled back to Salisbury in disorder.[18]

After his arrival at Bath the king sent Dodington further reinforcements of foot and two guns. Woodhouse contained less than a hundred men under a Warminster watchmaker named Wansey—'a person of equal quality with many of the rebels' officers', Sir Edward Walker revealingly comments— and its days were numbered. On the 19th the place was taken. Twenty of the defenders were killed in the assault, and Dodington had hanged another fourteen before the disgusted Hopton put a stop to it. Before the executions Sir Francis is said to have assaulted one of the victims, striking him 'so many blows upon the head, and with such force', says Ludlow, 'that he broke his skull, and caused him to fall into a swoon'. Dodington's excuse was that the men were royalist deserters and that he was merely retaliating for the hanging of six Irish prisoners by the roundheads at Wareham not long before. But there is no doubt that Dodington was violent and vindictive. He had hanged prisoners after the fall of Wardour Castle, and he was the subject of other atrocity stories. 'Who art thou for, priest?' he bellowed at a passing minister on the highway near Taunton. 'For God and his gospel', the cleric replied, whereupon Dodington shot him dead.[19]

On the day Woodhouse fell, the king's army rendezvoused near Nunney and Charles moved from Mells to Sir Charles Berkeley's house at Bruton. During the march, says the royalist officer Richard Symonds, 'abundance of the Country came to see the king, which was rare before'. Charles then advanced to Ilchester, still attracting great crowds; the town, a local gentleman noted, was 'full of varlets'.[20] A serious attempt to raise the Country for the royalists was now to be made; warrants were sent out summoning a general meeting on the nearby King's Moor.

On 23 July the countrymen streamed into the moor from all parts. The king's arrival was greeted with 'general shouts and acclamations', and he was followed by large throngs wherever he went, more out of curiosity than affection, Sir Edward Walker suspected, 'for a king had not been seen in many years before in that county'. In a speech read for him in various parts of the field, Charles said that he had come to Somerset to relieve the inhabitants 'from the violence of a rebellious army'. All he wanted was peace and the settlement of disputed issues in a free parliament. He called for support against the Scots, whose recent entry into the war had transformed the military balance in the North and made possible the great parliamentarian victory at Marston Moor. To beat the Scots and the English rebels he needed his people's 'hearts, and hands, and purses'. Volunteers would soon be released to return to the harvest; in the meantime the high sheriff and county commissioners were to collect necessary supplies, and thus reduce the danger of plundering by the soldiers.[21]

The king's speech was carefully designed to appeal to local sentiment. It was followed by a proclamation calling on the men of the eastern division of the county to enlist under Sir Edward Rodney, those of the western under Sir John Stawell. A thousand men already listed under Rodney came forward. The rest of the great crowd, 'having seen their sight', says Walker, went home again. When Stawell tried to implement the proclamation in a western division meeting at Bridgwater a week later, the outcome was no better. There was a large attendance, but Stawell found them 'very unapt to engage themselves'. Even the gentry were apathetic, though in the end they reluctantly agreed to raise 2,000 men and £2,000 in contribution-money.[22]

Reinforced only by Rodney's 1,000 and by 800 foot from Bristol, Charles left Ilchester on 24 July. He spent the night at the house of the Catholic Sir Robert Brett at Whitestaunton, and the next day his army marched from Chard into Devonshire and onward to deal with Essex. Although he had not succeeded in raising the Country, Charles did instil some energy into the Western Association. At Exeter he was met by Lord Poulett and other commissioners, who made elaborate plans for provisioning the army as it advanced westward. 'Large proportions of victuals' were to be raised in Somerset; a brigade of horse was stationed at Chard to secure the commissioners from interruption by the enemy at Lyme and no doubt to make their arguments with the local population more persuasive. During his march the king had sent out warrants imposing special levies. Wells was charged with £500 on 18 July and received another demand for money for horseshoes three days later.[23] The commissioners would ensure that these were more than occasional exactions. And those who escaped them were likely to receive similar demands from parliament's garrisons at Lyme and Taunton.

While the king tightened the noose around Essex at Lostwithiel, Somerset, though well to the rear, was nevertheless in a state of turmoil. The commissioners gathered quantities of provisions, but their proceedings were interrupted in August by 2,000 parliamentarian horse and dragoons under the Scot, Lt-Gen John Middleton. This new force had been hastily sent from Hampshire to take some of the pressure off Essex, and to harass royalist supply-lines and recruiting. Middleton was soon adding to the demands on the county: the citizens of Wells were called on for sixty horses or their equivalent on 16 August, for another £500 a week later. Vainly they protested that they were ruined and that 'divers of the chief inhabitants... are now gone from the town'. The royalists sent their supplies, with Dodington in charge, to the shelter of the Bridgwater garrison. In the early morning of 14 August 500 of Middleton's horse fell on the convoy at North Petherton. At first the parliamentarians did well, capturing several of the waggons, but reinforcements from Bridgwater came to Dodington's aid; the roundheads were driven off and the waggons recovered.[24]

Middleton withdrew to Ilchester. He was reluctant to advance into Devonshire because of the danger that in his absence the Somerset royalists would raise yet more men and money. Dodington was now in the western part of the county recruiting his regiment—evidently with some success, because at the end of the month he advanced from Minehead into north Devon with 1,000 horse, and on 13 September he took Ilfracombe. Meanwhile there was skirmishing on other borders of the county. At sunset on 4 September Col Edward Massey appeared before Bath with a small party from Gloucester, but decided not to attack when he heard of threatening royalist movements in his rear. Ludlow's Wiltshire forces took Stourton in a night attack and then forced the Witham garrison to surrender. Nearly a hundred of Hopton's cattle in the park, Ludlow recalls, 'served for the payment of my soldiers'. A few days later the survivors of Essex's horse, who had slipped away from Lostwithiel by night before the foot capitulated, straggled dejectedly through the county. Some of them made contact with Middleton's brigade near Taunton, and both parties then turned south-east, towards Sherborne and Dorchester. On the way, in the bitter frustration of defeat, they smashed windows and monuments and destroyed the organ in South Petherton church. 'Rude and most ungodly', the royalist Sir Humphrey Mildmay thought them, a menace to all men of property. Visibly, as well as economically and politically, the county was being ruined by the war.[25]

* * * *

In the evening of 23 September the vanguard of Charles I's victorious army again entered Somerset, on the return march from Cornwall. For a week they quartered, some 10,000 strong, at Chard and in the villages to the east. Richard Symonds, billeted at South Petherton, spent the time studying the nearby village churches, regretfully observing the damage inflicted by Essex's horse. The county enjoyed the situation less than did the visitors. Fresh burdens were being imposed: the commissioners were told to raise another £3,000 plus clothing for 3,000 soldiers. Quartering produced the usual complaints. 'You old rogue, do you give us your hog's wash?—we will have roast meat', a cavalier quartermaster roared at one old man who had meekly shared his boiled meat and broth with the unwanted guests. Some people suffered more than abuse. Henry Hodges of Haselbury, one of the ship money sheriffs, was murdered and his cattle and goods stolen by 'lewd persons pretending to belong to his majesty's army'.[26]

While his army rested, the king made some necessary military dispositions. Forces had already been assigned to block up Lyme and Taunton. Maurice had threatened Taunton with a party of horse a few days earlier, but found Blake too strong to be challenged. Taunton would have to be besieged. Command over the siege was given to Edmund Wyndham: his Bridgwater forces were joined by Rodney's local foot regiment and men from Francis Wyndham's garrison at Dunster. Charles's real plan may have been to go into winter quarters at Oxford; however, parliament sensibly took seriously his announced intention of exploiting his recent victories by advancing on London. Waller and Haselrig were therefore sent to delay the king's advance while Essex's army was rebuilt. By the end of September Waller's force was at Shaftesbury, and forward patrols of the two armies were occasionally skirmishing in the Yeovil area. At last on 30 September the king left Chard, and after dining with Lord Poulett at Hinton advanced into Dorset towards Waller and Haselrig, who withdrew before him.[27]

As he left Somerset, the king made another attempt to raise the Country. A proclamation again stressed the king's desire for peace, and defended the advance on London as a means to persuade parliament to come to an accommodation. Loyal subjects living near the army's route were to arm themselves and accompany him; Charles promised them their own gentry as commanders. The proclamation was read, a parliamentarian sneered, only at 'the high cross of two or three market towns in Somersetshire, before some petty country audience assembled about the more weighty affairs of eggs and butter'.[28] But though it may not have inspired a great wave of new recruits, some of the Somerset gentry took the proclamation seriously. Sir John Stawell in particular seems to have read aright the lessons of the previous July. The king could only succeed, Stawell thought, if he appropriated the Country position more convincingly than heretofore, and enabled the royalist gentry to regain the confidence of the freeholders. The way to do it, he argued, was to launch a vast new propaganda campaign, stressing more firmly than ever that on the king's side lay the cause of peace, and to rely on war-weariness to ignite a great grassfire of royalism among the common people.

A petition was quickly circulated in Somerset and presented to Charles at Sturminster Newton. In language echoing the recent proclamation, the petitioners asked for permission to march with the king towards London; 'at a nearer distance of place' they would petition parliament to accept the royalist peace offers. On 14 October there was a public meeting at Wells to chart the next step. The petition to parliament was drafted, calling on the Houses to forget imaginary fears of popery and arbitrary government and join the king in making peace. And a declaration was adopted, announcing that anyone who opposed the forthcoming march would be proceeded against as 'an enemy to peace'. The war was to be ended by a quick victory for the king, but the appeal was to men who were tired of fighting, to all 'who have any bowels left towards their bleeding country, any sense of pity and desire of peace, or weariness of war'.[29]

To combine an ostensible call for peace with a demand for a military solution is a common technique of war propaganda. Stawell was sincere enough, but the king and his officers wanted victory before negotiations. The peace campaign, indeed, was used to justify yet more military pressure. In his answer to the petitioners at Sturminster Newton Charles gave the sheriff and county commissioners power to summon the inhabitants as a *posse comitatus*. This could be interpreted as authority for a general impressment; a roundhead pamphlet reports that as a result many people 'were fain to fly from their dwellings'.[30] Stawell had learnt the lesson, but the king had not. Once again the royalist gentry failed to regain the willing co-operation of the freeholders.

The king departed eastwards with few recruits. The left wing of his army, Maurice's horse, had reached Wincanton by 8 October. Rupert and Hopton were at Bristol raising more men, but had made little progress by the time Charles suffered inconclusive defeat at Newbury on the 27th. After the battle the main royalist army retreated to Oxford, but the king himself returned briefly to Somerset, riding through the night and reaching Bath on the afternoon of the 28th. Two days later he set off to Oxford, leaving Somerset for the last time.[31]

The county's chief military concern in the autumn of 1644 was the siege of Taunton, where Blake remained vigilantly on guard against Wyndham's forces. The town was not well fortified: Sir Anthony Ashley Cooper reported the defences as 'but pales and hedges and no line about the town'. But the spirit of the Taunton men burnt high, and in a godly covenant they swore never to surrender. Cannon were brought from Bridgwater and Exeter, but two attempts to storm were beaten back. Wyndham abandoned the close siege and placed his troops 'round about the town at a mile or two distance'.[32] Early in November Blake offered to give up the town but not the castle; Wyndham rejected this unless the castle was included, relying on the presence of starving civilians to generate pressure for a total surrender. Blake had to dip into his precious supplies, but still he held out, aided by frequent sallies in which the garrison somehow extracted provisions from the denuded countryside.

At last parliament acted. Sir William Waller, striving to reduce a weak and mutinous army at Newbury to order, was told to detach 1,000 horse for the relief of Taunton. 'Under a persecution from the perpetual clamour in the West', he collected half that number, who were sent off under the command of Maj-Gen James Holborne. Forces from Dorset under Ashley Cooper and from Wiltshire under Ludlow were added to Holborne's cavalry, and on 9 December the relief party entered the county. The royalists raised the siege and also abandoned Wellington; on the 14th Taunton was relieved. The castle was still well supplied, but Cooper thought it a miracle that the town had held out. 'Like the burning bush amidst a country full of fiery flaming swords': so the preacher John Bond witnessed to Taunton's fame as the western bastion of puritanism.[33]

Waller and Haselrig thought that north Somerset still contained 'as fruitful parts as are in England to quarter in'. But in the southern and western parishes a trail of ruined villages and gutted mansions proclaimed the desolation of war. 'Alas, poor helpless, and almost hopeless West', sighed Bond as he appealed to London citizens to contribute to a relief fund.[34] Already the royalists were finding it difficult to raise money and provisions. The supplies ordered in September were still not collected months later. In December the royalist commissioners, in session at the *Crown* at Wells, were still bullying the city to produce the rest of the 500 pairs of shoes and stockings which the mayor, a shoe-maker named Richard Casbeard with a sharp eye for a war contract, had agreed to provide if he was reimbursed by the corporation. Nor had the citizens been any less obstructive when the king's excise officers came to raise money that same autumn. After consulting the county commissioners, Casbeard refused to publish the proclamation; while one of the alderman declared, the officers complained, 'that he would pay no excise, and another, that we came to rob and devour the people'. Two of the excise commissioners, George Trevelyan and John Bourne, had already refused to serve, and the county commissioners, led by Edward Kirton, would do nothing to help the officers. Resistance to centralisation and war taxation was beginning to infect even the royalist gentry.[35]

As the realisation spread that they had failed to regain the Country, doubt and demoralisation increased among the royalist leaders. Personal jealousies and angry rivalries erupted. There had already been signs of this when the king was at Chard. Edmund Wyndham refused to serve under Hopton, who had 'disobliged' him, but was given command over the Taunton siege in preference to Hopton's nominee, the ill-tempered Dodington. The 'divisions and factions' of the Somerset cavaliers, says Clarendon, greatly hampered them during the siege.[36]

Hopton was sent to compose matters after the siege was raised. His arrival did not help. He now held a commission as field-marshal of the West, which included command over all the Somerset forces; but inevitably he saw their role in a wider context than Wyndham, whose horizon was bounded by Taunton and Bridgwater. Wyndham protested indignantly to Rupert. Until Hopton's return, he complained, he had been 'absolute master of the field', with command over 4,000 men—enough to have driven the roundheads out of Somerset. He did not explain his failure to take Taunton, and indeed after its relief his generalship was fumbling and ineffective. He initially withdrew to Chard, where he could keep an eye on the parliamentarians at both Lyme and Taunton. There was some skirmishing with the Taunton garrison; early in 1645 some of Holborne's cavalry raided Col Amyas Poulett's quarters at Ilminster, taking prisoners and 150 horses. After the row over the command Wyndham's forces dispersed. The Devon contingent went home when Hopton arrested one of their commanders. Others marched away to Langport, where Hopton established a garrison under a newcomer to the county, Sir Francis Mackworth. Fuming at Hopton's 'impossible projects', Wyndham returned angrily to Bridgwater. Hopton began a new, energetic round of impressment, but by now reinforcements had reached Holborne at Taunton: another detachment of Waller's army under the German professional, Col Vandruske.[37]

It was time for the royalists to make a fresh start. Early in March 1645 the young Prince of Wales was sent to Bristol with a council of his own and a commission as general of the Western Association. The fourteen-year-old prince was too young to exercise authority; the object, as his father put it, was to 'unboy him'.[38] But the presence of such responsible men as Hopton and Sir Edward Hyde among his advisers gave some hope that the king's affairs in the West might now receive more purposive and intelligent direction. Unfortunately for the prince, and for Somer-

William Strode of Barrington

Robert Blake

set, his arrival in the West coincided with that of General George Goring.

Notes to this chapter are on pages 202-4.

F

5
The Battleground
March-July 1645

The war's miseries seemed endless. For month after weary month the armies fought and foraged, pillaged and plundered, reducing a fruitful countryside to ruin and desolation. To most people the issues in dispute lost whatever relevance they had ever had, taking second place to the preservation of hearth and home. The real enemy was the plunderer; the commander who kept his men under control and paid for their quarters could be tolerated, perhaps even helped. All over southern England in the spring of 1645 the apathetic neutralism of farmers and men of modest property flamed into resistance. First came isolated, sporadic attacks on soldiers of either side. Then came a second stage: organisation in a mass movement. 'Peace-keeping associations' appeared in many counties, whose members came to be called clubmen, for the weapons they used. Royalists and roundheads alike competed for their allegiance, and strove to disperse them if they could not obtain it. Although in Dorset and Wiltshire the clubmen tended to be better disposed to the king than to parliament, most of their Somerset counterparts in the end took the opposite position. The Somerset yeomen, as we have seen, could acquiesce in royal government if it followed accustomed paths of legality and avoided undue taxation; but of those who had any clear political views, a majority had always favoured the cause of 'Liberty and Property'. A more immediate reason for Somerset's distinctive behaviour was the outrageous conduct of the king's troops in the county, especially those under Goring.

When Prince Charles arrived at Bath on 6 March the clubmen were still in the future. The royalists' immediate problems sprang from the growing factionalism of the local gentry and the rivalries of competing commanders. Apart from the region around Taunton, where Holborne and Blake held sway, the cavaliers nominally controlled the entire county. But Wyndham was still sulking at Bridgwater; Sir Francis Mackworth, Hopton's man at Langport, was disliked as an outsider; and the county commissioners were showing no inclination to raise either men or money. Worst of all Goring's army, unpaid and out of control, had been moving west through Wiltshire and Dorset. Early in March they entered Somerset and established themselves near Chard and Crewkerne, still committing 'horrid outrages and barbarities'.[1] No one wanted Goring, but he had an army of 4,500 men. To avoid trouble, and hoping to control the intruding general by diplomacy, the prince's council decided not to insist on Hopton's superior authority.

Lord Goring, as he had become by the promotion of his father to the earldom of Norwich, was a man remarkable for both his talents and his excesses. On occasion a brilliant cavalry officer, as he had shown at Marston Moor, and possessing a military genius that produced intermittent bursts of strategic originality, he was nevertheless a disaster to the cause he served. Ambitious and irresponsible, Goring was determined to be the king's chief commander in the West, and cared little how he achieved that goal. Whatever abilities he displayed, controlling his men and winning the confidence of the countrymen among whom they operated were not among them. His own drinking-bouts were legendary, and his staff joined in what one of his officers called 'strange debauches'. His soldiers' 'continual butcheries, rapes and robberies' implanted their memory deeply in the county's consciousness. 'The name of Goring's Crew is even now remembered with abhorrence', the Bridgwater historian John Oldmixon declared almost a century later.[2]

Throughout the early spring the armies continued their ruinous manoeuvres. Holborne tried, at first successfully, to gain 'enlarged quarters' around Taunton—a wider area from which he could draw provisions. Royalist forces moved from Bristol and Bridgwater towards Taunton, to block up the town again, and at Wells on 24 March emissaries from the prince's council tried to persuade Goring to commit his army to the siege. Goring agreed to send his infantry and artillery; they were to be joined before Taunton by forces from Devon and Cornwall under Sir Richard Grenville.

A
COPIE OF THE

Kings Meſſage ſent by the Duke of *Lenox*.

Alſo the Copie of a Petition to the King from the Inhabitants of *Somerſetſhire*, to come with him to the Parliament.

A Declaration by the Committee of Dorſetſhire, againſt the Cavaliers in thoſe parts ; declaring how ſixe French Papiſts raviſhed a woman one after another: She having been but three dayes before
delivered out of Child-bed.

Alſo, how a Gentleman at Oxford was cruelly tortured in Irons, and
for what they were ſo cruell towards him.

And how they would have burnt down an Ale-houſe at the Briil , be-
cauſe the woman refuſed Farthing tokens ; And other cruelties of the
Cavaliers, manifeſted to the Kingdome.

Publiſſhed according to Order of Parliament.
LONDON, Printed by *Iane Coe.* 1 6 4 4.

A roundhead propaganda tract

The bulk of Goring's horse would remain on the Wiltshire and Dorset borders, to cover possible thrusts by Waller and Oliver Cromwell, who had come into the West with a makeshift army. Grenville was at Chard with 3,000 men by the 27th, but Holborne eluded him. Leaving Blake to hold Taunton with a substantial garrison, Holborne marched south with his main force to Axminster, skirmishing with Grenville as he went, then east through Dorset to join Cromwell and Waller near Cerne Abbas. This convinced Goring that the Taunton project ought to be suspended until the roundhead concentration had been dispersed by his and Grenville's combined armies. Sir Richard, however, was as awkwardly independent as Goring himself and refused to co-operate on the ground that his men had been promised that they would not be employed so far east. Early in April he sat down before Taunton.[3]

By this time Goring had moved to the Bruton area where, it was noted, 'the villages were thick, and great store of forage for horse'—good country for plunder, in other words. Waller was at Salisbury, with his forces strung out towards the Somerset border, in more sparsely populated country. Several times Goring's patrols beat up their quarters in night attacks, taking prisoners and doing other damage; Sir John Digby led a particularly successful raid at Cucklington, near Wincanton. Eventually Waller and Cromwell were stung into action and sent 2,000 horse and dragoons in small groups into the enclosed region around Bruton, forcing Goring to retreat towards Glastonbury and Wells. But neither side had foot enough to risk a battle in the lanes and hedges. Goring soon returned to Bruton, Cromwell's men to Salisbury.[4]

The countrymen suffered heavily from both sides. A Somerset ballad well expresses their plight:

> I'ze had zix oxen tother day
> and them the roundheads stole away,
>   a mischief be their speed.
> I had six horses left me whole
> and them the cavaliers have stole,
>   God zores they are both agreed.[5]

But, horses or oxen, the royalists were worse. Goring and Grenville took free quarter and competed for contributions with the Bridgwater and Langport garrisons. Besides supporting Mackworth's troops, the inhabitants of Langport were also having to produce food for Grenville's commissary to take to the leaguer at Taunton. Lympsham was having to find over £7 a day as 'pay to the Lord Goring'—an enormous sum for a single village. Even royalist sympathisers were being alienated. At Queen Camel Sir Humphrey Mildmay was several times plundered, 'abused by knaves', and his house virtually ruined. Soon after his arrival before Taunton Grenville arbitrarily imposed a fine of £1,000 on John Symes of Poundisford, one of the most experienced and respected of the king's JPs. Sir Ferdinando Gorges encouraged the constable of Long Ashton to organise the villagers against attempts to collect assessments for the Bristol garrison.[6]

Events in the villages near Brent Knoll in the fortnight before Easter provide a good example of the state of affairs in the county. Troops from Col John Tynte's regiment of horse had been quartered at South Brent (the village of Brent Knoll as it is now called) earlier in March. On the 24th they came back in larger numbers. Riding down from Bristol, they passed through Axbridge during the fair. After being abused by bystanders in the village street, one of them drew his sword against a Cheddar man, who defended himself with a staff, broke the soldier's sword, but was then beaten over the head 'very dangerously'. Order having been restored, the soldiers continued on their violence-strewn way. They robbed a butcher on his way home from the fair and killed a poor labourer they encountered on the highway. When they reached South Brent, a reign of terror began. Among other misdeeds they seized a 'fat bullock' a farmer had bought at the fair, savagely beat the servant who allowed the owner to recover it, put a rope round his neck and threatened to hang him unless they were given money. The South Brent tithingman did his best to satisfy them, but they searched his house and promised to 'tie him neck and heels together' if he did not bring more the next day. At Lympsham they told the villagers to 'lie upon straw: ... the soldiers should lie in their beds'. At Berrow they wrecked William Lush's house, took clothing and bedding, and when the poor man protested, told him that they would burn the house and kill his wife if he did not keep quiet. Others 'with execrable oaths' swore that they would burn the whole village if the inhabitants did not co-operate.[7]

John Tynte, the nominal commander of these bullying thugs,

was a local gentleman from Chelvey, near Nailsea. But he was not present at South Brent, and most of the regiment were outsiders, some of them Irish.[8] This may not have made much difference, for his own kinsman, Lt Henry Tynte, exhibited a flagrant contempt for the villagers: 'the Country were fools, and ... good for nothing but to be made idiots'. When at last orders came from Hopton for the regiment to march away and join Goring, they refused to move until the villages produced yet more tribute. It was the last straw. The lead was taken by John Somerset, a popular and amiable gentleman from South Brent, whose very name was a telling symbol of resistance. With his encouragement, the villagers of the entire region took up arms—pikes, staves, and muskets—and attacked the soldiers on Good Friday, 4 April. No one seems to have been killed, but several troopers were wounded. An officer, 'shot through the thigh with one musket shot and seven smaller shot', came beating on Thomas Gilling's door for shelter against the mob. Gilling (a friend of Somerset's) kept the door locked and shouted 'begone, begone'. The ringleaders were not roundheads: John Somerset had served as a captain under Edmund Wyndham.[9] This was a spontaneous village rising—a rising of the Country—against plunderers. There were, almost certainly, other such episodes in Somerset at about this time which lie unrecorded.[10] They were a natural preliminary to wider combinations for similar ends.

Retribution was not long delayed. Gilling and John Somerset were imprisoned at Bristol. The county commissioners were sympathetic, but even after a gift of partridges to Wyndham it was weeks before they got out on bail. More troops came from Bristol to levy fines of £30 each on the offending villages, and after their release Somerset and Gilling were still 'daily prejudiced and infested with unruly soldiers'. The four villages of South Brent, Berrow, Burnham, and Lympsham claimed to have suffered over £600 damages in the whole affair, quite apart from what they were having to pay to Goring.

Some of the local leaders, Sir John Stawell foremost among them, realised that this was no way to recover the trust of the Country. When the idea of sending the prince to Bristol had first been discussed, Stawell had gone to Oxford with a delegation from the western counties. The prince, Stawell urged, should rely on the freeholders' longing for peace, and stimulate another

popular movement for the king as peacemaker on the lines of the
one attempted in October 1644. Once again the counties would
send a peace petition to parliament; 'many thousands of the most
substantial freeholders' would accompany it to London, united
under the slogan 'One and All'. Stawell's naive reliance on the
Country was received with polite scepticism, but the king could
not actively discourage him, especially in view of the delegation's
offer to raise money and a guard for the prince's person. Peace
negotiations between king and parliament at Uxbridge in February soon made the 'One and All' scheme less pressing, but Stawell
and his friends did little to implement their promises of men and
money. When the Somerset commissioners met the prince at
Bristol on 11 March they showed no interest in making a new
military effort and instead insisted on discussing the county's
grievances. There was a chorus of indignation against the Bridgwater and Sherborne garrisons for conscripting the populace to
work on their fortifications, and the usual complaints about the
'riots and insolences' of Goring's men.[11]

It was obvious that even the gentry were losing their enthusiasm for the royal cause. In the weeks that followed no progress
was made towards forming Stawell's popular association, and the
project, Clarendon says, served only to 'cross and oppose all other
attempts whatsoever'. Nothing, the prince's council concluded,
could be expected from the 'flatness, peremptoriness, and un-
activity of the gentlemen of Somerset; . . . till . . . that county could
be driven and compelled to do what was necessary'. Driving and
compelling, however, was not the way to placate the gentry and
freeholders. In a meeting between the prince and the Western
Association leaders at Bridgwater on 23 and 24 April the whole
course of royalist policy was discussed at length. Stawell was still
fervently committed to the 'One and All' plan. But he was outmanoeuvred and reduced to a minority of one, the other commissioners all admitting that until Taunton was taken there could
be no relaxing the military pressure. The association agreed to
raise a new army immediately, to be levied in the counties 'according to their several known proportions'. The national viewpoint
of the prince's council had prevailed over Stawell's Country
position. Instead of an appeal to the people, Somerset would face
more taxation, impressment, and outrages from Goring's crew.[12]

*   *   *   *

By now the siege of Taunton was in full swing. Grenville at first copied Wyndham's tactics of the previous autumn, blocking up the town from a distance and clearing the district of provisions. But Blake had been building up his supplies in preparation: in March, for example, men of Edward Popham's regiment seized 100 sheep and fourteen cattle belonging to the royalist George Trevelyan at Nettlecombe.[13] Two half-hearted attempts to storm were repulsed with loss, the garrison having by now dug in behind a strong line of earthworks. On 10 April Grenville moved in closer and the real siege began, with the cavaliers in turn building entrenchments from which to pour musket and cannon fire into the town. The royalists were still hampered, however, by their generals' rivalries. The prince's council ordered Goring to implement the original plan of sending his foot and guns to Grenville, while he covered them from the Wiltshire border with the horse. Goring complied to the extent of sending his infantry to Taunton, but he himself retired petulantly to Bath, peeved at not being given command over the siege. Then, after Grenville was wounded in an attack on Wellington House, which the Pophams had garrisoned, the command was given to Sir John Berkeley. Grenville went to Exeter to recover, but took care to prejudice his officers against Berkeley before he left.

While the royalists bickered and alienated the Country by their excesses, parliament had been making preparations for Taunton's relief. The ineffective campaign in Wiltshire by Waller and Cromwell in March had been only a holding operation to contain Goring while a great new army, the New Model, was mustered under Sir Thomas Fairfax. The feebleness of the half-hearted aristocratic generals—Essex, Manchester, Denbigh—under whom the parliamentarian armies had floundered in the previous year, had led in the winter of 1644-5 to the passage of the Self-Denying and New Model Ordinances. At last parliament had an effective army under a resolute general, supported by a proper establishment for regular pay. The New Model's fighting qualities were unknown, but were soon to be proved triumphantly. Fairfax's first task was the relief of Taunton. Waller's eastward retreat in April, Blake was told, was 'in no sort to desert you, but that there may be a speedy and more effectual relief sent unto you'.[14]

Fairfax left Windsor for the West on 30 April. By this time Blake was in serious trouble. A probing attack had been repulsed on the 25th, but Goring had at last been given the command and was investing Taunton with 8,000 men (some of them admittedly unreliable local levies). Just as Fairfax began his march, Goring was ordered to take his horse to Oxford and join the king, who was planning to combine with Rupert for a new northern campaign. For once Goring obeyed immediately: the absence of his cavalry made it impossible for the royalists to intercept the relief force as it approached. By 7 May Fairfax was at Blandford. He was then told to bring his main force back towards Oxford because of Charles I's threatening movements, and to detach only a brigade under Col Ralph Weldon to Taunton. Supplemented by various horse regiments and by foot from Lyme, Weldon's force amounted to about 6,000 men. Events now moved quickly to a dramatic climax.

Hopton, who had taken over from Goring, had been surprised by the speed of the New Model's advance, and heard nothing of it until Fairfax was at Salisbury. On the morning of the 8th Fairfax left Blandford and at first continued a westward march, confirming Hopton's impression that he was to be opposed by the whole New Model. But it was a clever feint: Fairfax soon turned east again, while Weldon continued towards Taunton, and news of Fairfax's later movement did not reach Hopton until the next day. By now Taunton was suffering terribly from Hopton's artillery. On 6 May the royalists had attacked on the east side, capturing an outwork known as the Vicar's House. The next day they attempted a bastion outside the east gate, but after a fierce bombardment were driven back by musket fire, stones, and boiling water. On the 8th Hopton fruitlessly tried deception: a sham fight between two royalist parties firing blanks, intended to lure Blake into a sortie in the hope that the relief force was at hand. News then arrived that Fairfax had left Blandford, and it was decided to make one last effort to storm and burn the town. At seven that evening a general assault began. The royalists were beaten back at the west gate, but on the other side Blake's men were driven from their entrenchments and part of the town, East Reach, was taken. An attempt to start a fire that would burn the whole town failed, however, through an adverse change of wind.

On Friday the 9th the cavaliers were encouraged by news that Fairfax's main force had turned east, and that Goring was on his way back from Oxford. Again they attacked, fighting their way through barricaded streets against desperate, house-to-house resistance. By evening half the town was on fire; the defenders held only the castle, St Mary Magdalen church, 'Muyden's fort', and an entrenchment in the market place. That same day Weldon's brigade had reached Chard, sending word to Blake that they would fire ten cannon shots to signal their approach. Slowly, too slowly, they advanced through the narrow lanes towards Pitminster, with the flames of Taunton beating against the night sky. On Saturday morning royalist agents made a last unsuccessful attempt to fire the small part of the town that still held out. Three of them were caught and lynched; one, a woman, by the women of Taunton. Hopton sent in a final call to surrender, to receive Blake's famous reply that he would eat three of his last four pairs of boots first. In the afternoon Weldon's advance guard reached Orchard Portman, surprising a royalist outpost, while Blake, who had never faltered in his belief that the Lord of Hosts was with him, observed them from afar. Salvation had come. By four o'clock the royalists had raised the siege and were retreating, felling trees across the roads to hamper Weldon's pursuit.

On Sunday 11 May, a day long kept in the town as a day of thanksgiving, Weldon entered Taunton. It was an awesome scene: 'heaps of rubbish ... consumed houses ... here a poor forsaken chimney, and there a little fragment of a wall'. Two-thirds of the houses had been destroyed and the rest stripped of thatch to feed horses; more than a hundred of the defenders had been killed, twice that number lay wounded. But Taunton had come through the fire, and the men of nearby villages who had left their homes during the days of terror came out of hiding and gazed in wonder. As the eminent local puritan George Newton proclaimed in his 11 May sermon a year later, it was 'a day of gladness: ... The God of Heaven shewed himself for Taunton this same day'.[15]

*   *   *   *

Blake's resolute resistance was a crucial factor in the outcome of the Civil War in Somerset. By tying down much larger royalist forces for several months, Taunton forced the cavaliers into the unpopular position of living off the country. And at the end of it the successive efforts of Grenville, Berkeley, Goring, and Hopton had all been defeated: psychologically even more than militarily the relief of Taunton was a roundhead triumph. Weldon's timely arrival, to be sure, did not mean that the parliamentarians had won the county. Their forces could operate towards the Blackdowns and the Dorset border, but Taunton was all they held securely. Goring, moreover, arrived back from Oxford, joyfully waving the independent command he had so long coveted, on the very day of Weldon's entry into Taunton. Weeks of hard fighting lay ahead, during which Goring's troops completed the transformation of an angry, riotous peasantry into purposefully organised groups of clubmen.

Goring was now in effect general of the king's forces in the West, subject to the advice but not the orders of the prince's council, and with full powers except that he could not grant commissions to officers of the Western Association. But the association was a broken reed. Scarcely a man had been raised of the new army promised at Bridgwater. Impressment was arousing open resistance: in several places conscripts were 'rescued by force'. If the gentry did not provide an army they could control, Goring would provide one they could not. For a time his warm geniality won some converts and enabled him to build up a faction among the commissioners. There were plenty of people, like the Wyndhams at Bridgwater, who were jealous of Hopton's authority and willing to listen to Goring's assurances about maintaining discipline and curbing the demands of the garrisons.[16] Such illusions were quickly dispelled.

Goring's return had temporarily restored the advantage to the royalists. On 17 May his army rendezvoused, 8,000 strong, on King's Moor near Ilchester. Weldon, with a much smaller force, was a few miles away at Martock. He had emerged from Taunton, leaving an augmented garrison behind, with the dual object of observing Goring's movements and avoiding being confined in an area already stripped of provisions. Now, in danger of being trapped, Weldon retreated towards Ilminster. Confidently the royalists moved in pursuit. Weldon ought to have been destroyed, but thanks to Goring's mismanagement the chase ended only in comedy and frustration.

On 19 May Goring's army came marching down the Fosse Way from Ilchester. Weldon had broken down Petherton Bridge, leaving a rearguard to harass royalist repair work. Goring promptly detached 1,000 horse and dragoons under Sir William Courtenay to cross the Parrett a few miles further south, at Merriott, and take Weldon in the flank while the bridge was repaired. After some evening skirmishing, Weldon's rearguard withdrew under cover of darkness, and not until dawn did Goring detect their departure. The royalists patched up the bridge and crossed the river, Goring leading the advance with his own brigade of horse and the 'Irish tertia'. But his orders must have been unusually incoherent, for the remaining regiments marched south towards Crewkerne instead of following their general to Ilminster. Near Crewkerne they encountered what they took to be part of Weldon's force, and there was a brisk and bloody conflict for nearly two hours before they discovered that it was Courtenay's party— their own men—that they were fighting. Meanwhile Goring had further weakened his brigade by detaching a regiment to deal with another party of roundhead horse on his flank. When he at last overtook Weldon near Ilminster, he was in no condition to press home an attack. Weldon's rearguard of horse twice beat back the cavalier forlorn hope, and although Goring himself led a more successful third charge, the absence of his infantry meant that he could not challenge the musketeers who covered Weldon's retreat through the winding lanes. Weldon got his men back to Taunton almost intact.[17]

While the king stormed Leicester and marched to disaster at Naseby, Goring showed no sign of taking the initiative. Ordered to join the king against Fairfax, he got the prince's council to certify that he could not be spared because of the danger from Weldon. In fact, although he again blockaded Taunton, he still did not press a close siege. On 17 June the defenders enlarged their quarters by a successful sortie. Soon Goring was complaining that lack of powder and provisions might compel him to withdraw. The shortage was real enough. Even the better organised Bristol garrison could levy only a fraction of its assigned contributions, and in an otherwise optimistic report to the king Hopton admitted the Country's lack of co-operation and 'inclination to comply with the rebels'.[18] Parliament, meanwhile, was again collecting forces to deal with Goring. Col Edward Massey, the hero of Gloucester, had already been appointed to command the parliamentary Western Association. Troops were recruited from the south-eastern counties as well as from Gloucester, and the revived association was given power to impress local levies. Massey took his time, but by 29 June he was at Shaftesbury. Fairfax was also marching west with the whole of the victorious New Model. Time was running out for Goring.

A possible reason for Goring's lethargic inactivity in June may be that he hoped to win over the clubmen, who first appeared in Somerset at this time. There had already been outbreaks elsewhere: in March, for instance, a great throng of countrymen had assembled near Hereford to demand compensation for their losses.[19] But by June the most intense centre of 'club' activity was the region where the three counties of Somerset, Dorset, and Wiltshire come together. It was an area long affected by food shortage and depression, and with a history of riots against enclosure and disafforestation. The disorders of 1629-31 were still remembered and they had been followed by sporadic outbreaks in the Wincanton–Gillingham area in the early days of the war. The typical clubman was a yeoman or less affluent farmer; in the nature of things he might accept the leadership, if it was offered, of minor gentlemen, clergy, or even lawyers. The clubmen were in fact the Country, shorn of its upper echelon of politicised gentry. Isolated attacks on plunderers, of the Brent Knoll type, were now being replaced by combined action over a wider area.

The first sign of organised neutralism in the West was a huge assembly of countrymen from Dorset and Wiltshire at Gussage Corner, near Wimborne St Giles, on 25 May. A 'peace-keeping association' was formed, whose principal aim, its members declared, was to 'preserve ourselves from plunder and all other unlawful violence'. The association intended to petition both king and parliament for peace; in the meantime parish leaders were to be elected to muster their neighbours for self-defence and round up plundering soldiers. Bands of farmers with white ribbons in their hats (often inscribed with such mottos as 'Peace and Truth') were soon defiantly demonstrating against both sides. Communication between villages was maintained by ringing the church bells when marauding soldiers approached. Men armed with 'fowling-pieces, pikes, halberds, great clubs, and such-like' interposed themselves between cavalier and roundhead patrols and made them drink together instead of fighting. The clubmen wanted peace. But as one of their banners proclaimed:

> If you offer to plunder or take our cattle,
> Be assured we will bid you battle.[20]

The flame spread quickly into Somerset. On 2 June 5,000 countrymen, many of them armed, gathered near Castle Cary. A petition denouncing the 'intolerable oppression, rapine, and violence' of Goring's soldiers was adopted and a delegation elected to present it to the Prince of Wales at Wells. In reply the clubmen were given some promises of improvement, but also sternly reminded that such public meetings were illegal and dangerous.[21] The warning was ignored. During the weeks that followed, with Goring's crew still fattening on the countryside, there were similar meetings at several other places in Somerset.

Obviously the clubmen were dangerous; still, it might be possible to win them over. So thought Sir John Stawell, to whom they seemed to provide a potential foundation of the 'One and All' movement which he had for so long been recommending. Stawell had his agents among the countrymen, and he strove busily to divert the club agitation into royalist channels. In this he was less successful than the cavaliers of Dorset and Wiltshire, where the club leaders included many beneficed clergy and vaguely royalist minor gentlemen like Thomas Hollis of Salisbury and the Bennetts of Pythouse. Such men had no objection to collecting money for the king's garrisons in return for promises of the soldiers' good behaviour.[22] Only a few identifiable Somerset royalists co-operated with the Wiltshire and Dorset men, most of them from the disturbed south-eastern corner of the county: Capt Edward Davies of Lamyatt and the Bruton attorney Thomas Jervis, for example.

In central and north Somerset, as we have seen, popular feeling tended more towards parliament than the king, even if only a minority of people below the educated élite had strong enough views to accept the risks of commitment. Most of the clubmen were genuinely neutralist. But they were ready to take action against plunderers; and the plunderers were Goring's men, a situation that was bound to reinforce or reawaken submerged parliamentarian sympathies.

Much depended on Goring's ability to keep his troops under control. At first he pretended to do so, courting the royalist commissioners, requesting prayers for his success, and promising the clubmen that his men would desist from plunder if contributions were regularly paid. Temporarily Mackworth at Langport replaced him as the chief target of club hostility. Goring had deliberately starved Mackworth of supplies, and when the Langport garrison tried to collect them by force, there was immediate resistance. Soldiers were taken prisoner by clubmen who then advanced menacingly on Langport, forcing Mackworth to retaliate with a cavalry charge which dispersed them with some loss of life. Goring promptly reprimanded Mackworth, and continued to ingratiate himself with the clubmen even when the prince's council asked him to prevent their meetings. In fact his conciliatory attitude was a sham. Contributions were duly paid, but Goring would not, or could not, stop the plundering. The clubmen not surprisingly felt cheated, and acted accordingly. Goring blamed their increasing hostility partly on Mackworth, partly on the blow to royalist morale given by the defeat at Naseby: the clubmen, he argued, would always support the stronger side. On his own role in determining their allegiance he was silent.[23]

*　　*　　*　　*

By 4 July Goring had raised his half-hearted siege of Taunton. Fairfax was at Beaminster after a rapid march through Salisbury and Dorchester, making contact with Massey's slower-moving brigade, which was now between Axminster and Chard. The combined parliamentarian armies totalled some 14,000 men; Goring had barely half that number. On the 5th the New Model entered Somerset and established its base at Crewkerne. Goring had to keep the roundheads from advancing towards Bridgwater and the other Bristol Channel ports through which he was being supplied from Wales. Massive Welsh reinforcements were on the way: 1,500 landed at Uphill a few days later and others were expected at Minehead and Watchet. 'This is our unhappiness still', a roundhead newsbook lamented, 'Bristol for ammunition, Wales for men.'[24] Some early arrivals were taken prisoner during the advance from Dorset; at Crewkerne on Sunday the 6th the Welsh puritan Walter Cradock preached to them in their native tongue. Awaiting his reinforcements, Goring occupied the line of the River Yeo from its junction with the Parrett near Langport south-east towards Ilchester. In spite of his numerical inferiority, Goring had good hopes of using the rivers at least to delay Fairfax's offensive.

With methodical professionalism, the New Model went immedi-

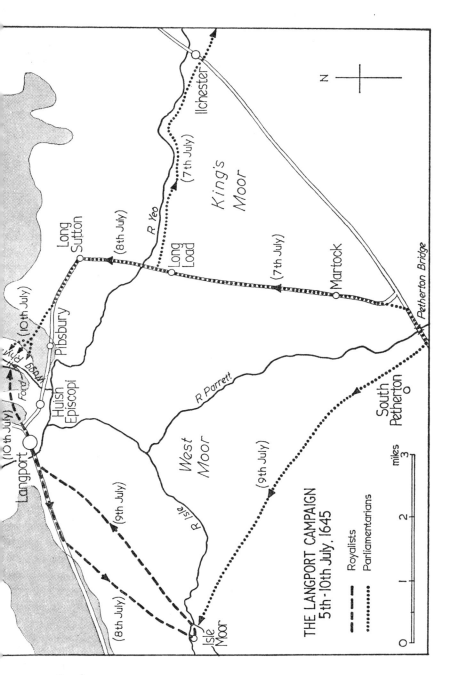

THE LANGPORT CAMPAIGN
5th - 10th July, 1645

Royalists
Parliamentarians

Langport
Huish Episcopi
Pibsbury
Long Sutton
Long Load
Ilchester
Martock
South Petherton
Petherton Bridge
Isle Moor
West Moor
King's Moor
R Yeo
R Parrett
R Isle

(7th July)
(8th July)
(9th July)
(10th July)

G

ately into action. Col Fleetwood took 2,000 horse and dragoons to secure Petherton Bridge, recently repaired. The royalists broke it down again, but Fleetwood restored it and drove the defenders back towards Ilchester. More parliamentarians under Edward Mountagu moved up to occupy South Petherton and Martock, thus protecting the bridge and Fleetwood's lines of communication. Fairfax was across the Parrett.[25]

Refreshed and inspired by the sabbath rest at Crewkerne, on 7 July the New Model's main force resumed the advance. The bridges over the Yeo were all down. Those at Long Load and Ilchester were too well guarded to be attempted, so Fairfax sent a force of infantry to Yeovil to gain the third one, which Goring evidently thought was the responsibility of Sir Lewis Dyve's Sherborne garrison. The royalists withdrew without resistance: Fairfax was across the Yeo. The cavaliers quickly abandoned both Ilchester and Long Load, enabling the parliamentarians to repair the bridges and get their horse across.[26]

Goring's strategy had collapsed, and his tactics now betrayed his desperation. On the morning of Tuesday the 8th he sent his bibulous brother-in-law, Lt-Gen Charles Porter, with most of the cavalry to make a thrust towards Taunton. Fairfax immediately sent Massey's brigade in pursuit. Some time the next day Porter's men were relaxing in the meadows of Isle Moor, some asleep, others bathing in the River Isle or strolling along its banks. The officers, as usual, were drinking, and no scouts had been sent out. The peaceful summer scene was ruined by the sudden arrival of Massey's force, who rounded up 500 startled prisoners and pursued the demoralised remnants across the moors. Goring brought new forces out of Langport to help them, but although he got some of the survivors across the Parrett to safety, he himself was slightly wounded and angrily blamed Porter for his negligence. The entire cavalry, Goring admitted, was 'very much shattered with the disorder that day'.[27] It might have been even worse: Fairfax could hear the distant firing across the levels, but the rivers prevented him from cutting off Goring's retreat. Still, as the New Model moved through Long Sutton on that Wednesday evening, Goring was in poor shape for a battle. He considered an immediate general retreat to Bridgwater, but this would have involved the risk of being thrown into disorder by an attack from the rear. A delaying action was imperative until more of the

Welsh arrived. When night fell, therefore, Goring sent off his heavy guns to Bridgwater and prepared to fight to cover a gradual, orderly withdrawal.

The battle of Langport was fought on Thursday 10 July 1645. Unlike Lansdown, which was prolonged, bloody, and indecisive, Langport was short, overwhelming, and caused mercifully few fatalities. In the early morning Goring drew out his army just east of Langport on Ham Down, the southern extension of Ham Hill. Fairfax established himself on another low hill nearly a mile further east, with his headquarters by the windmills that then existed at Pibsbury, just north of the modern A 372 road. Between the two armies lay a shallow valley through which a small stream, the Wagg Rhyne, runs south-west towards the Yeo. Nowadays neither the stream nor the slope of Ham Down look like serious obstacles, but there had been a good deal of recent rain (though the day itself was dry and dusty), and the rhyne could only be crossed at a ford from which a narrow lane ran uphill towards Goring's position.[28] Goring lined the lane and the hedges of enclosed fields on his side of the brook with musketeers; his two remaining cannon commanded the ford, while his cavalry awaited Fairfax's attack on Ham Down. Against his 7,000 men Fairfax could put roughly 10,000 into action. Massey's brigade had not yet recrossed the Parrett; Montagu's foot, who had supported them, were also still on the way. In fighting efficiency and morale, especially since the fiasco at Isle Moor, there was no comparison between the two armies.

The battle began with the silencing of the two royalist guns by the powerful roundhead artillery; the cannonade also prevented the royalists sending relief to their men in the valley as the New Model infantry advanced. But Goring's musketeers fought stoutly from their hedges and it was almost noon before the parliamentarian foot got across the rhyne. Sensing the decisive moment Fairfax sent three troops of horse under Major Bethel in a charge across the ford and up the lane beyond. Against a resolute enemy it would have been suicidal—the cavalry could ride only four abreast in the lane—but Fairfax's confidence in his men was not misplaced. They splashed through the ford, ran the gauntlet of musket-fire as they galloped up the hill, and charged bravely at the front ranks of Goring's horse. For a few minutes— 'whilst you could count three or four hundred', the chaplain of

Whalley's regiment, Richard Baxter, recalls—there was a hectic struggle at swordspoint, before the dispirited royalists began to retreat. Bethel pursued too far and was in danger of being surrounded, but he pulled back in time to the top of the lane. Then, joined by Disbrowe and several more troops of horse, he attacked again, Bethel taking the royalist centre, Disbrowe the left.

By this time Goring's musketeers had been flushed from their cover and the New Model foot was advancing up the hill. Suddenly panic set in among the royalists to the rear. Baxter watched in fascination from the opposite hill as the flight began and gradually spread to the forward ranks nearer the action. Soon the whole royalist army broke and fled and the jubilant roundheads pressed forward in pursuit. Next to Baxter stood the exuberant puritan Major Thomas Harrison. As the cavaliers gave way, Baxter heard him 'with a loud voice break forth into the praises of God with fluent expressions, as if he had been in a rapture'. Once more the Lord of Hosts had been with them.

The royalists fled in small parties towards Bridgwater. Mackworth abandoned Langport, firing the town before he left, and his troops joined the fugitives, as Fairfax's men went after them down the blazing main street. Some reached the shelter of the Burrowbridge garrison, others made a brief stand in Aller Drove; many more threw away their arms or lost their horses in the rhynes and were captured by clubmen. Only 300 were killed in the battle, all but a score of them royalists, but Fairfax took 2,000 prisoners and quantities of arms, including the two cannon. Many of the foot got away to Bridgwater, but the cavalry were virtually destroyed. The defeated general escaped to Dunster and tried to minimise the disaster, but even he admitted the great 'terror and dejection amongst our men'.[30] It was the end of Goring's crew.

Notes to this chapter are one pages 204-5.

6
The War's End
July-September 1645

After Langport only mopping-up remained. The royalists had no field army in Somerset and no prospect of recruiting one. Stragglers from Goring's army, with help from the cavaliers of Devon and Cornwall, could do no more than annoy the western parts of the county. There also remained royalist strongholds on the borders: Bristol, Bath, Dunster, and Sherborne, the first and last particularly threatening because of their strength and their potentiality for stirring up the neighbouring clubmen. But Bridgwater was even more dangerous: strongly garrisoned, open to reinforcement across the Bristol Channel, and still a barrier to communication between the eastern and western parts. To Bridgwater, therefore, the triumphant New Model immediately directed its attention. Besides the obvious military results, its reduction was to have significant political consequences, through its impact on the clubmen.

By the time Langport was fought and won the clubmen of central Somerset were already beginning to swing towards parliament. Remembering what had happened in Dorset, Fairfax had at first been highly suspicious of them. The Dorset farmers had fallen on Massey's troops at Sturminster Newton towards the end of June, and had attacked the garrison at Lyme, with casualties at both places. When Fairfax received a club delegation a few days later he found their leader, Thomas Hollis, 'most peremptory and insolent in his carriage'. On the morning of the battle Hollis turned up at headquarters outside Langport and again uttered some rash threats. Fairfax had him arrested, but he escaped before the day was over. The Somerset men from the Wincanton-Bruton area had thrown in their lot with Hollis's association and were tarred with the same royalist brush. And Stawell was still busy, receiving some encouragement from the prince's council in a scheme to enlist the clubmen en masse for the king. Early in July a club meeting at Wells adopted a distinctly royalist petition. Influenced, parliamentarian pamphlets sneered, by 'a malignant conjunction of the lawyer and the clergyman' and understanding no more of politics than 'ploughmen do Greek', the farmers blamed parliament for the failure of the Uxbridge peace talks, and some of them had co-operated with Goring before Langport.[1]

Not all the Somerset men were taken in by Stawell's agents. Many assisted Massey in the action at Isle Moor. They felled trees to obstruct Porter's flight across the levels and disarmed or captured many royalist prisoners. After the battle the next day others helped to round up the beaten fugitives. 'They stopped provisions from our army, and killed some of our men', Goring complained.[2] An important factor, undoubtedly, was the contrast between the outrageous conduct of Goring's men and the punctilious discipline of the New Model. Bringing the news of victory to the House of Commons, Lt-Col John Lilburne recalled the villagers' astonishment at being offered payment for quarters when the army first entered Somerset, 'divers of them telling us that they never knew what it was to finger soldiers' money'. His men's ability to pay had 'infinitely gained the Country'.[3] A victorious army which might end the war in a few weeks, which actually paid its way and refrained from plunder, was a very different proposition from Goring's rabble.

Yet behind this simple, immediate explanation of the roundhead trend among the Somerset clubmen lurks a more fundamental one. The yeomen and clothworkers had more to gain from a parliamentarian than a royalist victory, and if left to themselves, without interference from cavalier gentry and clergy, they knew it. These after all were men of the same type as those who had driven Hertford out of the county in 1642. A London newsbook stressed their consistency, contrasting the Wiltshire and Dorset clubmen with those of Somerset, 'which indeed at first were active clubbers against Hopton, Stawell, and the rest of the incendiaries of the western parts'.[4] Nowhere was this submerged parliamentarianism more evident than among the clubmen of the western Poldens and the surrounding levels. Their history is an interesting one, not least because they threw up the one outstanding leader of the Somerset clubmen, the one articulate spokesman for the silent thousands in the middle and lower reaches of society.

Humphrey Willis came of a Woolavington yeoman family, though one that was moving up in the world. His father aspired to the rank of 'gentleman'; he had no real claim to the title, but after his early death his widow, Humphrey's mother, married successively a Londoner, Robert Smith, and one of the Huntworth Pophams, the older but now hopelessly declining branch of that family. Humphrey must have had some education, for he was capable of stringing together a pamphlet and expressing his generally conventional ideas in doggerel verse. The most interesting feature of his background is that the Willises were tenants of the Pyms, who owned the manor of Woolavington. Humphrey grew up in a family long accustomed to standing up for their rights in lawsuits against the great John Pym himself.[5]

By the end of June Willis had emerged as the undisputed 'general' of the mid-Somerset clubmen: 'Lord' Willis, Sir Humphrey Mildmay ironically described him when one of his kinsmen was captured and taken before him. On the 30th, while Fairfax's army was still in Wiltshire, there had been a great meeting at Pensy-Pound on Sedgemoor. In a long speech Willis presented the countrymen with a list of 'queries' regarding their future organisation. He proposed that they follow the Wiltshire and Dorset model: elect their own officers, choose a group of 'sufficient men' to present their peace petitions to king and parliament, and lay down rules for listing men and rating the parishes for contributions. But they should avoid the mistakes made in the other counties and steer clear of any cavalier entanglement. In fact the royalists, with their garrisons at Bridgwater and Burrowbridge, were the worst burdens on the county: freedom of trade across the Parrett was the least they should ask of the governors. To avoid infiltration from either side, gentry and clergy already committed in the war should be discouraged from joining the association, though the ministers might be asked to read a club declaration from their pulpits. The whole programme shows a degree of political sophistication that reminds us that however humble, these were men of independence, long familiar with processes of self-government.[6]

After the Sedgemoor meeting Willis continued to resist royalist

overtures, and encouraged his supporters to assist Fairfax and
Massey. On the day after Langport he had his first encounter with
Fairfax. On that 11 July, in preparation for the investment of
Bridgwater, the New Model's scattered formations rendezvoused
on the same Pensy-Pound where the clubmen had met a fortnight
earlier. While the general was inspecting his troops large crowds
of countrymen, carrying white banners made of sheets and aprons,
were sighted on Knowle Hill, two miles away beyond Bawdrip.
Sir Thomas rode over with an escort to see what they wanted.
Willis stepped forward with a friendly welcome and to explain
the purpose of the gathering. It was, he said, 'for safeguard of
their goods, and for peace, to which purpose he produced a petition for a treaty'. A rival spokesman tried to read the royalist
petition from the Wells meeting, but was shouted down. Fairfax
made a conciliatory speech in his turn, appealing for help against
Bridgwater and promising to pay for supplies needed for his
army. As his party left the hill on their way back to headquarters
at Chedzoy, the clubmen fired their muskets in salute, a disorderly
volley which some of the officers admitted shook them more than
all the fighting at Langport.[7] Willis was still a neutral, but he and
his friends were obviously becoming better disposed to the New
Model than to the royalists.

The noose was tightening around Bridgwater. Willis's clubmen quietly co-operated with Fairfax, provisioning his forces and
cutting off Wyndham's supplies. Their strength in the countryside
to the north-east made it impossible for Wyndham to break
out towards Bristol, even before the New Model completed its
encirclement of the town. Methodically, confidently, Fairfax made
his preparations. The small garrison at Burrowbridge, the last
royalist outpost in the moors, surrendered to Okey's dragoons
on 13 July. Holborne took Sydenham House, a mile north-east
of Bridgwater, where there was another strongpoint; Weldon
occupied Hamp, to the south, and posted batteries on an adjoining
hill. Wyndham's last hope of reinforcement from Wales soon van-
ished. Parliamentarian ships were cruising in the Bristol Channel
between Penarth and the Holms; they intercepted several small
vessels carrying supplies for Bridgwater, and sixteen 'Welsh barks'
intended for transporting soldiers.[8]

In spite of Fairfax's formidable strength and his own men's
low morale, Wyndham was still in a strong position. Bridgwater

was surrounded by a tidal ditch, ten yards wide; the old walls, fifteen feet thick, were plentifully studded with cannon and barbed with forts, especially on the eastern side; to the north was the castle with even higher walls. The muddy Parrett, which still has a considerable tidal range at Bridgwater, divided the town in two, but posed more problems for the attackers than for the defenders. During a preliminary tour of inspection Fairfax and Cromwell came close to drowning when they were surprised by the incoming bore while crossing the river at Dunwear. Eight movable bridges, forty feet long, were constructed for crossing the ditch, and at a council of war on the 16th it was decided to storm early the following Monday morning, the 21st. The main assault was planned for the northern and eastern sides. The regiments drew lots for the honour of leading the attack; on Sunday they were fortified in their zeal by militant sermons from their chaplains, Hugh Peter in the morning, Edward Bowles in the afternoon. Fairfax sent Wyndham a last call to surrender and received a defiant refusal. As evening drew on, the storming party paraded in the fields near East Bower and Horsey; once again Hugh Peter provided a vigorous oration.[9]

In the dark morning hours of 21 July the storm began. Massey's brigade made a diversion on the south side, while Lt-Col Hewson led the main assault from the north-east. The movable bridges were put down, the ditch around Castle Field crossed, and the royalists driven back towards the town centre. A party under Capt Reynolds got over the ditch near St John's and pressed on through East Gate and into Eastover, the district east of the Parrett. In the broadening daylight they fought their way through the streets to the river, pushing the survivors of Sir John Stawell's regiment across the bridge. But the bridge was barricaded in time and the drawbridge at its centre raised. Royalists in the sector near the church and the market place were under fire from their own captured guns, but they retaliated by firing grenades and red-hot cannonballs into Eastover; the whole district was soon in flames. To cross the river would be a major operation, so Fairfax prudently decided to regroup and resume the attack the next day.

On Tuesday morning the parliamentarians opened a heavy fire from all sides, forcing the defenders to abandon their line to the south and south-west and retreat to the shelter of the walls. At two o'clock Fairfax gave the garrison two hours to send out their

women and children; in the words of one of his officers, 'a whole
regiment' of them, including even the stout-hearted Mrs Wyndham, soon came streaming out of the town.[10] When the ultimatum
expired, the guns opened up again, this time with red-hot projec-
tiles. Big fires were started in Cornhill and several other streets
and spread quickly, fanned by a high wind. Surrounded by terri-
fied townsmen crying 'Mercy, for the Lord's sake', Wyndham
could only capitulate. A town in flames had not been enough to
defeat Blake at Taunton, but his relations with the inhabitants
had been far different from those of Wyndham with the men of
Bridgwater. Hostages came out in the evening twilight, and early
the next morning the surrender of Bridgwater was completed.
Vast quantities of arms and ammunition, thirty-six cannon, and
over 1,000 prisoners were taken, while more than another 2,000
men were allowed to march away without arms. More important,
Fairfax had destroyed the royalists' last hope of communication
between Rupert at Bristol and Goring's demoralised forces further
west.

*   *   *   *

The end was inevitable, but there still remained some hard fighting. Fairfax's council of war debated two alternatives: to march
west and complete the destruction of Goring, or to deal first with
the remaining royalist strongholds—Rupert's at Bristol and Sir
Lewis Dyve's at Sherborne. The first decision was to move against
Goring, leaving Massey to contain Rupert and 'disturb the clubmen if they frequented meetings as formerly' in Dorset and east
Somerset.[11] On 26 July the New Model marched south-east to
Martock, resting there the next day, Sunday, for a great thanksgiving service. However, Fairfax was worried about the royalist
garrisons in his rear, and he now overruled his council of war and
turned back, detaching a brigade under Col Pickering to watch
Dyve at Sherborne. On the 28th the army reached Wells in
preparation for an attack on Bath. Rupert was to be isolated.

The prince was having his troubles: the plague was spreading
in Bristol and he was short of supplies. Apart from a raid on an
outlying detachment of the New Model under Sir Robert Pye at
Wells on 16 July, he had done nothing to take the pressure off
Bridgwater while it was being invested. His hopes of manpower

from Wales were being frustrated by the enemy warships off the Holms, and when ships carrying several hundred Welsh and Irish soldiers slipped through the blockade to Portishead, clubmen prevented the men from landing. Some of them got ashore at Pill, but it was clear that Rupert had a hostile population to contend with. It was apparently at about this time, too, that the villagers of Worle, Milton, and Weston-super-Mare attacked soldiers under Sir Thomas Aston when they came to plunder.[12] Rupert had several fruitless encounters with the clubmen of north Somerset and south Gloucestershire, one of them on Lansdown. A meeting on the hills near Wraxall ended acrimoniously. The prince arrived with 1,000 men, but the clubmen refused either to fire a volley in salute or to allow him to 'march through their body'. The royalist squire Sir Edward Gorges tried to win them over in a speech that contained some instances of roundhead depravity, including the allegation that in a nearby village a prayer book had been torn up. This was denied by a man from the village in question, who said that Gorges 'lied like a knave'. The war was producing a disturbing lack of respect for social superiors.[13]

The garrison towns, too, were restless and defeatist. When Fairfax advanced to Wells on the 28th, Rupert sent a party of horse to reinforce Bath, with one of his officers as a replacement for the governor, the local man Sir Thomas Bridges. There were angry protests from the citizens, who were also upset by fear that the soldiers might bring the plague with them. When they discovered the nationality of the reinforcements, they were even more resentful and there were shouts of 'No Welsh! No Welsh!' The next day resistance collapsed. Fairfax sent Col Nathaniel Rich over the Mendips with two regiments of horse and some dragoons, in what was intended only as a probing operation. In the evening light they came riding down from Odd Down and had almost reached the bridge before they were halted by a volley from the defenders. After a brief exchange of fire Rich sent in a summons to surrender and this was accepted early the next morning, even though there was nothing to prevent the garrison from escaping to the north. Bridges and his officers were allowed to march away to Bristol.[14]

Fairfax now decided to dispose of Sherborne and the club royalists of Dorset. Four regiments were left at Bath, which, the general told his father, 'with the assistance of the county with the

well-affected thereabout I hope will straighten Bristol very much'.[15]
On 2 August the army left Wells and marched by way of Queen
Camel to Sherborne. On the same day the club leaders from Dorset, Wiltshire, and east Somerset met at Shaftesbury to consider
Dyve's urgent request for assistance. Fairfax sent Fleetwood with
two regiments to surround Shaftesbury and arrest them. There
was an angry buzz of protest in the villages. Church bells were
rung, and messengers came flocking in demanding their leaders'
release. On the 4th a great crowd of clubmen assembled on Ham-
bledon Hill, towards Blandford, with white colours, drums, and
weapons. Cromwell persuaded one group to disperse peacefully
as he approached the hill with 500 dragoons, but the main body
defied him, so he charged and scattered them. Twelve countrymen and three soldiers were killed and many wounded. It was the
ugliest episode of the whole club movement, but the firm show of
force put an end to any further trouble. The leaders were soon on
their way to London in custody, while the Somerset clubmen
quickly disowned them. 'The moderate party [of the clubmen]
(especially about Somersetshire) do much deride their folly', a
roundhead pamphlet noted.[16]

Fairfax now closed in on Sherborne Castle. Siege guns were
brought from Portsmouth and a group of experienced Mendip
miners came to tunnel under the defences. On the 14th a breach
was made and the next day the tenacious Dyve surrendered. Sherborne lay just outside the county's borders, but since 1642 it had
been a place of sinister significance for Somerset parliamentarians:
'That first western nest of the cockatrices' eggs', John Bond de-
claimed, 'the cradle of cavalierism, the very bag of the western
imposthume.'[17]

Only Bristol remained. On 18 August the New Model came
marching through Castle Cary and Shepton Mallet to settle
accounts with Rupert. On the way Fairfax detached a force under
Col Thomas Rainsborough to take the small castle of Nunney, a
few miles east of Shepton. Nunney's owner and governor, the
recusant Richard Prater, commanded a garrison of eighty men,
most of them Irish, and also provided shelter for a number of
Catholic refugees who must have watched in alarm as Rainsborough's men entered the village. Fairfax came to inspect operations,
and Rainsborough's cannon soon made a small breach in the
castle walls. Prater quickly surrendered.[18] The next day, the 21st,

Fairfax advanced towards Bristol; in two days the city was surrounded, with the general's headquarters established at Wild
House in Stapleton. Rupert had some 2,000 men, but they were
not of the best quality, and the citizens were demoralised and
apathetic. For a few days, until their line was established, the
prince kept the attackers off balance. His horse raided parliamentarian quarters, taking prisoners (the dragoon officer Col Okey
was the best known victim), and burning Bedminster village. He
had long since swept the surrounding countryside clear of cattle,
and was well supplied, but the odds were overwhelming.[19]

In addition to the formidable power of the New Model,
Fairfax had the Country on his side. Advised by John Ashe, on
25 August the general issued warrants to Sir John Horner, parliament's high sheriff, 'to raise the power of the county'. What
Stawell had been unable to accomplish in the name of a royalist
peace movement, Horner was to achieve in the name of a parliamentarian victory. Soon the countrymen were flocking in to be
listed and armed. A large force of clubmen assisted operations
against the fort at Portishead, which surrendered on 28 August.
Early in September Horner's efforts produced a great meeting on
the hills near Chewton Mendip. It was 1642 over again, with
many of the same participants. On this occasion the countrymen
were greeted by Ashe and by a delegation of officers headed by
Oliver Cromwell. The volatile chaplain, Hugh Peter, gave them
a 'short exhortation' and was soon boasting that 'with that one
sermon [he] increased their army with 3,000 men'. True or not,
and even allowing for the very different circumstances, it was a
significant contrast to the response the king had received when
he tried to raise the Country in 1644. Cromwell also made a short
speech, thanking the countrymen for their good affection. A few
days later he and Ashe had a second meeting with the clubmen
on Dundry Hill; they recruited 2,000 auxiliaries who, an army
chaplain records, 'marched with 36 colours in the face of Bristol,
had quarters assigned them, and kept guards'. They were given
two cannon to amuse them, and either then or later Alexander
Popham was put in command.[20]

While he recruited the countrymen, Fairfax had been preparing
for an assault, building a temporary bridge over the Avon to improve communication between the Somerset and Gloucestershire
sides of the city. After a spell of heavy rain, on 3 September the

weather improved and a storm became feasible. Before it was attempted, Rupert was sent the customary last call to surrender, in a letter well calculated to appeal to the local populace. 'Let all England judge', Fairfax concluded it, 'whether the burning of its towns, ruining its cities, and destroying its people, be a good requital from a person of your family.'[21] There were some ineffective negotiations, but Sir Thomas soon decided that Rupert was merely playing for time. In the early hours of 10 September the storm began.

Like Fiennes before him, Rupert simply did not have the men to withstand the attack of an overpoweringly superior army; the king's angry reaction when he received the news of his nephew's capitulation was the unreasonable response of a beaten and disappointed man. The assault was concentrated on the southern and north-eastern sides of the city. Weldon's brigade, like the Cornishmen in 1643, were repelled near Redcliffe, but on the north-east troops under Rainsborough and Mountagu smashed through the royalist line; cavalry following up advanced along Kingsdown and St Michael's Hill to stop the defenders falling back behind the Frome. A counter-attack by Rupert's horse was contemptuously brushed aside. The northernmost fort at Prior's Hill was cut off and after two hours' desperate resistance its defenders were overwhelmed and slaughtered. The royalists tried to fire the city, but Rupert already saw that the game was up and that further resistance would mean annihilation. He sent out to Fairfax asking for terms, articles of surrender were quickly agreed on, and all was over. The next morning the garrison gave up their arms and marched away to Oxford, Rupert to disgrace and exile. The prince, who had replaced Goring as the chief object of local hatred, was pursued by the angry shouts of the country folk: 'Give him no quarter! Give him no quarter!'[22]

Dunster Castle still held out, and Goring still threatened the western parts of the county from Devon, but effectively the war in Somerset was over. With the plague still raging, Fairfax left only a small garrison in Bristol, withdrawing most of his troops to Pensford and other villages to the south. For a few weeks the New Model regrouped and recruited its weary forces, awaited the arrival of pay from London, and prepared to advance westward for the last campaign. At the end of September the army was at Chard, muttering about the lack of pay, but by 11 October, the money having arrived, Fairfax was on his way to Tiverton and the final victories. Goring's outriders occasionally caused trouble in the Exmoor villages and even plundered Minehead in one daring raid. Francis Wyndham, meanwhile, hung on at Dunster with gallant resolution. Local forces kept him quiet and protected the western border from Goring's patrols. Among them were Alexander Popham's clubmen, now respectably established as parliamentarian forces and paid from a rate levied on the parishes: 'club money', village accounts often labelled it. Farleigh Castle, the last royalist outpost on the eastern border, fell on 3 October. Hopton, steadfast to the end, fought on courageously in Devon and Cornwall, but to salvage honour, not victory. While Fairfax hunted him down, Blake moved in to besiege Dunster. A midwinter attempt to storm was repulsed; Blake did not waste his men's lives again, but left the outcome to the inexorable logic of time. After the fall of Exeter to Fairfax there was no hope for Wyndham, and on 20 April 1646 he surrendered.[23]

*   *   *   *

It had been a long time since Marshall's Elm, but the war had come full circle. In 1642 the yeomen and clothworkers of northeast Somerset had risen overwhelmingly to drive out Hertford's cavaliers. In 1645 they turned out in even larger numbers against Rupert. In the three intervening years their enthusiasm for parliament had often been tepid. Like most Englishmen then and always they had no liking for military service and a natural preference for self-preservation in times of danger. If the royalist gentry would govern in the old way, as on the whole they did between August 1643 and the early summer of 1644, they were not likely to rebel. Active commitment to parliament was confined to a politicised minority, most of whom left Somerset to continue the fight elsewhere when the county was conquered. It took the massive strength and discipline of the New Model to convince the freeholders that their best interest lay in helping parliament to finish the war quickly. Still, the royalists had dominated Somerset in 1644 just as totally as the roundheads did a year later, yet the king's appeals evoked nothing like the response that Horner, Ashe, and the Pophams obtained in either the first year of the war or the last. In so far as they had political preferences, the men of north-east and central Somerset were parliamentarian.

There were, of course, important differences in the outlook of other parts of the county. The south-east corner around Bruton had produced royalist outbreaks in the winter of 1642-3, and at the end the clubmen of this region turned to the royalists of Wiltshire and Dorset, not to Willis's more parliamentarian group. Apart from the clothing towns and the Vale of Taunton, the hilly western parishes were much less strongly for parliament than the north-east, both in 1642 and later. Pyne had raised only a few hundred men there at the outset, and although in the spring of 1643 he enlisted larger numbers, they displayed no inclination to fight against the Cornishmen.

In 1645, too, the clubmen of west Somerset were far less sympathetic to parliament than those who turned out at Bridgwater and Bristol. In July a 'peace-keeping association' emerged in west Somerset, as in other regions. Pyne and Blake tried to get them to adopt a strongly roundhead petition. Besides the usual Country denunciations of plunderers, their suggested draft contained demands for the prosecution of 'Irish rebels, delinquents, and incendiaries', and promises to support Fairfax's army in rooting out 'popery, superstition, and idolatry' and to accept whatever 'reformation in church and state' parliament should impose. At a meeting at Triscombe in the Quantocks on 30 July the clubmen flatly rejected the proposed draft. Instead they adopted a petition to parliament calling for peace by negotiation, not conquest, through a renewal of the Uxbridge treaty. They wanted the preservation of royal prerogatives as well as parliamentary privilege, a return to the protestant religion as in Queen Elizabeth's time, and altogether a moderate, conservative settlement.[24] In this they were probably not very different from Humphrey Willis's friends; but they trusted their royalist gentry, not the New Model army, to lead them to it.

Why were the south-eastern and western parts of Somerset so different? Some of the contrast can be explained by leadership, by the ability of Berkeleys, Stawells, and Trevelyans to command greater local loyalty than people like Pyne and Wroth, neither of whom could rival the influence of the Horners and Pophams in the north-east. In 1645 much can be attributed to central Somerset's sufferings at the hands of Goring's army—but the Bruton area also suffered severely and the western parts even more during the protracted operations around Taunton. Once again it seems clear that we have to look at variations in the economic and social structures of the several regions of the county to explain their differing political behaviour. The parliamentarian areas were those in which there were large numbers of clothworkers (the north-east, Taunton, Wellington—the term 'Wellington round-head' was proverbial);[25] where people's lives had recently been disrupted by disafforestation or enclosure (the Frome area, parts of the moors—yet much of the Bruton region was royalist); or where the yeomen were unusually independent (in Martock, it will be recalled, there were no resident gentry). Obviously there were neutrals and adherents of both sides at every social level, scattered throughout the county. Nevertheless the western parts with their more traditional social structure, more exclusively agrarian economy, and fewer wealthy yeomen to challenge the gentry, tended naturally to royalism.

The war had been fought between two minorities, struggling in a sea of neutralism and apathy. And the further down the social scale we penetrate, the more neutralism and apathy we encounter. The greater gentry may have been largely royalist, but even among them were many like William Basset and John Symes who put local loyalties above national ones. Among the lesser gentry and yeomen, too, the Country outlook enabled men to acquiesce in the rule of each side in turn; sometimes, as in the case of John Somerset, to lead riots against soldiers ostensibly of their own side. We should not expect to find widespread political involvement below the yeoman level: the poorer farmer and cottager, like the typical peasant in all ages, tended to regard government as part of a remote natural order which he was powerless to influence. He might in the end revolt against plundering and oppression, but only if there were determined men to lead him, and even then with no distinct ideology to guide him. In an occasional village, to be sure, an effective preaching minister might ignite a signifi-cant puritan awakening, as the two Richard Allens did at Ditcheat and Batcombe. But such places were exceptional.

In the towns, with Taunton to the fore, puritan zeal was more common. Yet many townsmen were just as apathetic as the rural population. The compelling ties which always united men nom-inally on opposite sides are well illustrated by the attitude of the corporation of Wells in 1643. The previous mayor, Robert Mor-

H

gan, had co-operated with Hertford during the brief royalist occupation, but during the winter had clearly committed himself to parliament. When the royalists arrived, he was imprisoned in Taunton Castle and Hertford demanded his expulsion from the corporation. His embarrassed successor went to Taunton and urged Morgan, 'if it should be his hap to put the said command in execution, that he would not be offended with him'. Morgan replied that he quite understood his colleague's difficulties and 'was contented to be put forth of his place ... with all his heart'. Morgan and another roundhead member were thereupon expelled 'until it be further considered of'—until the times should alter.[26]

Only among a minority in town or countryside did puritan, parliamentarian feeling predominate, and often even then only in a negative way. There were many who knew what they were against—popery, arbitrary government, commissioners of array— without being able to define their objectives any more positively than by the vague slogan 'Liberty and Property'. Humphrey Willis is a good example, with his simple view of the dual purpose of the war: first 'our church to purify/from all the dregs of popery', and secondly to uphold parliament 'lest arbitrary power/should state and liberty devour'. Ideas like protecting 'the ancient and fundamental laws of the kingdom' may seem conventional and naive, but they were held strongly enough to inspire the great bulk of parliamentarian sympathisers.[27]

Throughout Somerset society Country attitudes were tenaciously held. They influenced leading partisans in the war—Stawell and Horner, for example—as much as they did men like Basset, Symes, and the Hunts of Speckington, hovering on the brink of neutrality. They comprehended the entire political outlook of the great mass of lesser men—minor gentry, yeomen—who collectively made up the Country. In 1645 in most of Somerset parliament had won over the Country, partly through the greater appeal of its own policies, partly through the actions of the king and his armies. If parliament was to retain the active loyalty of the Country, it would have to avoid the king's mistakes: maintain low taxes, reduce the visibility of the army, achieve a moderate reformation in church and state, leaving the essential framework of both intact. The vision of the good old days, the comfortable harmony of Queen Elizabeth's time, was largely mythical, but it constantly inspired the ordinary Englishman through the dark days of civil war—everything to be, as the Quantock clubmen put it, 'as in former time'. Although they might go further in espousing the replacement of episcopacy by a presbyterian form of church government, in all other respects the moderate parliamentarian leaders—Strode and Horner, for example—were not far in advance of this position. The war had ended in victory; now it was time for a compromise settlement with the king, a return to stability and order.

But the Country-oriented parliamentarianism of men like Strode and Horner had been outflanked. The war had generated a militant minority who would stop at nothing to achieve the puritan New Jerusalem which it was their God-given duty to impose on the reprobate majority. Their strength in the New Model army, especially among Cromwell's regiments from the old Eastern Association, was already worrying men like Richard Baxter before the end of the war. The heady millenarian excitement of Major Harrison's outburst at Langport expressed a far less compromising spirit than the sober constitutionalism of a Strode or a Horner. And there was a radical minority in Somerset, too, which was willing to bypass even the parliamentarian gentry if they lacked the necessary zeal for godly reformation.

Certainly it was a small minority. Most Somerset men, as we have seen, would have been content with the church as in the old queen's time, with episcopacy shorn of Laudian extravagances. An energetic programme of political education was needed, three roundhead officers told Speaker Lenthall soon after the fall of Bridgwater, 'the Country hardly believing you intend them either Liberty, Property, or Religion, especially since you take away the common-prayer book, which every soldier doth practice to do'. Puritan clergy were drifting back in the wake of the New Model— George Newton to Taunton, for instance—but most of the pulpits were still occupied by active or passive supporters of episcopacy. Even in Bristol, it was said in November 1645, the people 'sit in darkness and the collegiate men still chant out the common-prayer book to the wonted height, and in private parishes they think of no other discipline, here being hardly three sermons in the whole city on the Lord's day'.[28]

In these circumstances it was clear that the minority who wanted extensive changes—radical puritan reform, a tough policy towards the king—would have to govern, if they governed at all, by force and by reliance on the army. The aim of the Somerset radicals was the same as that of their counterparts at Westminster and throughout the land: to keep the army on foot until a godly settlement had been achieved and the last vestiges of episcopacy and royal power rooted out. They could not rely on public opinion, for minority government meant military rule, quartering, high taxes, centralisation from London—all the things responsible for Charles I's failure to win over the Country.

The radical minority—the 'godly gang', as Clement Walker was soon to label them—quickly found themselves as far out of touch with Country opinion as the royalist gentry had been in 1642, with the added disability of having no support among members of the old power structure of the county. Inevitably they had to govern through makeshift institutions like the new County Committee, while they purged and remodelled old ones like the Commission of the Peace. At all levels they were confronted with reluctance and resistance. Without an absolute and total social revolution, for which there was no mass support, in the end their rule was bound to end in failure. Even in the short run they needed the leadership of a ruthless and determined personality. The hour produced the man.

Notes to this chapter are on pages 205-7.

7
The Committee and the County
1645-6

John Pyne of Curry Mallet had not been a man of great prominence in Somerset before the war. But his family was reasonably
affluent and well connected, related to the Pophams, the Rogerses
of Cannington, and other magnate clans. Pyne sat for Poole in the
turbulent parliaments of 1625-9, acquiring a violent antipathy to
the Court, at least equal to that expressed by his vehement uncle
Hugh. After eloping with his cousin, a wealthy heiress, he settled
down to the law in London, keeping chambers at Middle Temple.
Elected to the Long Parliament, once more for Poole, he attached
himself to the most extreme group of 'fiery spirits', the 'war party'
as it came to be called after 1642. Tough talk, as is so often the
case, concealed military incapacity. Pyne ran away at Marshall's
Elm, failed ingloriously against Hopton's Cornishmen, and did
nothing notable thereafter. Pyne was no soldier. His moment came
at the end of the war: he was a politician and above all a local
one.

Pyne first achieved notoriety early in 1645. Like the rest of the
war party he had originally welcomed parliament's alliance with
the Scots. But the Scots proved to be allies of doubtful value, more
interested in the export of theocratic presbytery than in parliament's constitutional programme. Pyne soon turned against them.
He was 'the first incendiary ... between the kingdom of England
and Scotland', his enemies charged, dispersing anti-Scottish
'speeches, reports, and letters' in the county. One such letter, to
Edward Popham early in 1645, was intercepted and gleefully
published by the royalists to pour oil on the flames of division
in parliament. The letter spoke scornfully of the peace party
hero Essex, hoping 'to see him and his accomplices laid aside',

as they soon were in the Self-Denying Ordinance. Pyne also warned Popham of some 'sour Scottish ale a-brewing' with the peace party, an intrigue allegedly aiming beyond the establishment of presbyterianism to encompass a total betrayal, a sell-out to the king.[1] Publication of the letter had its intended effect and further deepened the breach between the parties. Scandalised moderates insisted that Pyne be summoned before the Commons to explain himself. He was a marked man, though he escaped without punishment.

Besides being a determined advocate of military victory and of restrictions on royal prerogative, Pyne was also ardently for godly reformation. His puritanism was indeed inseparable from his politics: parliament, he later declared, stood for 'the privileges and freedom of the people both in civils and spirituals'. Horner and the other leading moderates were also puritans. But for them godly reformation had to be advanced legally, using the traditional institutions—king, parliament, JPs—and without disturbing the hierarchical political structure. Pyne was different. If the parliamentarian magnates would not co-operate with sufficient energy and ruthlessness, then he would seek other allies. He found them, naturally, among the radical puritans of the county, men for the most part of lower social rank than the traditional governors. Pyne himself may not have been anything more than an unusually militant presbyterian—certainly the minister he installed at Curry Mallet, John Baker, was one, and many other presbyterian ministers looked to him as their protector. But like Oliver Cromwell, Pyne was willing to tolerate and encourage men of more extreme views than his own—Independents and baptists, for instance—provided they had 'the root of the matter' in them. He was also acutely conscious that the godly were 'a very small remnant' elected by God to combat 'the corruptness of man's unsanctified nature'.[2] It was as the leader of a radical minority that John Pyne confronted his county in 1645.

*   *   *   *

It was a ruined and ravaged county. The plague raged alarmingly; at Wells, Yeovil, in a wide arc from Bristol to Frome, at Taunton, and in moorland villages such as Othery. At Wiveliscombe 'many poor distressed people' had been 'driven to extremity'. Poverty was widespread, food prices high, and trade hampered by the wartime disruption of already primitive communications. Even in 1649 many damaged bridges had not been repaired.[3]

The operations around Bristol had brought especially severe suffering to the northern parishes. Many people, an official report noted, had had 'their cattle driven, their houses fired, their goods spoiled by the enemy, and that little remainder eaten up by the great confluence of people coming to the leaguer'. Red tape often prevented the army commissioners from giving quartering allowances because the victims did not know 'whether our army or the club armies eat up their provisions'. Quartering continued long after the departure of Fairfax's main force. In February 1646 the Bath corporation petitioned parliament against the evil. 'Our houses', the mayor wrote to John Harington, 'are emptied of all useful furniture, and much broken and disfigured; our poor suffer for want of victuals, and rich we have none'. Yet there were 400 soldiers in the town and more expected: 'God protect us from pillage.' Harington obligingly arranged for his son's company to be sent to replace the outsiders, but the place was still in chaos. 'We have no divine service as yet', the younger Harington was told, 'the churches are full of the troops' furniture and bedding.' Generous compensation was essential, the army commissioners urged, so that 'the conquest we have made over the clubmen by payment of our quarters may not be blasted'.[4]

But the military burden could not be reduced. Before Fairfax marched away 2,000 men were levied in Somerset to recruit the New Model. A home guard of clubmen provided some protection against Goring's last incursions, but against Dunster more troops had to be raised; all men of the hundred of Williton Freemanors were summoned to enlist in October 1645. These and other local forces had to be supported by levies on the parishes; there were contributions to the upkeep of the Bristol garrison; and worst of all the weekly assessment payable to London—£1,250 a week for Somerset—was revived.[5]

Meanwhile the whole local government system had been shattered by the war. There were no legally commissioned JPs, and through the disqualification of the royalists a virtual power-vacuum existed at the top of the county hierarchy. Many royalists had been able to come home under articles of surrender but others were in prison or had left the county. When the war ended in

Cornwall, Hopton joined Prince Charles in Jersey, and went from there to Holland and permanent exile. Sir William Portman was captured at Naseby and died in the Tower later in the year. John Stocker was at Oxford until the surrender and then retired into Wales. Prisoners taken in the last campaign were still in gaol in London months later: John Bull of North Cadbury, taken at Langport; Edward Dyer of Sharpham, Humphrey Walrond of Sea, and the lawyer Thomas Warre, all captured at Bridgwater. Lesser men who had escaped at the war's end were rounded up by local forces, often, like the two Trevillians, John of Kingsbury and Robert of Midelney, spending months in captivity.[6] But whether in prison or at large, the cavaliers were excluded from government.

In these circumstances parliament's County Committee was the one effective local institution, and soon after the war it was brought firmly under Pyne's control. At first, it will be recalled, the committee had been dominated by the leading roundhead families—mostly gentry, with only a few new arrivals like Ashe and Strode, and a handful of townsmen like Blake and George Serle. In 1642-3 they had governed the county with tolerable unanimity. When they came back in 1645, however, it was a different matter. Time had brought to the front many men of far less eminence than the original MPs and deputy lieutenants. And there was a bitter outbreak of faction fighting from which Pyne emerged victorious.

Some of the changes of membership did little to alter the committee's character. Old Sir Francis Popham and John Fraunceis were both dead, but the former's two famous sons were active committeemen and the latter was quietly succeeded by his son Thomas. Other changes had been made necessary as the war revealed the unreliability of such neutralists as Bassett, Bull, Harbin, and John Hunt. Harington and a few others had dropped out for less obvious reasons. Among the replacements were men of substance and authority: Sir Edward Hungerford, Samuel Horner, and Alexander Pym of Brymore, for example. Others were prominent lawyers like Lislebone Long of Stratton, the excitable, verbally prolific William Prynne, and the Bridport MP, Roger Hill of Poundisford. But most of the newcomers were men of striking obscurity who before the war could never have aspired to the upper reaches of county government. Henry Bonner of Combe St

Nicholas and Edward Ceely of Creech St Michael were reasonably solid minor gentry, but far below the level of the old establishment. The Taunton physician John Palmer was the son of an apothecary, Jonathan Pitt of Curry Rivel and Nicholas Sandys of South Petherton both merchants' sons. Matthew Clift was a Bath draper; Robert Morgan, the former mayor of Wells, an attorney with interests in the malting business. The father of Richard Trevillian of Midelney had been a yeoman, while the origins of Thomas English of Podimore Milton, Henry Minterne of Chiselborough, and Christopher Pittard of Martock were little more exalted.[7]

The factions which now split the committee reflected the general disintegration of the hitherto united parliamentarian cause. On one side stood Pyne and all who wanted rapid progress towards godly reformation, and a tough line towards beaten royalists and episcopal clergy. On the other stood moderate leaders like Horner and Strode, who looked for a compromise settlement with the king and a restoration of the old harmony of county society. Precisely how Pyne engineered their defeat is unknown, but it is clear that moderates still attending the committee in the autumn of 1645 were soon afterwards outmanoeuvred and shouldered aside. Some general reasons for Pyne's victory are obvious enough. For one thing, although many of them soon let him go his own way, Pyne had powerful allies: the Pophams, Sir Thomas Wroth, Blake, Henley, and Roger Hill. The leading moderates were influential too, but they were fatally divided by memories of the great wartime quarrel between Strode's friends and the Horners, and these antagonisms were heightened by the county election in the winter of 1645-6, which will be described later. Prominent men who might have helped, like John Harington, stayed out of the conflict. John Ashe was preoccupied by his Westminster responsibilities. Perhaps more important, only Pyne's friends were genuinely devoted to the policies the committee had to implement, willing to do the dirty work in the county and accept the necessary subordination to London. Their rivals shared the typical Country distrust of the central government and the military, and flinched from a vengeful hounding of old friends and neighbours. The Somerset committee, Sir Edward Hungerford sighed, was 'very hard to the gentry'.[8]

But Pyne was also a master of political tactics. The committee had a nasty habit, Prynne complained, of adjourning whenever he came down from London to 'examine and reform the abuses and grievances which the county generally complain of'.[9] Under the ordinance of 19 August 1644 the committeemen, too many in number for efficiency, were supposed to sit in rotation as a standing committee of seven. If this practice had been followed consistently it would have made Pyne's ascendency impossible, as his allies would never have been in control for long before their fortnightly periods of duty were over. It is clear from John Preston's papers that the rotation system still affected some members in 1647. But Pyne's faction had long since been exempt from it. Analysis of committee documents confirms a later charge that Pyne and his henchmen—Ceely, Clift, English, Minterne, Morgan, Trevillian, and 'two or three more of mean quality'—were the only ones who attended regularly and that they alone really did the work.[10]

So Pyne ran the committee. Meetings were routinely held at Bridgwater, Ilchester, Ilminster, Taunton and Wells, occasionally at Axbridge, Langport, and Somerton. The members received a weekly allowance of £2 for attendance, and were guarded by a 'committee troop' which in 1646 was commanded by Nathaniel Barnard of Fivehead, with John Barker of High Ham as his lieutenant. They quickly enlisted a new local bureaucracy, drawn mostly from the towns. Thomas Blackbourne, a Mells clothier, was treasurer for the eastern division, Samuel Whetcombe of Taunton, also a clothier, for the western until he was succeeded by the elder Roger Hill, uncle of the MP. The solicitor was another of the Hill clan, the MP's brother William. The auditor was Francis Tuthill of Bridgwater, of which town he was soon to be mayor, as his father had been before him. The marshal, responsible for the committee's prisoners, was David Barrett, a fiery baptist shoemaker from Wells.[11]

The committee's principal business was the sequestration of the estates of defeated royalists, for both fiscal and punitive purposes. They thus employed a tribe of sequestration officials, of whom there were two or three in each hundred. Most of them were men of some obscurity, often clients of greater ones, like Richard and William Collier of Curry Mallet, presumably appointed by Pyne himself. Only one, Captain Thomas Baynard of Blagdon, sequestrator of Winterstoke hundred, went on to achieve anything notable: he became a presbyterian elder, a JP, and held other county offices. The most famous, both because of his zeal and because his accounts have survived, was Edward Curll, from puritan Batcombe, who was sequestrator of Catsash hundred. Curll obviously enjoyed his work, hounding royalist landlords and uncovering attempted evasions by the use of paid informers. Estates under his management were ruthlessly exploited, and during the years 1645-7 he was bringing in over £650 a year to the committee. Gentlemen who tried to protect royalist friends or tenants were baffled by Curll's incorruptible resolution. George Horner told him to 'cease to trouble' Arthur Johnson of South Barrow: the sequestrator took no notice and put up with the 'ill words' he received for the public service.[12]

The cavalier gentry suffered severely. Anyone convicted of delinquency—which could mean helping the king with money as well as actually taking up arms—had to submit a particular of his estate. If this was accepted (and the sequestrators were quick to scent undervaluations or omissions) it was used by the Committee for Compounding, at Goldsmiths' Hall in London, to calculate the offender's 'composition' fine. The fine, which might be a tenth, a sixth, or a third of the value according to the degree of the offence, had to be paid before the estate was recovered. In the meantime the profits of the still sequestered property were received by the County Committee. Composition fines on the other hand were paid only in London, after which the local committee had no further claim on the land; it was obviously in their interest to prolong sequestration for as long as possible.

Many royalists were protected by having surrendered on articles of war promising them composition at lenient rates, and these bargains were usually kept. How much the cavaliers lost through sequestration is impossible to estimate. Composition fines are better documented, and those paid by Somerset men range from Sir William Portman's £4,600 all the way down to Henry Barlow of Wells, who paid a mere 6s 8d. Lord Poulett's fine would have been even larger than Portman's but fortunately his son, Sir John, was married to Fairfax's sister-in-law. The general several times intervened in the case and obtained substantial reductions. Others who paid large fines include George Speke of White Lackington (£2,390), William Basset (just under £2,000), William Helyar of East Coker and George Trevelyan of Nettlecombe (both over

£1,500). Titheowners often got their fines reduced by settling annual incomes on local ministers: in effect composition on the instalment plan. Rodney, Sir Charles Berkeley, and Sir Thomas Bridges all accepted terms of this kind.[13]

Coming on top of an expensive war in which many had spent freely and been plundered by friend and foe alike, sequestration and composition were disasters for all but the most prosperous. In 1651 Bridges deposed that he owed £5,545. Edward Berkeley, Sir Edward's son, was in Ilchester gaol for debt and must have encountered many familiar faces. Humphrey Walrond sold up and emigrated to Barbados; he was there by June 1647, when he appealed to his old friend John Preston to protect the family he had left behind. Some of the leaders were not allowed to compound: Hopton and the war-criminal Dodington were the most noteworthy. Sir John Stawell's obstinacy got him into even worse trouble. In July 1646 he went to London to compound on the Articles of Exeter, but stubbornly refused the necessary initial step: subscribing the Covenant to resist innovations in religion, and the Negative Oath to refrain from assisting the king. John Ashe, chairman at Goldsmiths' Hall, offered to help, Stawell says, if he was allowed to buy one of Stawell's farms at a low price. On Stawell's refusal to sell, Ashe brought him before the House of Commons and had him committed to Newgate and tried for treason. Long years of imprisonment for Stawell lay ahead.[14]

The committee's functions were not limited to sequestrations. It paid allowances to wartime hardship cases, for instance using Dodington's estates to compensate victims of his atrocities, including a Shepton Mallet woman 'whose husband and son were hanged at Woodhouse'. Until June 1647 it supervised the collection of taxes, both under the ordinance for weekly assessment and under separate measures for local garrisons. It took charge of the county's militia forces, and had general responsibility for law and order until new JPs were appointed. Committeemen issued orders against unlicensed alehouses, commanded the rating of parishes for the relief of plague-infected towns, and performed other magisterial duties. They also weeded out 'prelatical' clergy (one of them, by an odd coincidence, was Prynne's chaplain), made recommendations to the national Committee for Plundered Ministers for the augmentation of under-endowed livings, and supervised the payment of these sums out of sequestered estates.[15] The committee ruled the county. And John Pyne ruled the committee.

*   *   *   *

But the committee was not the only focus of county politics. In
the year after the war Somerset was plunged into a stormy series
of parliamentary by-elections which affected, and were affected by,
the conflict in the committee. By 1645 fourteen of Somerset's
sixteen seats in the Commons were vacant through death or the
expulsion of royalists: only Alexander Popham and Serle survived, though Pyne, Hill, John Ashe and a few others still sat for
places outside the county. Even after a civil war the old familiar
politics of family pre-eminence still continued. But in a few constituencies—Ilchester, for instance—a new kind of politics can be
detected, in which a seat became one of the stakes in a nationwide
party conflict over issues and principles as well as personalities.
Somerset in fact felt reverberations of the bitter parliamentary
struggle of presbyterians and Independents, as the old peace and
war parties were now rather confusingly coming to be called.

Pyne's position was clear. Though a presbyterian in religion,
he was an Independent in politics, not an unusual combination.
Such central co-ordination of his party's electioneering as existed
was provided in London by the Devon lawyer Edmund Prideaux,
through his triple offices: postmaster-general, commissioner of the
Great Seal, and chairman of the Committee of the West. Pyne was
his Somerset agent. 'King of the West Saxons', so Clement Walker
described Prideaux, with Pyne his 'viceroy or lord deputy for the
county of Somerset'. There was an immediate stirring of political
excitement when writs were issued for the vacant Somerset seats
in the autumn of 1645 and candidates were plentiful: '3 or 4 for
one place', John Ashe noted.[16]

The county election was held first and it threw Somerset into
turmoil. Prideaux could control the issue of the writ, but neither
he nor his Somerset allies could control its disposition. Conduct
of the election from this point was the responsibility of the high
sheriff, in this case Sir John Horner, the least likely of all men to
do Pyne's bidding. Horner knew all the options open to a sheriff
in an election, as he had shown during a previous tenure of the
office thirty years before. He was now determined to get his son
George elected as one of the knights of the shire. Three other

candidates soon emerged: the pious and well respected John Harington, the pugnacious presbyterian William Strode, and the committee's candidate, Henry Henley of Leigh.[17]

Harington had always kept out of faction struggles and had few enemies; he was an acceptable second choice for both the Horners and the committee. Strode, on the other hand, was unacceptable to both. Politically he was like Horner a moderate, already openly hostile to the radical committee. But the old quarrels of 1643 still festered: Strode would get no help from Horner. His chief advantages were his great wealth and his immense popularity among the freeholders. During the war he had been an admired and successful officer, and had indeed been the clubmen's first choice as their commander, though the committee had circumvented him by appointing Alexander Popham. Henley appears to have attracted little support outside committee circles. More than any of the others, Strode was the candidate of the Country.

In the weeks before the election the Strode and Henley factions canvassed energetically. George Horner, it was pointed out, was a 'known neuter, if not worse' who had lived quietly at Mells and Cloford during the royalist occupation. Committeemen grimly passed the word that anyone rash enough to support Strode would be in danger of sequestration. Charges of financial irregularities, of favour to royalists, and even an absurd story of Strode's 'inclination to independency' were scattered abroad. Shortly before the election the committee transferred its sessions to Ilchester, and Henley arrived at the head of the county troop.

By the morning of the election, Monday 1 December, Ilchester was crowded with freeholders, in spite of a weekend snowstorm ('the weather and ways were extreme ill', one observer comments). Strode's adherents swarmed noisily around the cross. The sheriff's clerk called the county court into session, but then immediately adjourned it to Queen Camel, four miles away, on the pretext that Ilchester was infected with the plague. There was a confused uproar and by the time order was restored the legal hour for the election had passed. Still shouting 'A Strode! A Strode!' the crowd gradually dispersed. Both Strode and Henley seem to have decided that their best tactics would be to boycott the election, fearing that Horner would repeat the adjournment indefinitely to tire out the opposition if the freeholders followed him to Queen Camel. When the sheriff opened the proceedings in the village the next morning, there was no visible opposition; George Horner and Harington were elected by a handful of voters. The committeemen spent the day drawing up a protest to the House of Commons; it was signed by Pyne, Edward Popham, and other leading radicals, but also possibly by a few Strode supporters. It was then carried to London by the army preacher Hugh Peter, an inveterate election agent, who had been an interested spectator.[18]

Pyne and Henley had been outwitted. But there still remained the boroughs. The first to make returns were Bath and Milborne Port. The Bath corporation wanted to elect their neighbour Harington, but after his return for the county they chose the lawyer James Ashe, John's son, in preference to Edward Popham. The Ashes were politically slightly more moderate than the Pophams, but the Bath election was probably affected more by personal considerations than ideological ones. At Milborne Port, according to a presbyterian newspaper, there were some curious happenings. The bailiff was a sequestered royalist and prisoners were brought out of gaol to vote. This odd electorate returned Harington's nephew, William Carent, and Thomas Grove. The Carents, of Toomer in Henstridge, were an old family, but one not recently very prominent in county affairs. Nor was Carent an active politician, though his later token appearance in the Rump suggests that he may have been acceptable to Pyne. But Grove, who lived at Ferne House in Wiltshire, was certainly hostile, a strong presbyterian in both religion and politics.[19]

When after a long delay Horner released his warrants for the other boroughs, the committee's candidates filled both seats at Bridgwater and Minehead and the single vacancy at Taunton. At Minehead Edward Popham inherited his father's old seat, in a borough where his Luttrell relations had long been dominant. The other new member was a Yorkshireman without Somerset connections: Walter Strickland, parliament's ambassador to the Dutch republic and a consistent radical, whose candidacy may well have been arranged by Prideaux. Both the victors at Bridgwater were local men and both close to Pyne: the war hero Robert Blake, and the recorder Sir Thomas Wroth. Puritan Taunton also presented few difficulties, returning the committeeman Dr John Palmer.

These were all committee successes. But at Wells the results were mixed and at Ilchester they were disastrous. The committee was preparing the ground at Wells in December 1645 when the recorder, Christopher Dodington, brother of the notorious Sir Francis, was the target of an investigation. In the end the city elected the committeeman Lislebone Long, but also chose Clement Walker, whose contempt for the 'godly gang', Pyne included, was soon to receive vitriolic expression in his famous *History of Independency*. The Ilchester voters were under constant committee pressure for weeks before the election, but the town's bailiff, John Lockyer, obstinately returned Strode and his ally Thomas Hodges of Wedmore. The committee proposed Alexander Pym for one place; for the other the puritan zealot, Major Harrison, and Henley were successively put forward and then dropped before (at Prideaux's suggestion) they settled on the Yorkshireman Sir William Selby, Fairfax's brother-in-law. Pyne used every known trick, bullying the bailiff and even appropriating the warrant during a night alarm over a fictitious royalist raid. But Lockyer held fast, and although a second election carefully supervised by the committee produced a rival return, the Committee of Privileges confirmed Strode and Hodges after a lengthy investigation.[20]

Political excitement was still at a high pitch. The county election dispute aroused intense partisanship in the Commons, but at last a neutral committee resolved that the sheriff's conduct had been illegal. On 5 June 1646 Harington and George Horner were unseated and a new election ordered. To reduce the passions in the county the Commons summoned all Somerset MPs to attend the House forthwith, thus removing them from the campaign. Pyne protested indignantly and his faithful committee declared that his departure would be 'a very great disheartening unto the best-affected people'. But there were rumours that if he did not leave, a troop of horse would be sent to fetch him, and in the end he complied.[21] Horner and Harington were already hard at work. After rejecting Horner's proposal of a formal alliance Harington rode busily about the county seeking support. He met with Pyne and Henley at Wells and dined with the Pophams at Hunstrete several times, hearing Alexander repeat his preference for Henley and 'complain of Sir John Horner's unkindness'. Other candidates, too, were stirring. Strode still coveted the greater prestige of the county seat (if successful he could resign Ilchester) and once more he had the clubmen behind him. During the summer there were club meetings both on the Poldens and near Castle Cary, osten-

sibly to protest against quartering by the Taunton and Bridgwater garrisons. Humphrey Willis was much in evidence, boasting
that he could deliver 500 votes for Strode. But he was summoned
before the 'great and over-topping Pyne', who quickly silenced
him by consigning him to prison at Weymouth.[22]

On 13 July the county court again convened, this time at Castle
Cary. Before the day was out Harington and George Horner had
again been elected, though not without some more irregularities:
much of the poll was taken in private in the sheriff's chamber,
while he was at dinner. And there had been changes of allegiance
since the previous December. In the first election John Preston
had supported Henley, but at Castle Cary he went over to the
Horners, and Henley suspected him of being responsible for having the poll taken in private. There was a blazing row in the
committee when they got back to Ilchester and even talk of a
duel.[23] Once more the failure to elect Henley showed that in the
traditional institutional framework the committee could be defied
by a powerful family like the Horners. The Somerset by-elections
were over, and Pyne had been only partly successful. Of the fourteen new MPs six were committee nominees, three were tolerable
allies (Harington, James Ashe, and Carent), and five were outright
opponents. The elections had raised the political temperature and
hardened the lines of division. The conflict in the committee can
be the more easily understood.

*   *   *   *

Throughout 1646 the Country's alienation from parliament and
committee grew ever deeper. Was this what they had fought for—
higher taxes than ever, continued military oppression, government by unfamiliar, upstart bureaucrats instead of a return to the
old, comfortable ways? The gentry's restiveness was in part an
expression of resentment at being governed by men of relatively
humble origins. Social deference was still strongly ingrained, so
many commoners also felt contempt for their new governors and
looked back nostalgically to their 'natural' rulers. Humphrey
Willis made a virtue of his origins—a 'gent. sprung from a fig'—
and was full of scorn for the 'blue apron-blades', the 'blue-new-
made-gentlemen' whose sole aim was 'to keep the gentry under'.[24]

Much of the hostility was engendered by inevitable postwar

J

Times VVhirligig,

OR,

The Blew-new-made-Gentle-
man mounted.

A Committee-man.

Take him Marshall.

Heu quantum mutatus ab illo!

Written by a faithfull Servant and true Lover
of his Countrey,

Hum. Willis, Esquire.

Feb: 9ᵗʰ Printed in the Yeare, 1647. 1646

Humphrey Willis denounces Colonel Pyne

difficulties for which the committee was not responsible. But as the immediate, visible authority it was naturally blamed for them. Discontent was almost as widespread as in Goring's time. In March clubmen again raised their heads in the Bruton area and a manifesto was circulated calling a mass meeting near Hornblotton churchyard. Persons attending, it was suggested, should avoid being 'overtaken in drinking'. The messenger tried to swallow the document when he was arrested, but could not conceal that the purpose of the gathering was to obstruct impressment for the army.[25] Plundering soldiers were still all too common. During the summer the worst culprits were the men of Massey's brigade, who were awaiting disbandment after months without pay. To the normal excesses of unemployed troops they were adding organised highway robbery and murder, and although Massey hanged an offender at Ilminster, discipline was little improved. Fairfax, on leave at Bath, wrote to support a county petition, and eventually the brigade was paid off. Later in the year troops on their way to Ireland by way of Minehead caused similar trouble. 'If they lie above a night in a place the Country rise', Thomas Piggott of Long Ashton noted, 'which has much lessened their numbers, neither are the committees or governors here apt to redress it.'[26]

Pyne was well aware how the military burden affected the committee's reputation. In February 1645 he had denounced 'the great insolencies and pressures of the soldiers', and bemoaned the 'miserable pressures on our poor county' by Holborne's men. In 1646 the committee complained that the free quarter taken by the Taunton and Bridgwater garrisons was a major cause of 'the exasperating the Country against the committee'. The resurgence of the clubmen before the second county election was provoked by this quartering, and by the time Willis was arrested there had been two serious riots near Bridgwater in which enraged countrymen had 'beaten the soldiers out of their quarters'. In one of these or a similar riot a soldier of the committee troop was killed. Other grievances also led to violence. There were demonstrations against the newly imposed excise at Taunton, Bruton, and Somerton, still smouldering unrest in Selwood, and an epidemic of rioting and murder at Pilton, where repeated investigations failed to discover the perpetrators.[27]

Many things for which the committee was blamed were not its fault; but some were. Pyne's conduct was certainly not endearing.

He was accused of imposing oaths which compelled witnesses to incriminate themselves and of sitting 'as a committee himself, in his chamber', drawing up orders which were rubber-stamped by his underlings. Clement Walker affected to believe that he was often drunk in committee, 'inspired with sack'. Humphrey Willis provides a graphic description of Pyne's style:

> How do you swell and bluster out. . . . Then begins nothing but 'What are you? Who sent for you? Is this any business of yours? What made you here?' But if the man will not be daunted for this, then 'Who knows this fellow here? Where doth he dwell? Hah— speak, man'. And if this fail too, then 'Did he never take up arms against the parliament? How stands he affected? Sirrah, you are a peremptory jack, but we'll take a course with you well enough ere you go. Have you taken the oath yet? Reach hither the book. Come hither sirrah—will you take it?'[28]

The committee's tyrannical reputation was not based solely on its chairman's bluster. Financial pressure made it impossible to make adequate allowance for people's losses; the committee insisted on 'great contributions' even from those who had suffered badly in the war. Outrageous behaviour by sequestration officers also contributed to the discontent. Richard Short and Charles Hooker, sequestrators of Wellow hundred, put in a new minister at Combe Hay; after nine months the poor man had to leave because the officials were appropriating his stipend. Sequestrators and soldiers assaulted Edward Burgh of Priston during a dispute over his composition and dangerously wounded his pregnant wife. Joan Strode, a Stoke-under-Ham widow, had done nothing worse than sell corn to royalist garrisons and had indeed maintained three of her sons in the parliament's service. She compounded, but the County Committee again seized her estate, which they leased to one of their officers. Repeated orders by Goldsmiths' Hall to leave her alone were ignored, and the case dragged on for years before the committee's proceedings were voted 'irregular and not according to law'.[29] Even more notorious was the murder of the dean of Wells, Dr Walter Ralegh, one of the classic royalist atrocity stories. Ralegh, a nephew of the great Elizabethan, had been imprisoned in the old bishop's house at Banwell, where the marshal, Barrett, was in charge of the committee's gaol. There are several versions of the affair, but all agree that Barrett ran the dean through with either a sword or a knife and that he died a few days later. Needless to say, Barrett was never convicted.[30]

In November 1646 there was an outright confrontation at Bridgwater. Three months earlier, the Commons had ordered that the Taunton and Bridgwater garrisons be disbanded and the fortifications dismantled. This must have caused rejoicing in such places as Woolavington, where Alexander Pym had tried to evade the rate levied for the soldiers' maintenance. 'You will not expect that your poor tenants should bear it all and your farms go free', his steward reproved him. Early in November the committee, attended by the usual troop of horse, came to Bridgwater to begin dismantling operations. Enthusiastic crowds collected and offered their services. Some of the local gentry also came to watch, and urged the countrymen to finish the job by levelling the works around the castle, which the committee argued were not included in the official order. There was an ugly scene and the committee troop charged the crowd, 'knocking countrymen in the head for doing as they bid them', Willis complained. Several were killed, 'poor men', Clement Walker lamented, '... whose bloods were shed like the blood of a dog'. The committee arrested a certain Henry Cheeke as the ringleader. He in turn sued Minterne and others allegedly responsible for the soldiers' violence, but to no avail.[31]

Like the cavaliers before them, parliament's officers had alienated the Country. 'No county, that I can understand, hath had such a hard measure afforded it by their committee', Willis declared. Encouraged by similar complaints from other counties, presbyterians in parliament denounced the committees' 'oppressions and illegalities' and tried unsuccessfully to abolish them. 'Great disorders', the Lords resolved, 'have been occasioned by the continuance of them.'[32] It was time for a counter-attack by the moderates. Pyne in the end turned it back, and his victory swept Somerset onwards to revolution.

Notes to this chapter are on pages 207-8.

8
Conflict and Revolution
1646-9

One February day in 1647 a royalist colonel named Thomas Gallopp encountered William Strode, journeying down to Somerset
from London. The talk soon turned to politics. The news at
Westminster, Strode confided, was that 'we are now about to
disband Sir Thomas Fairfax's army'. Gallopp was dumbfounded,
but Strode dismissed his objections; there were precedents, he suggested obscurely, in the Wars of the Roses. If the soldiers would
not disband they would be hanged or sent to Ireland. 'We will
destroy them all', Strode declared, '...Fairfax will be deceived,
for part of his army will join with us, and besides, the Scots are
very honest men and will come to assist us.' Strode vowed that he
would 'never fight more, unless it were against this Independent
army'. The radical politicians were also marked down for destruction: 'we are resolved not to leave one of the Independent party
to live in this kingdom'. The county committees were equally
bad, Strode continued—'all rogues'. Somerset's was the worst, but
it would not long survive the disbandment of the army. 'As for
Pyne', Strode concluded, 'I make no doubt but we shall have him
hanged and then what will become of the rest? The Country will
rise and knock them all in head as soon as their guard is gone, and
that shall be done very speedily.'[1]

A new political wind was blowing. It was no longer the cavaliers
but the army, the Independents, and the county committees who
were now the worst enemies of the parliamentarian moderates.
Strode accurately forecast the tactics his presbyterian friends in
parliament, led by Denzil Holles and Sir Philip Stapleton, were
about to follow. Backed by a Scots army and new forces raised in
London and from Massey's defunct brigade, they intended to send

part of the New Model to Ireland under more submissive officers and get rid of the rest. They would then negotiate a settlement with Charles I which would restore constitutional government: abolish the committees, revive the power of the gentry JPs, and impose a presbyterian religious system, thus defeating the radical sects' hopes of toleration. In the spring and summer of 1647 this programme led to the radicalisation of the New Model as it united in resistance. It also provoked a partial military coup. The army impeached the presbyterian leaders (the 'Eleven Members') and occupied London.

These remarkable events had inevitable repercussions in Somerset. The presbyterians were not moved solely by a selfish desire for power. Indeed, their whole programme reflected the universal Country dislike of military rule and centralisation. In 1647 Somerset, like other counties, seethed with discontent. Troops on their way to Ireland were again largely responsible. The behaviour of Col Townsend's regiment was so bad that it inspired a grand jury petition at Taunton Assizes. John Turberville, a London lawyer who lived at Tolland near Wiveliscombe, had some of them quartered on him: 'such uncivil drinkers and thirsty souls', he grumbled, 'that a barrel of good beer trembles at the sight of them, and the whole house nothing but a rendezvous of tobacco and spitting'. Whenever Townsend's men quartered in north Somerset they were attacked by clubmen, often with the connivance of the local authorities. Richard Cole, who had succeeded Horner as high sheriff, even summoned the neighbouring villagers to meet on Dolebury Warren to assist in apprehending the marauding soldiers. In London John Harington was troubled by exaggerated rumours of a full-scale local insurrection. The disorders declined during the summer, but by September a new anti-military petition was circulating in the county, and a month later the JPs again complained to parliament of the 'heavy pressures and burdens by free quartering'.[2]

Disbandment was politically popular, but the radicals knew that it had to be avoided if their power and their hopes for godly reformation were to be preserved. In February Roger Hill confided to Pyne his fears of the 'dangers and calamities' which might follow the early votes against the army. The fates of Bridgwater and Taunton, whose garrisons had survived the previous year's dismantling, hung in the balance. The ministers, Hill thought, could help by promoting a petition for a firmer establishment of church government; then some of the reliable gentry might sign, with an addition 'to touch upon the common fears from cavaliers and malignants and to desire a sufficient standing force to over-awe them'. But the petition did not materialise, and instead the Commons reaffirmed their earlier order for disbanding Bridg-water and reducing the Taunton garrison to a mere 100 men. The committee was told to employ the surplus troops to recruit a regiment being raised for service in Ireland.[3]

*   *   *   *

The military burden was thus diminished, but the hated commit-tee remained. To reduce its authority, since they could not abolish it, the moderates tried to strengthen alternative institutions. The most obvious one was the Commission of the Peace. The first postwar commission had been issued in the early summer of 1646; until then, it will be recalled, the County Committee had filled the breach. The new magistrates were appointed on recommenda-tions by MPs to the commissioners of the Great Seal. One might have expected Pyne's alliance with Lord Commissioner Prideaux to have enabled him to pack the commission with radicals, but county traditions were too strong—and the moderate gentry were much more anxious to serve as JPs than as committeemen. Active JPs included Pyne's friends Henley and the Pophams, but also his enemies Prynne and Strode and such non-partisan county worthies as John Buckland of West Harptree (whose wife was a Phelips) and Richard Jones of Chew Magna, both perennial magistrates through all the changes of the next fifteen years. Some additions in July included solid men like George Luttrell and William Capell, and even a former royalist, Charles Steynings. The only reliable Pyne henchman among the newcomers was Henry Bon-ner, though another future ally, Ludlow's brother-in-law Giles Strangways of Charlton Adam, came into the commission in 1647.[4]

The first postwar Assizes were held at Taunton in August 1646, the first Quarter Sessions at Bridgwater in October. There was much to be done before normal government could function. The sessions records had disappeared 'during the late combustions', no treasurers for maimed soldiers had been appointed, and the houses of correction at Taunton and Shepton Mallet stood vacant and neglected.⁵ For the present politics did not seriously affect either the appointment or the operations of the JPs. Through most of 1647 they seem to have acted in outward harmony, radicals and moderates alike combining in the October protest against quartering. But the JPs could not control the committee; at best their revival provided for the moderates a welcome sign of returning legality.

If Pyne could not be restrained by the JPs, perhaps he could by the new subcommittee of accounts. Unlike the County Committee, this was technically a branch of a national body, the Committee of Accounts in London, which had been established during the war to audit the accounts of all receivers of public money, from soldiers to sequestrators. The county subcommittees were supposed to perform the routine business of auditing local accounts. Such a body might be very embarrassing to the County Committee, uncovering damaging instances of corruption and abuse. In some places the subcommittees were in effect nominated by the county committees, who thus appointed their own watchdogs. This did not happen in Somerset, mainly because the most energetic member of the London committee was William Prynne. Full of righteous zeal for honest government and enraged by Pyne's misdeeds, Prynne named the Somerset subcommittee himself, probably with some help from his neighbour Harington. Most of the men thus appointed came from the Bath region—aldermen of the city or minor gentry from the surrounding parishes—though there were a few from as far afield as Backwell and Wrington.⁶

In the summer of 1646 the members went quickly to work. Meetings were held in the guildhall at Bath, at the *Swan* at Shepton Mallet, and in many of the villages. Constables, collectors of assessments, sequestration officials, and military men all turned in their accounts. Friction soon developed between the subcommittee and the County Committee, in Somerset as in other counties. The worst incident followed discovery of the crimes of the two Wellow sequestrators, Hooker and Short. The County Committee immediately protected its officers, forcibly interrupting the subcommittee's sessions. By this time Pyne had won over several members of the subcommittee, notably John Gay of Englishcombe, who according to Strode was 'in great favour with the committee of the county'. Nominally the committee backed down after being reproved from London and promised to desist from obstruction, but in return

the subcommittee abandoned the investigation of Hooker and
Short.

Apart from this episode the subcommittee had fair success in
the eastern division. But it was another story in the west, the heart
of Pyne's power. And Gay's clique deliberately delayed approving
Strode's accounts so that they could avoid moving on to a proper
audit of committeemen. There were repeated orders from London
that Pyne should be made to submit to audit, and that 'all the
treasurers' and sequestrators' accounts, as well in the western as
eastern division' should be scrutinised. Pyne responded with eva-
sion and bland indifference, at last condescending to reply that he
had kept no accounts and had 'utterly refused to finger public
money': a half-truth, to say the least. Sir Thomas Wroth was only
slightly more co-operative. Prynne's allies were simply not of sufficient stature to challenge the committee, even if they had not been
infiltrated by Pyne's agents.[7]

Parliament's appointment of a separate Assessment Commission
in June 1647 provided the moderates with another means of stem-
ming Pyne's power. That their representatives in the Commons
were aware of this is clear from the names of the men they
nominated. Pyne and other leading radicals were included, to be
sure: the MPs could scarcely be left out, while Henley and Preston
were also men of authority. But almost all the rest of the faction
—Alexander Pym, Richard Trevillian, Edward Ceely, and many
lesser men—were omitted. The new commissioners were nearly all
identifiable political moderates, men of substance who would put
the county's interests ahead of the national policies being imposed
from Whitehall through the committee. Several were in disfavour
with Pyne because of wartime neutrality or royalism: Harbin and
Richard Cole, for example. William Strode's son and the MPs
Grove and George Horner were open presbyterians, Buckland and
George Luttrell Country moderates by any definition. A signifi-
cant number of them came from the Horners' part of the county
and may have been their friends or clients: Thomas Bampfield
of Hardington, James Strode of Cranmore, and William Orange
of Foxcote all fit this description.[8]

The Assessment Commission appropriated some of the committee's fiscal powers, just as the JPs reduced its police and administrative functions. But Pyne retained formidable authority. The
committee still controlled sequestration business, still had ulti-

mate responsibility for security, and above all still commanded the militia forces. Moreover it played a central role in the reconstruction of the church in Somerset, both in the weeding out of royalist clergy and in the establishment of the presbyterian system which replaced the diocesan authority. Control of the pulpits, the vital media for circulating information and propaganda as well as spiritual truths, was an essential part of county government. But it was also a matter which attracted the attention of the moderates perhaps more than any other. They too had fought for godly reformation.

*   *   *   *

The first step towards establishing presbyterianism in Somerset was a circular letter from Speaker Lenthall in September 1645. This called on the county committees to divide their counties into classical presbyteries, and to appoint ministers and lay elders in each classis. Progress in Somerset was slow, no doubt because the committee first had to replace the royalist clergy before there were enough reliable ministers to create an organisation. In April 1647 Harington was still conferring with Sir John Horner; the committee's divisions must have hampered their work. At length in March 1648 the names of the ministers and lay elders were published in a letter signed by Horner, Prynne, Henley, and the divines Newton and William Thomas. Ideally, they thought, there ought to be nine classes in the county, but 'by reason of the scarcity of fitting ministers and elders' they had to be content with four, centred at Bath, Wells, Ilchester, and Taunton respectively. The lay elders included all the major roundhead gentry—Harington, Ashe, Strode, Pyne, Wroth, Henley, the Pophams, Horners, and the rest—as well as many lesser, but for the most part substantial men. Among the ministers were all the old puritan stalwarts: Crooke of Wrington, the Allens of Ditcheat and Batcombe, Newton of Taunton, and Thomas of Ubley, as well as Pyne's parson at Curry Mallet, John Baker.[9]

Legally presbytery had replaced episcopacy. But although individual presbyterians exercised great influence in their parishes, their organisation never really flourished in Somerset. Far more decisive was the clerical purge that followed the war. A combination of local initiative and action by the Committee for Plundered

Ministers in London swept the royalist clergy into temporary oblivion.

Some of the Laudian minority had already effectively removed themselves. Henry Ancketyll, rector of Mells, fought as a cavalier officer, became governor of Corfe Castle, and died of wounds as a prisoner of war. Henry Byam, rector of Luccombe and Selworthy, went into exile, first in Jersey, then on the continent. Many others, not all of them Laudians, were imprisoned by the committee; lurid stories of their miseries, some of them true, were assiduously collected years later by the martyrologist John Walker. Ministers who still used the Book of Common Prayer in the autumn of 1645, like Anthony Richardson at West Camel, were hunted down, sequestered, and ejected. Others declared themselves when they were called on to take the Covenant: Thomas Gauler of Chiselborough, for instance, who was ejected by a troop of horse and imprisoned for months. A few never emerged from captivity. Joseph Greenfield of Whitestaunton died in prison in London, Richard Long of Chewton Mendip in the committee gaol at Axbridge. Old scores were being paid off by disgruntled parishioners. At Compton Pauncefoot Hugh Collins was accused of 'lewd and scandalous behaviour', including cattle thieving, fathering a bastard child, and even, it was hinted, conniving at the murder of a parliamentarian soldier quartered in his house. Such allegations have to be taken with a large grain of salt; nevertheless, there is no doubt that many absentees, pluralists, and incompetents, as well as many pious and dedicated men were removed.[10]

Not all the sufferers were as badly off as John Walker's dismal picture suggests. Their replacements were supposed to pay them a fifth of the value of their livings, and although this provision was sometimes evaded, most of the ejected clergy received at least a minimal maintenance. Some conformed and moved on to new parishes in or outside the county. Matthew Law and Samuel Peryam, removed from Wedmore and Nynehead respectively, 'ran in with the times', and kept the other livings they had previously held in plurality. William Kemp went from Podimore Milton to the Lake District, serving several parishes there; others obtained livings closer to home, in Devon and Dorset. Yet others became schoolmasters or were sheltered by the royalist gentry; at Hinton Lord Poulett looked after the ejected rector of Dinnington, Robert Clement, even though his brother was a regicide. Some who had preached for the king were protected by influential parliamentarians. Pyne stopped the sequestration of his old tutor, John England, vicar of Isle Brewers, though he did not prevent the committee ordering him not to preach. Alexander Popham looked after Richard Long's family after the death of the Chewton Mendip parson.

Altogether upwards of 100 Somerset ministers were ejected in the years after the war; a large number, yet not more than a fifth of the parishes were affected.[11] The far more numerous survivors included many with no strong theological opinions, who took the Covenant and used the Directory so that they could go on serving their flocks, conformists who regarded neither episcopacy nor presbytery as divinely ordained. In 1647 Thomas Brooke reflected that he stood 'upon slippery grounds' at Weston Bampfylde, but added consolingly that 'in these casual times there are but few can promise to themselves any better certainty'. Suitable replacements were hard to find. 'Our committees', a presbyterian complained in July 1646, 'have filled many churches with vile wretched men, worse than some they put out.' True enough, no doubt, but it is also true that some of the intruders, as well as the wartime puritan appointments, were men of distinction. Benjamin Whichcott had been presented to North Cadbury by his college in 1643; a leader of the Cambridge Platonists, he was one of the outstanding philosophers of his time. Richard Fairclough, son of a well-known Suffolk puritan, accompanied Whichcott to North Cadbury and stayed to officiate when his friend was recalled to Cambridge. After the war Sir John Horner was so impressed by the quality of his sermon at the Assizes that he promptly installed him at Mells. Henry Jeanes, who acquired Chedzoy from the murdered Dean Ralegh, was another theologian and controversialist of more than average ability. Such names may remind us that the expulsion of the Laudians was not an unmitigated disaster.[12]

The puritan clergy had crucial roles to play in the campaign for godly reformation, and their sermons on public occasions were often highly political. Yet the early vindictive mood quickly evaporated. At the May 1646 commemoration service at Taunton, Newton preached violently against the royalists, those 'implacable and desperate enemies of God, and of his people'. A year later, however, Timothy Batt of Ilminster was far less political, contenting himself with denouncing sin and complaining that 'drunkenness, swearing, whoring, profanation of God's day and ordinances' were spreading again even among the godly people of Taunton. And soon the rise of far more radical sects swung the presbyterians sharply to the right. William Thomas regretted that ministers everywhere were being despised by men who claimed to be 'more perfect saints'. Threatened by the sectarian tide, in 1648 the Somerset ministers collectively attested the urgent need for stronger church government and denounced the prevailing toleration.[13]

Independents, baptists, and even more radical sects had indeed spread rapidly after the end of the war. Soldiers of the New Model set a contagious example. At Bristol in the autumn of 1645 a scarlet-coated lieutenant daily preached 'very strange things', including the mortality of the soul. Few Independents held Somerset livings, but there was one at Bath in 1646, sharing the abbey pulpit with a presbyterian, and holding 'Christ a king, and every new-moulded congregation his kingdom'. More dangerous to both religious and political stability was the voluntary formation of 'gathered churches', in which wildly heretical opinions were often expounded. Among them were the baptists, a byword for revolutionary excesses ever since John of Leyden. The 'first that sowed the seeds of anabaptism' in Somerset was a militant army preacher, Thomas Collier, who came from Westbury-sub-Mendip. A baptist took over the pulpit at Middlezoy in 1646 (he was arrested for preaching without a licence), and there was a congregation in St Mary Street, Taunton. Blake, however, showed them little sympathy. 'Our governor', one of them told Collier, 'does labour to beat us down', attributing their meetings not to tenderness of conscience, but 'damnable pride'. But discipline had gone with the ecclesiastical courts, the presbyterian settlement was still not completed, new and dangerous ideas were abroad. Many of the wilder sectaries were men who had been, and still were, the very backbone of the parliamentarian cause. One of them, a sequestrator, argued that 'adultery was no sin', and drunkenness merely 'a help to see Christ the better by'.[14] The lid was off.

＊   ＊   ＊   ＊

By 1648 radicals and moderates were on a collision course. The king, exploiting his enemies' divisions, had already signed his fatal alliance with the Scots. On 3 January the Commons retaliated with the Vote of No Addresses, suspending negotiations indefinitely. But these were the manoeuvres of politicians: all the Country wanted was peace and settlement. Smouldering hostility to centralisation and military rule burst into flame in the very heart of parliamentarian England. In a series of popular petitions, the south-eastern counties from Essex to Hampshire demanded a 'personal treaty' with Charles, as a prelude to the restoration of normal constitutional government. In May Kent exploded in rebellion against its tyrannical committee; Essex soon followed. The Second Civil War, culminating in the siege of Colchester and Cromwell's rout of the invading Scots at Preston, was at hand.

Somerset escaped open hostilities in 1648, but the county was not far from the brink. Indeed, there was growing tension throughout the West. Royalists recently returned from exile or imprisonment made common cause with Country localists. At Bath the growing number of visitors who came to take the waters included many of both kinds. Local firebrands encouraged a clergyman to use the prayer book and preach against parliament in St James's church. The place was packed and the mayor dared not arrest him; after the service the defiant cleric was escorted by an armed mob to the house of Henry Chapman, an ardent cavalier. Chapman also promoted regular bull-baitings outside the city walls to which, it was reported, large numbers of 'disaffected people flocked from the adjoyning counties'. When the magistrates held a meeting to stop the disorders, the culprits marched to it 'with a drum before their dogs' and insulted them. Prynne, who disliked bull-baiting as much as stage plays, had recently been elected recorder, but was powerless to intervene. The offences took place outside the city, and his jurisdiction in the county had been destroyed by his removal, at Pyne's instigation, from the Commission of the Peace.[15]

Bath was not unique in its disaffection. Throughout the county feeling against the committee was as strong as ever. When one of their troopers killed a royalist officer in a brawl, he was tried before a jury that the committee thought 'would have condemned all those that act for the parliament' and duly hanged. The committee's officers, it was said, could 'hardly pass two miles' without

'fear of a martyrdom by stoning'. In May Cromwell wrote anxiously to Fairfax from Gloucestershire: 'You hear in what a flame
these western parts are.' Rumours of royalist plots abounded.
Hertford and his son, Lord Beauchamp, were believed to be preparing for a rising of 8,000 men in the West, in which parliamentarian as well as cavalier officers were engaged. Hopton's old
friend Walter Slingsby was busy listing men.[16]

Pyne's committee went quickly to work to defeat this menacing
combination. On 23 May Alexander Popham was sent down from
London to raise a troop of horse; soon afterwards a regiment of
foot was authorised. Militia forces were being raised in many other
counties as the Second Civil War erupted, usually under new
commissioners broadly representative of the roundhead gentry.
Because of the county's divisions no such commissioners could be
appointed in Somerset, and the new forces therefore remained
under the committee's control. Popham's troop duly secured Bath.
Otherwise, however, the eastern division (the territory of Horner
and Strode, it should be noted) was not well protected. 'Some
in those parts', the committee told the Commons, 'your seeming
friends, . . . too much dishearten honest men from listing, and
favour and uphold your enemies.' In Pyne's western division, by
contrast, nearly 600 horse and 2,500 foot were raised, as well as
800 men at Taunton.[17]

There remained the problem of paying them. Apart from the
minority of puritan zealots, Somerset greeted the new military
moves with distaste. Sir Edward Hungerford successfully protested when the committee tried to put a garrison into Farleigh
Castle. Popham's men were paid by the committee 'as long as
they could procure money', but in spite of large outlays by their
commander they soon had to fall back on free quarter. The
larger western division forces were only part-time soldiers, receiving allowances only when they mustered. After a conference with
Cromwell at Monmouth in July, Pyne and Popham repeatedly
asked for authority to tax the estates of all 'malignants and
neuters' in the county. When their request reached the Commons,
there was a sharp debate. The word 'neuters', one hostile MP
pointed out, was 'of a wide signification, and would reach to all
the well-affected that are not of their crew, and indeed to almost
all men of the county'. The proposal to give the new forces a
permanent establishment upset even some of the committee's

former allies. 'We do not know any necessity of forces in the said county', four Somerset MPs declared. Two of the four, to be sure, were the violent presbyterians Strode and Clement Walker; but the others were Harington and James Ashe, both much closer to the committee. The Commons rightly decided that they, not Pyne and Popham, expressed the true state of county opinion, and on 23 October ordered the immediate disbandment of all the Somerset forces.[18]

*   *   *   *

All through 1648 Pyne fought hard to stem the counter-revolutionary tide. He began early in the year with a move against the presbyterian JPs. The Westminster radicals had been contemplating a general purge of the commissions of the peace, and although the necessary legislation never materialised, Pyne acted without it. Prynne and several others were dismissed and were soon blaming Pyne's 'mere groundless spleen' at their past efforts to expose committee misgovernment. The 'causeless, clandestine discommissioning of justices of peace' gave fresh fuel to Prynne's campaign against the committee, and to his argument that only a return to the rule of law could prevent renewed civil war. But Pyne's hold on the county magistracy was growing. In 1648 several more committeemen became JPs: Trevillian, Edward Ceely and his brother William, recorder of Bridgwater, among them. And Pyne was also reducing the moderate majority on the Assessment Commission, to which Trevillian, the Ceelys, Alexander Pym, and several other radicals were appointed.[19]

While strengthening his institutional power, Pyne was also trying to commit Somerset to the support of revolutionary policies. Humphrey Willis had long since accused him of wanting to have the Prince of Wales killed. Now the radicals were speaking openly against Charles I himself. Seconding the Vote of No Addresses, Sir Thomas Wroth passionately declared: 'From devils and kings, good Lord deliver me. It's now high time, up and be doing. I desire any government rather than that of kings.' Soon Wroth was insisting that Charles ought to be 'brought to his trial, and to give an account for all the blood that hath been spilt'.[20]

'Up and be doing': while his allies spoke out in parliament, Pyne mobilised support for them in the county. Local petitions

K

had often been used as ammunition in propaganda campaigns; moderates and radicals alike had promoted them. But there was a difference. Left to themselves the gentry and the propertied freeholders, the Country, could be relied on to support moderate courses. For radical petitions careful stage-management was needed. There were strong suspicions that the Independents' petitions were 'framed at Westminster' and sent down to the counties to be circulated by sequestrators or adopted by packed grand juries. This was particularly alleged of the series of petitions in February and March 1648 in support of the Vote of No Addresses.[21]

If juries were to be packed, the key man was the sheriff who selected them. The first two postwar sheriffs, Horner and Cole, had been moderates, but in November 1647 Cole was succeeded by John Preston, a committeeman. Pyne could now obtain the grand juries he wanted. Before the county spoke, however, the first shot in the No Addresses campaign was fired by Taunton. Given Taunton's militant reputation this is not surprising, though presbyterians sneered that the petition was subscribed only by 'a few sectaries'. More important was the county petition that soon followed. According to Clement Walker it made little headway in the eastern division, but in the west Pyne had it circulated by the sequestrators, who obtained signatures by the usual bullying. On 27 March the Assizes were held at Chard; with the encouragement of a radical judge, John Wylde, the petition was adopted by the grand jury as the sense of the county. It declared Somerset's approval of No Addresses, and called for further revolutionary steps: the county should be freed from the power of all 'malignants, neutrals, and apostates'. Walker supplies the correct translation: a purge of all 'presbyterians and moderate men'.[22]

Walker's charge that this was a packed jury of 'schismatics and sequestrators' was not off the mark. The survival of Preston's papers enables us to see how the packing was done. At the beginning of his year of office the names of qualified freeholders had been returned, as usual, by the constables of the hundreds; these were copied into a 'freeholders' book'. Later, however, numerous additions and interlineations were made, most of them being recognisably the names of men connected with the Pyne faction: committeemen (Edward Ceely, Clift, Minterne, Pittard); officials

(Blackbourne, Tuthill, William Collier); men who as militia officers, JPs or in other ways followed Pyne's lead (Richard Bovett, John Gay, George Sampson of Kingsbury). The March presentment was signed by nineteen jurymen, fourteen of them known radicals, and ten of them from the additions to the freeholders' book. Among the nine jurymen who were original entries in that book are four known radicals, including the former committee official Samuel Whetcombe, and George Smith of Ilchester, father of the wartime royalist constable. In one case the evidence for tampering with the freeholders' book is unanswerable: against the name of the Wells radical Thomas Mead stands the marginal note, 'Mr Pyne'. The March petition was thus the result of elaborate preparation. In no real sense was the grand jury the mouthpiece of the Country.[23]

By the time of the next Assizes, at Taunton in September, the Second Civil War had been fought and won. The moderates at Westminster had also reopened negotiations with the king in the Isle of Wight in a last desperate bid for a settlement that would return the kingdom to legality and mark the end of such local regimes as Pyne's. But the soldiers and their radical allies had come back from the wars bitterly determined to bring Charles I to judgement. It was time for a new petitioning campaign. Serjeant Wylde again presided at the September Assizes, and again Preston made careful preparations. Richard Bovett, a Wellington man who had moved to Taunton and was rising fast through his connections with Popham and Pyne, helped in the arrangements, bringing supplies from London and employing women to furnish and clean the hall. An obedient grand jury produced another radical petition, one of the first in a series from all over England to call for an interruption of the treaty and for justice against the king. Charles, said the petition, could never be trusted to observe any agreement, and the treaty would 'enslave all that had engaged for the liberties of the people'. Only one solution was possible: 'that justice be executed upon all delinquents, from the highest to the lowest, without exception'. Although no list of the September grand jury has survived, once again the circumstantial evidence that it was packed with Pyne's henchmen is overwhelming.[24]

The climax of the revolution was approaching and the political crisis deepened against a background of dissension and depression. The war had intensified the problems of the clothing districts; now a succession of harvest failures drove up food prices and worsened the plight of the poor. In the previous winter Wiltshire had been especially badly affected, and it is unlikely that conditions in north-east Somerset were any better. The JPs made their usual half-hearted gestures, trying to reduce the excessive number of maltsters and thus keep down the price of barley. But the summer of 1648 was the wettest for years and there was another appalling harvest. There were food riots, attacks on excisemen, and renewed outbreaks by clubmen were common throughout the autumn and winter. The military were as unpopular as ever. So permanent seemed their presence that a lease granted by one local landowner discharged the tenant from all costs of quartering 'any of the armies now in this kingdom'. The depredations of Sir Hardress Waller's brigade prompted a despairing cry by Charles Steynings: 'Our poor county is like to be exhausted, and indeed undone.'[25]

The only hope seemed to be at Westminster and in the Isle of Wight. As agreement neared with the king, the moderates in parliament optimistically prepared for a resumption of normal government. Among the measures proposed was a national militia ordinance, which would have taken control of local forces away from the upstart committees and put them under gentry commissioners chosen as the old deputy lieutenants had been—for status, not party loyalty. In the end it would have made the army redundant and eliminated quartering and high taxes. More immediately, it would have taken away the main prop of Pyne's power in Somerset. Pyne himself and the other radical MPs were named as commissioners, but the lesser gentry and townsmen who had dominated the committee—Bonner, Richard Trevillian, the Ceelys and the rest—were nowhere to be seen.[26] Coupled with a successful conclusion to the Isle of Wight treaty, the ordinance would have opened the door to reconciliation with the royalists, to an era of good feelings, to peace and settlement.

It was too late. The army and the radicals were determined to frustrate the threatened presbyterian solution. In October a Leveller petition against the treaty was on foot at Bristol and was said to be attracting support in the neighbouring counties. The army, too, was on the move. Among numerous military petitions calling for action was one from Sir Hardress Waller's brigade in the West. The army's main force marched to Windsor and at the beginning of December advanced on London, just as parliament was giving final passage to the Militia Bill. Prynne, recently elected MP for Newport, Cornwall, made a great three-hour speech in favour of settlement, and on the 5th, after an unprecedented all-night session, the Commons voted to continue negotiating with the king. But the time for speeches had passed. The next day Col Thomas Pride (a Somerset man by birth, incidentally) came to Westminster with a party of musketeers and the moderates were unceremoniously ejected. Prynne, Strode, and Clement Walker were imprisoned, and even John Ashe was temporarily purged. Harington was among the large number of non-party men who withdrew from parliament in protest. Being passed 'upon design to destroy the present army', the Militia Ordinance was repealed before it became effective.[27]

In Somerset as elsewhere the radicals were triumphant. Pyne was in an ecstasy when the news reached Curry Mallet. 'Inevitable ruin', he declared, 'must have befallen honest men without a purge'; if anything, Pride's action was long overdue. The arrest of Prynne—'as very a firebrand as his fellows in evil my country-men Mr Strode and Mr Walker'—was especially pleasing. Now it was time to act against the godly party's enemies in the country-side, and frustrate the 'very high design on foot in these parts to cut the throats of honest men'.[28]

Soon the county was being urgently beset with appeals to support the forthcoming trial of Charles I. Most people, royalist and roundhead alike, responded with shock and horror, but a petition was quickly drafted by the baptist leader Thomas Collier. Its promoters included Pyne, his minister at Curry Mallet, John Baker (who is alleged to have 'persuaded and threatened' people to sign), John Gutch of Glastonbury, the Shepton Mallet clothier John Blinman, and William Gapper, an illiterate yeoman from Sutton Mallet: not an impressive list, to say the least. After some pious preliminaries the petition asked 'that a reformation be speeded and settled, according to God's word', that the army be 'encouraged, duly paid, not laid aside', and above all 'that justice be done on great offenders (a second time brought before you) in satisfaction of the blood shed in your quarrel'. Even Pyne was not sanguine enough to submit this open call for regicide to a grand jury; in any case, immediate action was essential, so it was impractical to wait until the next Quarter Sessions in January. Rather unconvincingly, Somerset had spoken.[29]

Presbyterians indignantly declared that the Country 'disclaimed and protested against' this and other petitions as 'impostures and forgeries'. No doubt this was true: the mood was counter-revolutionary, not revolutionary. Still, there was a radical minority in Somerset and without it Pyne would not have been able to govern. During the critical weeks between the purge and the execution of the king he was constantly on the move: at Taunton on committee business on 28 December, at Wells for Quarter Sessions on 9 January, at Taunton again on the 18th. His presence was indispensable during a time of extreme tension and danger, and this may explain why he was not named to the High Court of Justice (though it is also possible that his nerve failed him, not for the first time). Like so many others he went to London only when the king was safely dead. He was there the next day and quickly performed the necessary ritual for qualifying as a member of the Rump.[30] But it was the corridors of local power that Pyne haunted, not those of Westminster. Backed by Waller's brigade, he could feel confident that the proclamation of the republic guaranteed his continued supremacy. By the recurrent demonstrations of his ability to mobilise the active support of the godly he had played his part in accomplishing the revolution. But even less than ever did he represent the Country.

Notes to this chapter are on pages 208-10.

9
The County and the Commonwealth
1649-53

The king was dead, monarchy and the House of Lords abolished. One Somerset man, young John Locke, spent the fatal 30 January in school a few hundred yards from the scaffold; his headmaster, the famous Dr Busby, kept the Westminster boys on their knees, praying for their murdered king. Far away in the villages, symbols of kingship were rapidly disappearing; at Tintinhull, for example, where the churchwardens employed 'one Parsons for striking out the king's arms'. For a militant minority, in Somerset as elsewhere, Pride's purge and the trial of the king marked the glorious dawn of a new day. 'The Lord hath raised up the spirits of all the honest party in this county', a Somerset radical exulted. Men were listed and an association with the godly of the adjacent shires formed; the Rump, as the purged parliament was now scornfully called, pronounced its blessing and put Alexander Popham in command. John Turberville thought the country was on the verge of wild, thoroughgoing, Leveller revolution, constantly expecting 'men and horses to be raised and the Agreement of the People to be sent into every parish for subscriptions'. In January, at a meeting near Taunton, great crowds of the 'well-affected' declared their readiness to 'sacrifice lives and fortunes' to defend parliament and army.[1]

Yet the republic dedicated to liberty could scarcely have been inaugurated in less promising circumstances. Depression and poverty stalked the land. Prodded by the Rump, the JPs did what they could to cope with the conditions of 'dearth and scarcity', but achieved little. There were alarming signs that the poor might be getting out of hand. Taunton paupers lodged in Hestercombe House in the postwar emergency were still there in April 1649, having defied repeated ejection orders.²

If the poor were restive, the propertied had even less reason to welcome the republic. Troops were everywhere. In April men of Harrison's regiment quartered in the villages near Bath, striking terror into landlords by wild talk of impending confiscation. Mutineers at Bath surrounded the mayor's house and threatened to imprison him for refusing them free quarter. Soon afterwards troops bound for Ireland descended on the area. Prynne, out of prison and now home at Swainswick, was singled out for special treatment. The soldiers, he thought, were the worst he had ever seen, worse even than Goring's crew. They

> roared, stamped, beat the tables with their swords and muskets like so many bedlams, swearing, cursing, and blaspheming at every word; brake the tankards, . . . abused my maid servants, throwing beef and other good provisions at their heads and casting it to the dogs, . . . searched the outhouses for turkeys, which they took for their eggs and young ones, veal and mutton being not good enough for them. They continued drinking and roaring before, at, and after supper, till most of them were mad drunk, and some of them dead drunk under the table.

The incensed Prynne wanted to 'raise the Country upon them'. He received many offers of assistance, but wisely did not make good the threat.³

Even the radicals were quickly disillusioned. It was soon clear that the revolution was not to end in liberty and social justice, but in the rule of a self-appointed oligarchy. High taxes bore as heavily on the godly as on their enemies. When the universal hatred of the excise exploded in riot at Frome, the demonstrators were described as not 'the scum and malignants of the town, but such as have faithfully served the parliament'. Intoxicated by wild millenarian dreams, many radical puritans came to regard politics as irrelevant. Some became Ranters, repudiating all moral constraints and believing that all they did was holy. There were Ranters at Wells. One of them, John Robins, 'was proclaimed the great God, [and] came to a shameful end', Thomas Collier the baptist sneered. In 1650 four of Robins's Somerset disciples heard a call 'to go and preach the gospel in Galilee'. They sold their estates, went to London to embark, and were never heard of again.⁴

Ranter excesses might be disgusting or ridiculous to sober puritans, but political extremists were more dangerous. When the army Levellers mutinied in the spring of 1649, there were distant echoes in Somerset, where a party (whether soldiers or local men is uncertain) rose in arms. While Fairfax and Cromwell hunted down the main Leveller force at Burford, Pyne and Wroth raised volunteers to deal with the Somerset rebels. The outbreak was soon quelled, but for months Pyne was worried about it. Too many discontented soldiers had still not received their arrears, and after the dramatic acquittal of the Levellers' popular leader, John Lilburne, by a London jury Pyne observed his local adherents to 'increase as well as insult and cry victory'.[5]

Like most revolutionary idealists who find themselves in power, Pyne's party soon discovered that their freedom of action was severely limited. Their difficulties were partly of their own making, the result of a reluctance to carry the logic of their convictions too far. They might kill a king and establish a republic, might wish to confine power to the hands of the godly. But they still retained the old belief in hierarchy, still assumed that authority belonged as of right to men of property. Pyne was willing to promote men of lower rank—to obtain reliable local officials he had no alternative—but he also accepted the services of many who were only outward supporters of the regime, conformists who regarded any government as better than none.

Pyne had to take his allies where he could find them. In 1649 there was grave danger that the magistrates might defect en masse. Even hitherto consistent radicals were dubious about the new government. Henry Henley, high sheriff of Dorset at the time, at first decided that his commission had lapsed with the king's execution, though he was soon reassured and agreed to serve again. In Somerset John Buckland made no public protest, though privately he shrank from the dangers of 'this slippery age'. Pyne kept a close watch over the magistrates, and for a time it looked as if a purge of JPs might follow the one in parliament. In the end, as was common under the Rump, there was more talk than action. The secluded MPs were of course removed, but Harington, Sir John Horner, and most of the lesser moderates survived. Pyne tried to swamp them by gradually adding new men and by elevating reliable JPs to the quorum: Carent, Serle, Palmer, and Preston were all promoted in April 1649. Two more confederates, Morgan and Alexander Pym, became JPs, but other additions included such moderates as the lawyer Turberville and the assize clerk Francis Swanton, who had a royalist past. Most of the new JPs were landowners, but their status was far less impressive than that of the magnates of the old days.

Some of the magisterial changes of 1650 were the result of the government's imposition of the engagement 'to be true and faithful to the Commonwealth'. Although subscription was less energetically enforced than the Rump at first threatened, the more obviously disaffected JPs were slowly weeded out. Pyne welcomed the new oath with enthusiasm and quickly began swearing in the constables and tithingmen. A few of his old allies were less happy about it. The mayor of Bridgwater, Francis Tuthill, had to be replaced along with three other members of the corporation. Even Preston delayed taking the engagement until January 1651 and in the following year he resigned from the Commission of the Peace. The disappearance of the radicals Richard Trevillian and Henley from the commission also reflects the serious soul-searching the engagement provoked.[7]

The presbyterian clergy, needless to say, were totally hostile. Although many reluctantly subscribed to retain their livings, a few refused and were ejected, suspended, or lost valuable augmentations; men as prominent as John Norman of Bridgwater and Thomas Lye of Chard were among those in trouble. In 1651 their colleagues were still denouncing the oath from their pulpits. The Commonwealth could govern, but except among a radical handful there was resentment or apathy. When the judges arrived at Chard for the Assizes in March 1651 they were welcomed by the sheriff and militia with the usual formalities. But most of the gentry who would have attended in normal times were conspicuously absent.[8]

*   *   *   *

There was resentment and apathy but there was little overt resistance: wise men usually prefer peace to bloodshed. The Rump's bitterest enemies, the royalists, were too cowed to do more than grumble and dream of better times. Some, like Sir Edward Berkeley, even took the engagement, no doubt with suitable mental reservations.

> Then let's subscribe, and go through stitch,
> As long as we are governed by a soldier's switch,

Charles Steynings cynically recommended.[9] Sequestration and half-completed compositions were universal afflictions, and the costs were high: in 1649 William Basset was selling off land to pay his fine. Curll and other sequestrators were still uncovering minor figures who had escaped their net, sometimes relying on very dubious evidence. Occasionally there was resistance: Curll more than once had to send for troops to help him. Without them he was liable to encounter the kind of defiance forcibly expressed by Richard Mogg, an ex-royalist who was Buckland's under-sheriff. Curll had seized and locked up Mogg's goods. Mogg broke down the door and chased a startled constable from the house, shouting, 'I care not a fart from the highest to the lowest of them all, nor for any man in England. Tis my house and my goods.'[10]

Early in 1652 the Rump passed an Act of Oblivion, pardoning all offences committed before the battle of Worcester. There were many exceptions and qualifications, but royalists who were no longer actually sequestered were freed from further trouble. Many men of second rank, John Somerset for example, obtained the benefit of the act; so did doubtful cases like the old committee-man Robert Harbin. Oblivion also rescued some whose estates were confiscated and put up for sale in 1651 and 1652. Many of the lesser victims of the Acts of Sale were chosen simply because they had refused or had been unable to compound. Usually the threat of sale persuaded them to do so, sometimes the Act of Pardon was successfully invoked. Influence in high places helped, but even this was not always enough. Richard Gay of Widcombe, in prison for debt in 1650, sought the aid of his powerful neighbour John Ashe, who recommended leniency. But two years later Gay was in the Act of Sale and his farm was sold to two Londoners.[11]

There were many better known victims: prominent cavaliers like Dodington, Hopton, and Stawell, recusants like Richard Prater, who had not been allowed to compound. Their properties were duly sold, sometimes to tenants, often to London speculators or favoured local officials. The most notorious case was that of Sir John Stawell. After four years in Newgate he was removed to the Tower and tried by a special high court of justice. The court merely referred Stawell back to the Rump, which disposed of his estates in the 1651 Act of Sale. They brought in almost £64,000, benefitting such loyal friends of the regime as Richard Bovett and John Barker, as well as the town of Taunton, which received £7,000 compensation for war damage. Stawell convinced even his enemies that he had been unjustly treated. But Sir John's plight was exceptional. Many forfeited estates were lost only temporarily. Often they were bought by friends or relatives and recovered by the owners' families long before 1660: Christopher Dodington, for example, acquired several of his brother's manors.[12]

Later legend may have often exaggerated their troubles, but it is true that Somerset royalists were too burdened by sequestration and composition to court further disasters. A few, like Steynings and Swanton, even managed to creep back into local government; many lawyers pliantly continued to practise. There were sporadic signs of defiance when disgruntled countrymen spoke indiscreetly in their cups of the king over the water.[13] But such real conspiracies as occurred usually involved men of two kinds: continental exiles, and younger sons with a thirst for adventure and nothing to lose.

Not all the exiles took part in stirring up their countrymen. Edmund Wyndham, for example, settled down quietly as Charles II's agent at Boulogne. Hopton, who soon left Jersey to settle in Holland, was more active. In the autumn of 1648 he took to the sea and in the following spring cruised off the Cornish coast preying on local shipping. His appeals to the western gentry to rise for Charles II aroused no response, though the authorities took suitable precautions. After Worcester even Hopton talked seriously about returning to England to regain what was left of his estates. It is unlikely that he would have been allowed to do so, and in any case in 1652 he died at Bruges.[14]

Although Hopton was unsuccessful, elaborate efforts were made to rebuild a royalist network in the West. The initiative came from the exiled Court. In October 1649 commissions and instructions to prepare for a general rising were sent from Jersey to a number of western leaders. Among them were Robert Phelips, now living at Salisbury, and Francis Wyndham. Phelips was a typical younger son without estates. Wyndham had more to lose, having acquired Trent by his marriage to Thomas Gerard's daughter, but he had long remembered his father's dying words: 'Though the crown should hang upon a bush, I charge you forsake it not.'[15] Wyndham had not forsaken it: at Dunster he had held out nobly to the end. In the dark days of 1649 Phelips and

Wyndham quietly discussed the possibility of action, as they hawked and hunted with their friends. They found few willing to risk their necks.

As the months passed, a number of minor agents made better progress, at least on paper. The most effective was a Dorset Catholic officer, Alexander Keynes, whose family also had lands in Somerset. In April 1650 Keynes travelled secretly through the West. Among the Somerset cavaliers who entertained him were Wyndham and Phelips. Later in the month, under cover of a race meeting at Salisbury, delegates from several counties formed a new Western Association under the command of Lord Beauchamp, the ardently loyal son of the old Marquis of Hertford. While Charles II went to Scotland and his allies fumbled to defeat at Dunbar, the western royalists prepared. There was much clandestine journeying by the lesser agents, and Sir Edward Rodney's brother went to the king with an account of the plans. Wyndham was toying with a design to recover Dunster and there was talk of an attempt on the Holms islands.[16]

One thing the cavaliers could not do was hold their tongues. At the very time of the Salisbury meeting, five minor figures spoke wildly at Wells about an imminent rising and looked forward to cutting roundhead throats; they were arrested and consigned to Exeter gaol. In August Sir Edward Rodney and several others were imprisoned. In February 1651 a certain Thomas Foster turned up at Trent; instead of going to see Wyndham, he blundered into the house of the puritan minister, where he foolishly blabbed about the cavaliers' plans before being arrested. And in April the Western Association was smashed when one of the king's key agents was captured in London and made a full confession. Beauchamp went quickly to the Tower; Rodney and Sir Edward Berkeley were imprisoned at Taunton. Wyndham and Phelips escaped detection, fortunately for Charles II as it turned out.[17]

Presbyterian malcontents were equally efficiently disposed of. Nothing, to be sure, could be done to improve the temper of the ministers. 'Lord', one of them prayed in 1649, 'ever be good and gracious unto those who according to our covenant engagement *ought* to bear rule over us.' They consistently ignored the Rump's fasts and thanksgiving days. After Dunbar, so far from giving thanks, the Taunton clergy 'prayed indirectly to the contrary', and a few months later one roundly declared that the present regime was 'against Jesus Christ'. Pyne read them some stern lectures but otherwise treated them with remarkable leniency, presumably because he knew that any alternative occupants of the pulpits would be even worse.[18] Most of the political presbyterians kept their feelings to themselves. Strode was in trouble for refusing the engagement; he was twice disarmed and his horses were seized, but he was not arrested. Prynne and Clement Walker were less easily silenced. Walker's invective in the second part of his *History of Independency* sent him to the Tower in 1649 and he died there two years later. Prynne, meanwhile, was imprisoned at Dunster, where he occupied himself in cataloguing George Luttrell's manuscripts and drawing up a protest against the dismantling of the castle fortifications. In the summer of 1651, being thought too friendly with Luttrell, he was removed to Pendennis Castle in Cornwall.[19]

Thus the Commonwealthsmen dealt firmly with their enemies. But the greatest prize eluded them. On 12 September 1651, nine days after Worcester, Charles II slipped secretly into Somerset, disguised as Jane Lane's groom. After three days at the house of George Norton at Abbotsleigh, the king rode over the Mendips to Castle Cary, where he was sheltered by Edward Kirton. The next day he moved to Francis Wyndham's house at Trent, and for almost a month thereafter he was in the care of Wyndham and Robert Phelips. Their loyalty was impressive, though no more so than that of Wyndham's servants and other humble people who might well have been tempted by the £1,000 price for Charles's capture. From 17 September until 5 October, apart from a two-day trip to Charmouth and Bridport in an unsuccessful effort to find a ship, the king lay concealed at Trent. It was an anxious time, for the region swarmed with soldiers on their way to take ship for an attack on Jersey. The minister at Trent, Thomas Elford, was a fervent Independent, and as Charles himself admitted, most of the villagers were 'fanatics'.[20] On one occasion a rumour that the king had been killed threw the village into a frenzy of jubilant celebration.

Secure passage being unobtainable at Bridport, Robert Phelips was enlisted. Lord Wilmot, Charles's cheerful, reckless companion, rode over to Salisbury and was directed to Phelips and John Coventry. At first Phelips was suspicious—Wilmot's presbyterian connections were well known—but his attitude changed when he learned the identity of the person he was to assist. He failed to find a ship at Southampton but was soon in touch with Thomas Gunter in Sussex, who was more hopeful. At last Phelips rode back to Trent and conducted Charles to Hele, near Salisbury. While awaiting word from Gunter they explored Stonehenge, where, says the colonel, 'the king's arithmetic gave the lie to that fabulous tale that those stones cannot be told alike twice together'.[21] Soon Gunter was ready. Phelips escorted the royal fugitive towards Brighton and safety; nearing Brighton he was sent off to London to arrange for money to be awaiting the king at Rouen. Somerset royalists had played a major part in the 'miraculous preservation'.

*   *   *   *

Throughout the Commonwealth John Pyne remained securely in control of Somerset. There was an important institutional change when the County Committee was abolished early in 1650, but Pyne survived it brilliantly. The move was part of a general reorganisation of the sequestration system, and it involved Pyne in a struggle on two fronts, against London centralisers and local enemies. Although in many respects the committee had been the agent of Westminster, dragooning an unwilling county into obedience, it always had some independence, and Pyne guarded it jealously. The committee's existence depended on control of its own funds, in the shape of sequestration money. But in 1649 fiscal necessity compelled the Rump to tap the sequestration funds more directly and the county officials had to pay in their receipts to Goldsmiths' Hall. In the following January the new system was made permanent and all control over sequestrations passed from the local committees. In effect this spelt their abolition. There were loud protests from the counties, with John Pyne in the van. The committee, he pointed out, had formerly been able to pay the local forces at least part of their arrears. Deprived of these payments, the soldiers would be 'apt to turn Leveller', and only 'the old deceitful interest', the presbyterians, would benefit. In the dying months of its existence the committee hastily unloaded what funds remained as handouts to local supporters, rather than return them to Goldsmiths' Hall.[22]

The Rump intended to govern from London. Sequestrations

would now be handled by subcommissioners in each county, directly responsible to Goldsmiths' Hall. Pyne would normally have had no difficulty about ensuring that the new Somerset officials were drawn from his faction. But the retiring chairman at Goldsmiths' Hall, John Ashe, had other ideas. Before he left office Ashe got the jobs for his own men, and persuaded Alexander Popham to endorse them. Outwardly Popham had always co-operated with Pyne, but he was now beginning the slow retreat from Commonwealth principles which by 1660 converted him into a monarchist. Ashe's list included the uncontroversial JPs Buckland and Richard Jones. But it also included three men whose sole recommendation was that they were Ashe's own clients: Latimer Sampson of Freshford, Thomas Shute of Kilmersdon, and Benjamin Mason. Sampson was related to Ashe, had fought well in the war, and in 1647 had been deputy governor of Bristol, where he now resided. Shute had been employed by the old committee, but Pyne soon detected traces of royalism in his past. Mason was even more vulnerable. A Herefordshire man, he had served in Essex's lifeguard and had come to Somerset to marry the daughter of a royalist, a kinsman of Sir Francis Dodington.[23]

A glorious row resulted. The new sequestration system, Pyne decided, was simply a plot by Ashe to undermine his authority in Somerset; still, if subcommissioners there must be, they would be of his own choosing. Jones and Buckland prudently declined to serve, but by May 1650 the other three were bravely setting to work. Pyne now got Popham to change his mind and support a rival slate composed entirely of dependable radicals. The new Goldsmiths' Hall committee feebly tried to compromise. They found Pyne's charges serious enough to justify suspending Mason but retained Shute and Latimer Sampson, to whom they added three of Pyne's nominees: Bovett, William Ceely, and George Sampson of Kingsbury. Ashe was furious. He had carefully hand-picked men who would unmask the old committee's misgovernment; now Pyne, with the help of no less a personage than Col Pride, was about to circumvent him. Ashe had no love for soldiers, having recently been plundered by some of them at Freshford, but Pride (of whose purge he had been a passing victim) was a special enemy. All the men proposed, he announced, were Pyne's 'slaves and vassals'; even Ceely, the most impressive of them, was only a 'shuffling beggarly lawyer'.[24]

Monument to John Somerset

Sir John Horner

For months the struggle raged. There would be demonstrations by the 'honest party', Pyne warned, if Ashe's men were retained. Pyne told Mason that he could expect some mercy if he resigned but he was not to be frightened off.[25] There were icy stares when the two men were seated next to each other at the 11 May thanksgiving service at Taunton. Pyne had more success in London. His army friends, Harrison and Disbrowe, got the Council of State to dismiss Shute and Latimer Sampson as well as Mason. Ashe tried to save them, but in November they were all replaced. Pyne then had them arrested and charged with delinquency. Mason beat a hasty retreat to Hereford; the other two also retired from the scene. To save Ashe's face Ceely, Bovett, and George Sampson also had to resign. In their place were appointed five men acceptable to Pyne, including Humphrey Blake, the admiral's brother; John Gorges, son of a younger branch of the Gorges of Wraxall; and the former committee official Samuel Whetcombe. A well entrenched county boss with friends in the Council of State could defeat even as formidable an enemy as John Ashe.

The abolition of the County Committee thus made little difference to Pyne's authority. The sequestration system was soon in the hands of his clients, the Strodes and Horners had left the Assessment Commission, and the JPs were increasingly amenable. Most important, the new Commonwealth militia which took over the old committee's police and military functions was totally under his control. Although the Rump's Militia Bill was not passed until July 1650, the Council of State had approved a preliminary list of officers submitted by Pyne and Popham a year earlier and had authorised them to proceed soon after the bill's second reading in September 1649. Like the other county institutions of this era, the new militia was designed to defend the revolution, not to reflect the traditional power of the country gentry. When Col Disbrowe, who had taken over as army commander in the West, came to organise the Devon forces, he observed that 'few of the gentry appears in it'.[26] In Somerset few of them were even invited.

The militia was to be run by twenty-one commissioners, who were given wide powers of investigating suspected conspiracies, banning dangerous meetings, and disarming papists and 'ill-affected persons'. There was at first no provision for paying the soldiers, but eventually the horse were given two shillings a day, the foot half that amount. The money was raised by an assessment

L

on all persons with over £10 a year or £200 in personal property. Coming on top of the weekly assessment and the hated excise, the militia levy continued the process of alienating the Country. Nor did the choice of commissioners inspire much confidence. Apart from old Sir John Horner (who refused to act) they were all members of the Pyne faction, for the most part of lower rank. They were headed by Disbrowe and the three radical MPs, Pyne, Wroth, and Alexander Popham. They also included the inactive MP William Carent and one other man of stature, the sheriff Alexander Pym. Six were from the activist clique of the old committee and the rest also owed their prominence to Pyne or Popham. Such were Bovett, William Ceely, John Gorges and his lawyer brother Thomas, and George Sampson's father, George of Lopen, who was not even a freeholder. Apart from the MPs none had been in the gentry-dominated commission of December 1648, nor would they have had any chance of such eminence without Pyne's favour.[27]

The militia officers were also far less substantial than would have been conceivable in earlier days. Popham and John Gorges commanded the horse, Pyne and Edward Ceely the foot, with Bovett, William Ceely, and the younger George Sampson in subordinate commands. Some of the other officers were minor gentlemen, but among the captains were men of much lower status. William Venicombe was a South Petherton innkeeper, Francis Pyke the postmaster at Crewkerne, William Gapper an illiterate yeoman.[28]

By May 1650 training exercises were beginning. Pyne kept enthusiasm at a high pitch. In October his men declared their eagerness to march to Scotland if needed; in the following February his regiment again showed 'great forwardness'. Impressing recruits for Ireland, rounding up political suspects, supervising the dismantling of such fortified places as Dunster; in all such matters Pyne was indispensable, and he was repeatedly commended by the Council of State for his 'great pains and diligence in the public service'. When the Scots crossed the Cheviots in August 1651 the militia was quickly alerted. Disbrowe was ordered north with the regular forces. No successor was appointed (Blake was suggested but had to go to sea when the other Somerset admiral, Edward Popham, died), but Pyne was equal to the emergency. Horses were commandeered, the militia regiments brought up to strength and marched off towards Worcester; in view of Pyne's military prowess they may have been lucky to arrive too late for the battle. Alexander Popham raised a troop of dragoons, and the men of Taunton took arms 'with more than ordinary cheerfulness'.

There was not very much enthusiasm for the Commonwealth but there was even less for the Scots, and during the Worcester campaign popular feeling for once was on the side of the government. It was only half in jest that the fleeing king echoed a roundhead blacksmith's own opinion that the rogue Charles Stuart 'deserved to be hanged more than all the rest for bringing in the Scots'.[29]

But though the Country might rally against invasion, might prefer even Pyne to renewed bloodshed and disorder, this was a minority regime, alienating both yeomen and gentry by heavy taxation and military rule. The last remaining old families were disappearing from local government and being replaced by radicals and upstarts. The Assessment Commission was replenished with another batch of Pyne's henchmen such as Gutch and John Gay, new men like the lawyers Turberville and Thomas Gorges, townsmen like Thomas Mead of Wells and Thomas Wrentmore, whose family were Axbridge drapers. When the commissioners met at Somerton in July 1649, only eleven out of forty turned up. The Commission of the Peace tells the same story. Radicals like James Cottington of Frome and the former committeeman Thomas English became JPs in 1651, as did Col Thomas Pride a year later, though his connection with his native county was a tenuous one. Men of greater prestige—John Harington, for instance—were still active in their divisions, but rarely attended Quarter Sessions.[30]

There was, to be sure, some relaxation of the military pressure after Worcester. The new militia was allowed to lapse at the end of the year, and the garrisons at Dunster, Bridgwater, and Taunton were disbanded. The Dutch war brought increasing fame to Blake, and all Somerset gloried in his victories. But the war badly affected trade and there were the usual complaints about the excise, on one occasion leading to a riot at Norton St Philip fair. And the Rump was still bent on centralisation. A wholesale revision of borough charters was proposed which would have seriously reduced local independence. Bath and several other Somerset towns sent their charters to London, but fortunately for them the committee concerned never completed its work.[31]

*   *   *   *

The old view of the Commonwealth as a time of bigoted repression is no longer historically respectable. Milton and Marvell are sufficient reminders that not all puritans were graceless adherents of a negative, anti-life morality, rejoicing in the destruction of cathedrals and works of art. Much of the prevailing dislike of popular amusements was shared by all men of property, upset by the drunken disorders that followed fairs and revels: Hopton had been as opposed to churchales as Prynne. Thus when the Somerset JPs again prohibited revels and wakes in 1649 because of the 'divers quarrels, mutinies, and contentions' they provoked, they were doing nothing new. Nor were they when they closed unlicensed alehouses; such places pushed up grain prices besides being morally objectionable. The Rump's enactment of the death penalty for adultery has been held against it, but in fact meant that there were virtually no convictions. The recent abolition of the ecclesiastical courts paradoxically made the republic a better time for adulterers. In 1650 a woman was condemned at Taunton under the new act, but her partner was a priest: religious bigotry reinforced moral outrage. In anti-Catholic prejudice and superstitious fear of witches Somerset men were hardly unique; at least the county escaped the witchcraft hysteria that gripped some of the eastern counties in these years.[32]

Some puritans of course did smash stained glass, did deface statues and ornaments. When John Taylor the 'water poet' came to Wells in 1649 he found the cathedral in sad condition. Thieves were stripping the lead from the roof, and it was soon reported that the building was 'much ruined and leaky'. Officially the sequestrators ought to have prevented it, but they naturally did not take their responsibilities very seriously at a time when the Rump was known to be considering demolishing all cathedrals and using the proceeds for secular purposes. By now most of the episcopal property at Wells had been bought by the eminent presbyterian divine Cornelius Burges, who had decided to retire from London in the gloomy atmosphere of 1648-9. Burges was soon busily preaching in the cathedral and energetically exploiting his new estates. He partly demolished the bishop's palace, using the materials to remodel the deanery in which he resided. Local rumour had it that he even intended to take down the chapter house.[33]

Burges's arrival is a reminder that the Commonwealth did not lead to a sweeping replacement of presbyterian clergy by radical Independents and baptists. In fact the Rump had no coherent ecclesiastical policy at all and Somerset, like the rest of England, remained a patchwork of theological diversity. The presbyterian classis preserved a precarious existence, but in 1649 the Taunton elders were uncertain whether the sacrament could be administered in a still 'un-presbyterated church'. Opposition to tithes was widespread. The Claverton churchwardens refused to collect them, and even Richard Allen was unable to extract them from many of his Batcombe flock. Under pressure from army radicals the Rump discussed abolishing them altogether, but could never find a substitute. There was some redistribution of church revenues, a few livings were augmented by the Committee for Plundered Ministers, and in 1650 there was a general parish survey as a basis for future policy. Such local worthies as Harington and Buckland collected a great deal of useful information. Their returns were sent up to Chancery however, where they were pigeon-holed and forgotten.[34]

One obvious possible source of revenue to supplement endowments was largely neglected. Only trivial amounts went to religious uses when episcopal and dean and chapter lands were sold. As usual soldiers, speculators, and men with political influence got most of them. Roger Hill bought the rich manor of Taunton Dene and other property at Taunton; Bovett and Edward Ceely were also in the market. Perhaps the most energetic local speculator was the Bristol attorney John Casbeard, son of a former mayor of Wells. Like his father Richard, John Casbeard was an astute and ruthless operator. Having worked as a surveyor of the diocese of Exeter before the sales began, he had excellent backstairs contacts in London, which he put to good account. Casbeard bought parts of the manors of Wells and Westbury, other church lands at Banwell and Shipham, and royalist property near Bath. He did a profitable business as agent for other purchasers, speculated in Mendip lead, and had large investments in Cornwall 'and other remote parts'.[35] Men of his type were common in these years, happily profiteering on the fringes of the new bureaucracy.

Some of the property being sold consisted of market tolls and similar rights which corporations had long coveted. They now seized their opportunity. Through Serle and Whetcombe, Taunton bought the bishop of Winchester's rights in the borough. John Casbeard got the corporation of Wells to buy the bishop's royalties, involving it in a decade of bitter legal wrangles with Burges. Radicals like Mead and Barrett joined forces with the conservative localists who had always run the city; economic and religious feeling merged with the traditional antipathy between the city and the cathedral Liberty, which Burges now represented.[36]

Among Burges's enemies were the baptists, who prospered in the Commonwealth's tolerant climate. It was common, one of their critics complained, for baptists to come to church 'with a gang of soldiers and prate on a tombstone, while the minister preacheth in a pulpit'. Thomas Collier was still spreading the word. In 1652 he had a great debate with a local presbyterian cleric, Francis Fullwood, at Wiveliscombe. The church was packed, and when Collier arrived guarded by troopers, it looked as if there might be trouble. There was a lively argument, with the JP Thomas Gorges intervening on the presbyterian side, but it ended quietly with mutual congratulations. Fullwood was surprised to find Collier 'so sober and rational'.[37]

By 1653, in spite of Pyne's protection, the presbyterian clergy felt increasingly threatened. Harrison and the Fifth Monarchy men seemed to be pushing the Rump towards sweeping changes, and there was a corresponding rallying of conservative opinion. A petition to preserve a 'settled ministry' was circulating in the county in March; 'many hands are gained, but few well-affected', a newspaper reported. In April Cromwell threw out the Rump and there followed a new surge of the revolutionary tide. When the nominated 'Barebones' Parliament met in the summer Somerset had four representatives. Two of them—Blake and Henley—were religious presbyterians and by now appeared relatively moderate in politics. But the others—Pyne and the Bristol grocer Denis Hollister, a baptist soon to turn quaker—both supported plans to abolish tithes and reconstruct the universities. These alarming proposals were never enacted, but threw chills of horror down establishment spines. Locally, too, the baptists were still gaining ground. They annoyed Burges by interrupting his sermons and in May a group of them, headed by the fiery David Barrett, persuaded the Council of State to make him hand over the chapter house for their meetings. Their organisation was improving. During the summer Collier brought a number of westcountry congregations together in an association which in November held the first of several meetings at Wells.[38]

The change of government did nothing to soften the hostility of the republic's old enemies. Years of imprisonment had so embittered Prynne that he shocked Harington by hoping for a Dutch victory in the war. A few hardened royalists went further. Robert Phelips had been abroad, angling for a place at Court; failing in this he returned to England and took the lead in a crazy scheme to secure Poole and Portsmouth. A conspirator was bribed into betraying him, and Phelips soon found himself being interrogated by Cromwell and Sir Anthony Ashley Cooper. Cromwell greeted the prisoner courteously and spoke admiringly of old Sir Robert, 'commending . . . his great zeal for his country's good, expressed in his great bold speaking in former parliaments'. Phelips defiantly announced that if his father had lived 'he would have been of my persuasion'. Cooper, his Dorset neighbour, gave Phelips a 'very fair character', but thought him the 'forwardest man in all our parts to disturb the quiet of the state'. Phelips refused to confess or incriminate his friends and went to the Tower, but soon escaped into exile again.[39]

The Phelips plot was of minor importance. In 1653 all seemed set fair for the perpetuation of John Pyne's regime. Still more of his faction were becoming JPs: Barker, Bovett, and George Sampson among them. Only the lawyers Turberville and Thomas Syderfin, the durable Buckland and Jones, and a handful of others, appeared with them at Quarter Sessions. Another challenge to Pyne's power was easily brushed aside. John Gorges, the sequestration subcommissioner, began it by unwisely trying to uncover the misdeeds of some of the old committee's officials. Pyne retaliated with accusations that Gorges was taking bribes, was 'a professed enemy to the godly and well-affected', and was 'much cried out against' in Somerset. The Gorges brothers were both removed from the Commission of the Peace and on 14 December John was dismissed from the sequestrations post.[40] But the Barebones regime had already collapsed, and on the 16th Oliver Cromwell was installed as Lord Protector. The Pyne era was over.

Notes to this chapter are on pages 210-13.

10

A County Reunites
1654-60

The Protectorate was the first stage of a conservative reaction which culminated in the restoration of Charles II. There were setbacks: a relapse into puritan authoritarianism in 1655-6, a series of republican experiments in 1659. Cromwell brought only temporary stability. The impermanence of his regime was the result of its (and his) internal contradictions. Oliver the Huntingdon country gentleman might strive for 'healing and settling', but Oliver the puritan reformer could never entirely break faith with the Saints. His rule depended on the army, and although the officers became less puritan and more professional, there always remained a hard core dedicated to the republican Good Old Cause. To counteract their opposition to settlement Cromwell would have had to win massive support from former neutrals, presbyterians, and royalists. He tried, but there were plots, and the Protectorate's moderate beginning was interrupted by the rule of the major-generals. In 1657 he tried again with more success, and a good many of the old families began to drift back into local government. But a majority still held out; too much bad blood, too many old memories stood in the way of reconciliation.

In Somerset as elsewhere the Protectorate was a half-way house on the road to 1660. Pyne's Commonwealthsmen were in eclipse, but the pragmatic Cromwellians who replaced them never struck deep roots. A large standing army, heavy expenditures for war with Spain and for the occupation forces in Scotland and Ireland, all meant the continuation of high taxes. The Country was therefore never happy about the Protectorate, though it preferred it to either the radical minority regime of the Commonwealthsmen or the renewed bloodshed likely to accompany a royalist restoration.

The drift to anarchy after the republican interlude of 1659, however, convinced moderate men of all shades of opinion that Charles II was the only solution. Once this happened restoration no longer meant government by embittered cavaliers. The county community could reunite, confident that there would be no return to Laudian centralisation or tyrannical commissioners of array.

*   *   *   *

In 1654 the government of Somerset began to take on a more familiar look. The JPs again became the effective rulers of the county, guided by conservative assize judges like Chief Justice Henry Rolle, who lived at Shapwick. Radicals who survived as JPs—Bovett, for example—were now leaderless. Pyne would not serve the Protectorate: 'old Oliver' had betrayed the cause. He eventually reappeared at Quarter Sessions, but as one JP among many, not as the boss of an entrenched machine. Government was now in the hands of moderate men: Buckland, the younger John Harington (whose father died in this year), and trimmers like John and Thomas Gorges. The brothers had been saved by the fall of the Barebones regime and John was soon reappointed sequestration commissioner, though only to preside over the dismantling of the system. He was generally distrusted as a selfish careerist, but was the key man in the county. He had the ear of Whitehall and was willing to recruit anyone who accepted the Protectorate quietly. Once more friendship and connection became more important than ideology. When Robert Hunt was sworn in as high sheriff in December 1654, he resolved to give 'charity to poor people, right to injured persons'. But he was also very ready to perform 'civilities' for 'persons of quality'.[1]

When Cromwell's first parliament was elected in July, the MPs returned in Somerset were a mixed lot. Under the new constitution, the 'Instrument of Government', the county had eleven members and most of the borough seats were abolished. The new franchise—voters had to be worth £200 in either real or personal property—eliminated many of the poorer freeholders and replaced them by townsmen of moderate wealth. Disbrowe, the military overlord, was elected but chose to sit for his native Cambridgeshire; the Somerset vacancy was filled by the radical Barker. Samuel Perry, a Taunton mercer, and John Ashe may have represented the new urban voters. But all the other MPs were country gentlemen, though some were of lower status than the prewar knights of the shire. Sir John Horner and the younger Harington were accompanied by Buckland, Jones, Preston, Thomas Hippisley of Cameley, and the royalist Steynings. How many of the Somerset members were excluded from parliament for refusing the 'recognition' of the constitution is unknown. But no doubt most would have echoed the words of the disenchanted Alexander Popham (elected for Bath), who bravely told Cromwell that he came 'to do his Country service, and not his lordship'.[2]

The protector might hope to conciliate the gentry, but he was also anxious to preserve one of the few achievements of the revolution: religious toleration. Some form of church government was needed to replace the moribund presbyterian system, so a new body of commissioners was created to supervise the parish clergy. Independents like Thomas Elford and John Knowles of Bristol were joined by such staunch presbyterians as the Allens, Fairclough, Newton, and William Thomas. The lay commissioners included most of the leading parliamentarian gentry. Ministers of any orthodox persuasion (except open episcopalians) were appointed or confirmed as long as they were godly men. It was a step back towards a national church, modified by the protector's continued insistence on toleration. Baptists and other sects still flourished: Collier's association met at Wells again in March 1654; and new congregations were being formed, at Chard and Wedmore, for example.[3]

The middling and lower orders thus enjoyed the benefits of toleration. But they were soon reminded that this was a government of the rich, determined to keep order and protect the interests of its friends. Lord Broghil, a royalist recruit to Cromwell's regime, had acquired recently enclosed lands in Selwood Forest. His fences were repeatedly thrown down by rioting commoners, and just as often the Council ordered the Somerset JPs to eject the culprits. Other vested interests were busy. Sir Cornelius Vermuyden revived the Sedgemoor drainage project, though thanks to the commoners' opposition little progress was made. The countrymen were no more enthusiastic about the Protectorate than they had been about the Rump. As ever, taxes were widely evaded or resisted. Two collectors at Congresbury distrained a widow's goods when she refused to pay, but an assize jury awarded damages against them. Early in 1655 the assessment commissioners complained to the Council of their difficulties in meeting the county's quota; they were reminded that only punctual collection could avert the evil of free quarter.[4]

Before the Protectorate took root a handful of cavaliers determined to strike it down. Their plots were as unrealistic and ineffective as ever, attracting few besides the usual adventurous younger sons. After the debacle of 1651 there is no sign that magnates like Rodney and the Berkeleys, for example, risked their estates again. Stawell was in prison, Robert Phelips abroad, though his wife was a busy conspirator at Salisbury. A new organisation was secretly constructed; early in 1655 its members planned to take up arms. Although some bedraggled royalists assembled in other places, only in Wiltshire under John Penruddock did the outbreak even remotely resemble a rebellion, and Somerset cavaliers took little part in it. In February, near the time originally set for the rising, there was some loose talk by conspirators: a design on Taunton by Francis Wyndham was mentioned. Young Hugh Smyth of Long Ashton went to a meeting of the plotters at Salisbury, and at Ashcott a small group gathered who rode to Frome before they discovered that the action had been postponed. Smyth fled and Wyndham was soon arrested. There were alarmist reports from Bristol about movements by both cavaliers and Levellers, but Somerset was quiet when Penruddock announced his intentions by arresting the assize judges at Salisbury.[5]

The rising stirred up a few ripples in Somerset. Riding west from Salisbury, Penruddock's men halted to rest on Babylon Hill in the early morning of 13 March. The alarm was raised, and during the day, while a few hundred dispirited royalists trotted through Chard and Crewkerne towards inevitable defeat in Devon, messengers rode frantically to alert the local forces. Like Hertford's band in 1642, Penruddock's cavaliers were unwelcome outsiders—'tories', the countrymen were calling them—and they received almost no support. At Taunton nearly 3,000 old soldiers and militiamen turned out to oppose them. This pleasing display of unity was ruined, however, by an unseemly dispute between the Pyne and Gorges factions. Gorges claimed the command for himself, but the Commonwealthsmen dismissed him as 'a man but of yesterday, who hath not so fully born testimony against the cavaliers'. There was an angry scene and the Somerset volunteers were unable to march. Still, thirty-five rebel stragglers were taken in the county and lodged at Taunton and Ilchester. Among them were a Bruton shoemaker and a Kilmersdon farmer; a Yeovil tailor, a Bath servingman, and three minor Somerset gentlemen were imprisoned at Exeter. Somerset had shown no inclination to a cavalier restoration.[6]

The aftermath of the rising revealed the Protectorate's dual character: first moderation, then a dose of puritan militarism. The trials of the rebels were conducted with some regard for Country susceptibilities, so most of them got off lightly. Instead of appointing an emergency high court of justice, the common expedient for dealing with rebels since 1649, Cromwell followed the old way of assizes and local juries. Care was taken to select jurymen who accepted the legality of the regime, but this was standard procedure in any seventeenth-century political trial. Penruddock and about a dozen of his followers were executed and many more transported to Barbados, but there was nothing like the judicial carnage that Jeffreys directed thirty years later. This is the less surprising when it is noted that one of the judges was Francis Swanton, well known for his royalist leanings.[7]

Most of the prisoners were dealt with at Salisbury and Exeter, but one prominent man came up for trial at Chard on 25 April: Edward Phelips of Montacute. He had done no more than talk to the rebels, but this was enough for Disbrowe and he was committed to Ilchester gaol. However, Sheriff Hunt was happy to offer 'civilities' to a friend and took him into more comfortable custody at Speckington. Arrangements for defending the rebel leaders were made by Hertford's client, Seymour Bowman, and Phelips's son expected one of the judges, John Glyn, to be friendly; Glyn was, he noted, 'acquainted with my father, and pretends a great kindness to my grandfather'. But in spite of these useful connections there was anxiety at Montacute. 'Let not my mother know the worst of this business', young Phelips told the family steward. Bowman's lawyers were successful, and to Hunt's relief the jury brought in a verdict of *ignoramus*. Disbrowe still tried to keep Phelips in prison, but on Hunt's 'earnest importunity' at length released him on £2,000 security. Five of the other prisoners tried at Chard were sentenced to death, but only one was executed. Three received last-minute reprieves and one, Thomas Hunt, a Wiltshire man not related to the sheriff, escaped the night before he was to have been beheaded. His execution had been delayed because of 'the difficulty of procuring an axe', and there were suspicions that the neutralist sheriff had connived in the escape plot. But in spite of a letter to Cromwell 'stuffed with many notorious untruths put in by a gentleman in the country to do me mischief' (so Hunt complained), he was exonerated.[8]

The protector's law officers—Prideaux and the rapidly rising Roger Hill—had wisely steered a cautiously legal course. But the military had other ideas. The rebellion would never have occurred, the Council sharply told the JPs, if they had properly enforced the laws against vagrants and suspicious persons.[9] A new structure was needed, men like Disbrowe argued, to co-ordinate civil and military authority and instil new energy into the pursuit of security and godliness. Oliver fell for it and turned his back on settlement; the country was divided into military districts, each under a major-general.

Disbrowe was appointed major-general of the West in May 1655. A new Somerset militia was quickly formed under the command of John Gorges and Harington. The latter was disinclined to serve, but his royalist friends and kinsmen—Poulett, the Earl of Marlborough—pointed out that he might be able to protect the county from 'spoil and rapine', so in the end he took the commission.[10] Disbrowe was a formidable despot, but subordinates like Gorges and Harington made the new system far less fearsome to the gentry than the Pyne regime had been. Commissioners 'for securing the peace of the commonwealth' were appointed to assist the major-general; they too were relatively moderate. There was the usual difficulty about getting influential men to serve: the only active commissioners were Gorges, Hunt, and a handful of minor gentry like John Cary and Thomas Baynard. In collecting the 'decimation' which paid for the new militia—a tax of one-tenth of the annual value of cavaliers' estates— they showed none of Pyne's vindictive zeal. 'The gentlemen of this county act very mildly and will do my lord all the services they may', one of Hertford's bailiffs reported. People turned in absurd underestimates of their personal incomes but no one asked any awkward questions.[11]

The major-generals might have been worse, but the royalist gentry long remembered them. In the summer of 1655 Somerset cavaliers were systematically rounded up and imprisoned at Exeter: Lord Poulett, Francis and Sir Hugh Wyndham, William Helyar, and George Speke, to name only a few. They were released only on heavy security to desist from future sedition. Their movements were still carefully watched; they could not leave home without the major-general's permission and their journeys were recorded at a central office in London. They also had to dip into their pockets to pay the decimation tax. Most did so without resistance—not surprisingly in view of the commissioners' leniency—but the tax scarcely improved the Protectorate's popularity. A few got exemption by professing a change of heart. John Tynte of Halswell, for example, convinced the commissioners that he had conducted himself loyally when Penruddock was in arms.[12]

However mildly implemented, the major-generals' system completed the Country's disillusionment with puritan reform. It was worse than the 1630s, a police state with military despots instead of Laudian bishops. Disbrowe controlled the militia, the sheriff, the JPs. He nominated Taunton and Bristol puritans to the Commission of the Peace and made sure that only men of 'honest and blameless conversation' were selected for juries. At Chard Assizes in 1656 a grand jury presentment led to a whole series of reformist orders: proper enforcement of the laws regarding weights and measures, closing of unlicensed alehouses, the repair of Ilchester gaol and the houses of correction. For a time the JPs responded to Disbrowe's pressure and large numbers of vagrants and drunken royalists were rounded up.[13]

*   *   *   *

More than ever the puritan militants were a small remnant, struggling in a sea of ungodliness and apathy. At Pensford fair in 1656, at the height of the campaign for public morality, the petty constable (Edward Locke, the philosopher's uncle) was assaulted when he tried to keep order. In August the traditional 'revel feast' was held at Timsbury. A waggon-load of beer arrived from Bristol and a great crowd assembled at the cudgel match. There was much unseemly merriment, a disapproving puritan complained, following 'the sale of the said beer'. It was easy for resentment at attempts to suppress popular amusements to take on a political colour. In the *Black Boy* at Ashcott a carousing rustic burst into:

> Let us drink, let us sing
> Here's a health to our king,
> And it will never be well till we have one again.[14]

Sensible people avoided such reckless outbursts, but there was no mistaking the Country's dislike of the major-generals. There was the usual reluctance to pay taxes. At Meare the tithingman refused to return the names of defaulters and defied the collector to prosecute him. Declining trade added to the discontent. The war with Spain brought opportunity for venturesome mariners, though the great Robert Blake died at sea after the last of his victories, at Santa Cruz in 1657. But the war seriously interrupted business with southern Europe and even the Irish trade was affected. Minehead and other western ports complained of depredations by enemy privateers and asked for frigates to protect them.[15]

The reaction against military rule was clear in the elections of August 1656. The boroughs gave no trouble, but when the county voters gathered at Wells on 20 August, their feelings were plain. The Commonwealthsmen, Disbrowe noted, had been 'making parties' and were determined to 'overthrow all'. But it was Sheriff Hunt who set the tone in his speech from the market cross. 'Be wise and careful in your choice', he advised the crowd, and avoid radical enemies of the Protectorate: 'Do not cry up any man that cries down government.' Between the lines can be read Hunt's preference for men who would help to extricate Cromwell from his recent lurch into militarism, 'pious, sober, prudent, and peaceable men', who would bring the storm-tossed ship of state into the 'quiet harbour of a happy and blessed settlement'.[16]

The party that cried down government was decisively defeated. Buckland topped the poll with 2,374 votes, with the lowest successful candidate receiving 1,549. Pyne was laughably far behind with 457, while his allies—Bovett, Edward Ceely, Alexander Pym —did even worse. Nor did the military show any great strength in spite of Disbrowe's preparations. The major-general was elected along with John Gorges, but another army candidate, Col John Okey, got only a handful of votes. The victors were respect-

William Prynne

Francis Wyndham

able country gentlemen, many of them of distinguished family. After Buckland came Alexander Popham, turning increasingly to a Country position, Francis Luttrell, the judge's son Francis Rolle, Harington, and young William Wyndham of Orchard, grandson of the royalist Hopton. A few other parliamentarian notables were elected: old John Ashe, the lawyer Lislebone Long. But none preferred the major-generals to the Protectorate's earlier constitutionalism.[17]

When parliament met in September, Popham and Buckland were among the members excluded for their known opposition to military rule. But they must have watched approvingly when at the end of the year Cromwell bowed to public opinion and abandoned the major-generals. Soon the talk was all of 'settlement' again, and John Ashe rose to move that Cromwell 'take upon him the government according to the ancient constitution'. This, after all, was what they had fought for. Only monarchy, it seemed, could save 'our liberties and peace'. Cromwell rejected the proferred crown. But the 'Humble Petition and Advice' gave him the powers of a king without the title, power to name his successor, to appoint a house of lords; Alexander Popham was among those named to it, to remove him and other critics from the lower house. It was time, Cromwell told his officers, 'to come to a settlement and lay aside arbitrary proceedings, so unacceptable to the nation'.[18]

The new course was soon obvious in the county. In March 1657 the Commission of the Peace was drastically purged. Out went Disbrowe's nominees, out went Pyne's men—English, John Gay, Alexander Pym—out went the old rumpers Palmer, Serle, and Carent. In came the moderate gentry: the MPs Luttrell, Rolle, and William Wyndham, with others from solid parliamentarian families, like James Ashe and Henry Rogers of Cannington. Most strikingly, in came the sons of cavaliers, men too young to have fought in the wars, but undeniably royalist in their sympathies: Hugh Smyth, George Norton of Abbotsleigh, the younger George Trevelyan of Nettlecombe, whose father had died in 1653. As a new generation grew up, remote from the old quarrels, the old families were coming back into government, back to restore the unity of the Country. They might secretly prefer the king over the water and in the end they would turn to him with enthusiasm, but in the meantime the Protectorate offered stabil-

M

ity and settlement. The Assessment Commission was similarly reconstructed. Pyne's radicals were omitted and among their replacements names from the old families again loomed large: Wyndham, Luttrell, Trevelyan, Smyth, Robert Hunt and his son-in-law, William Lacey of Hartrow; even a Poulett, a Dodington, and a Berkeley.[19]

The gentry were closing ranks, basking in the fitful sunshine of settlement. And well they might, for the probable outcome if the Protectorate collapsed was all too clear. The radical sects were on the march, threatening magistracy and order in the name of the impending millennium. The baptists by now seemed comparatively harmless; far more menacing were the quakers, into whose ranks many baptists were drifting. Not yet the gentle pacifists they were later to become, the quakers defied convention whenever the spirit moved them, and put conscience above all things whatsoever. Their refusal to take oaths and remove their hats before magistrates seemed to express a mutinous contempt for authority. If the movement spread among the common people massive civil disobedience and bloodshed seemed inevitable. Many quakers were old parliamentarian soldiers; others had been officials under Pyne. Robert Wastfield of Brislington and James Pearce of Keynsham were former sequestrators; Jasper Batt of Street had been secretary to the County Committee, Christopher Pittard of Martock a committeeman. Old soldiers were of course notorious for all sorts of heresies. John Allen of Huntspill said that there would be 'as good scriptures made concerning the late war' as any in the Bible. He was obviously a Ranter ('let a man live as profanely as he would he should be saved if he thought himself to be in Christ'), but by 1656 it was common to attribute all ideas of this kind to the quakers.[20]

Somerset first woke up to the quakers in 1655. In May one created a disturbance in Bath abbey, and in September Robert Wastfield burst into Keynsham church, told the minister to stop seducing the people, and urged the congregation to abandon their 'false worship'. These incidents were the first of many and there were numerous arrests. Soon quakers were being imprisoned for refusing to pay tithes and other church rates, for keeping their hats on before magistrates, and for rejecting oaths. Often they were willing enough to do their public duty in other respects. Jasper Batt attended a court leet but was fined when he would not take the oath. James Hobbs of Walton came to serve on a sessions jury, kept his hat on, and was sent to prison when he would not pay his fine. Thomas Loscombe, chosen as surveyor of highways at Queen Camel, suffered the same fate when he rejected the oath of office.[21]

The most sensational episode was the visit of James Naylor in the autumn of 1656. A northcountryman and a former soldier, Naylor progressed through the West with messianic fervour, proclaiming that Christ was in him in language that indicated that he was the victim of blasphemous delusions. A disorderly crowd of disciples, many of them women, spread garments before him as he rode through Glastonbury and Wells. Puritans of all shades recoiled in horror. A 'new sort of Ranters', the baptist Collier exploded, and on his own doorstep too. Naylor was arrested and his case debated in parliament, where scandalised MPs competed in demanding ferocious punishments. 'Slit his tongue or bore it, and brand him with the letter B', Sir Thomas Wroth suggested, adding that the quakers were 'a very numerous party, and ought to be taken a course withal speedily'.[22]

The savage punishment accorded Naylor did not end the trouble, and frightened magistrates became increasingly intolerant. The quakers, Robert Hunt observed when he sentenced one of them, were 'in contempt of government', and here was the crux of the matter. Even for Cromwell toleration had its limits if public order was at stake, and most of the Somerset JPs were far less tolerant than Cromwell. In April 1657 Hunt and John Cary examined Thomas Budd, a former presbyterian minister who had held quaker meetings in his orchard at Martock. 'Mr Budd', said Cary, 'your friends are much grieved that you have been a man so much given to change.' Two years later, when a quaker drew up a list of 'cruel persecutors' in the county, almost all were the new Protectorate JPs: only Wroth, Bonner, and perhaps Cary had been Commonwealthsmen. Pyne, on the other hand, had been 'very loving and friendly' as had Bovett and several others.[23]

Quakers were frequently accused of provoking violence, but as often as not they were the victims rather than the aggressors. Angry parishioners beat up quakers who interrupted their services, and sometimes the violence was premeditated. One meeting in Budd's orchard was attended by several hundred sympathisers, eager to hear the itinerant preacher Thomas Salthouse. A delega-

tion of presbyterian ministers arrived, accompanied by an armed
mob—'wild brutish people' the quakers thought them—carrying
'cudgels, long staves, pitchforks', and other weapons. After an
argument with Salthouse the ministers left and the mob then
broke up the meeting. There was no doubt who fomented the riot,
yet it was Salthouse who went to Ilchester gaol. Wastfield argued
that the quakers had commonly shown more affection for the
Good Old Cause than persecuting magistrates like Hunt. He was
right, but irrelevant. The JPs spoke for propertied opinion. At
Chard Assizes in 1656 the grand jury warned against wandering
quakers, 'living often in idleness', and asked that they be severely
dealt with as vagrants.[24] Except to a minority of zealots, the
quakers were dangerous revolutionaries.

In Oliver Cromwell's last days the upper echelons of the
Country were reuniting. Old friendships were being renewed, old
enmities forgotten. There were only occasional bouts of repression, provoked by distant plots. In April 1658 Lord Poulett and
his brother Amyas, Lord Hawley (as Sir Francis had become), and
other cavaliers were imprisoned at Taunton. But John Gorges was
a 'handsomely moderate' gaoler (so one of their friends described
him), and they were released without bonds or conditions. Slowly
the cavaliers were being conciliated.[25] The clergy too were coming
together against the menace of sectarian anarchy. Old differences
were submerged as men of widely varying opinions joined in a
new ministerial association. John Gorges detected 'such a firm
bond of union that the names of presbyterian or Independent are
not mentioned here'. The Protectorate was even more generous
with augmentations than the Rump had been. It was 'a season',
John Devenish of Weston Zoyland rejoiced, 'that may be improved for encouragement of ministers'.[26] For all Cromwell's
toleration of the Saints, it was the gentry and the established
clergy who gained most from the Protectorate.

*   *   *   *

On the night of 2 September 1658 William Prynne slept uneasily
at Swainswick while a great storm raged outside. He dreamt that
he was urging the dying Cromwell (at Bath, conveniently) to
expiate his crimes by restoring Charles II and a lawful parliament.
Prynne awoke before Oliver's doubtless explosive reaction could

be made known; the real protector died a few hours later in Whitehall. The way was now clear for the outcome to which Prynne's wishful thinking pointed.[27] Richard Cromwell's peaceful accession, to be sure, seemed for a time to make the Stuarts unnecessary. The new protector's incapacity was not immediately obvious; he was in fact quite popular with people who wished to continue the trend towards legal government. But in turning to the moderate gentry without being able to control his puritan generals Richard dug his own political grave.

Before he fell Richard called a parliament, elected in the old constituencies on the old franchise. The Somerset results showed the strength of conservative opinion. Buckland and Hunt took the county seats and only one Commonwealthsman was successful in the boroughs: John Barker at Ilchester. The radicals tried hard at Taunton, where Palmer and Bovett claimed victory in a disputed election. 'The business was very foul on Bovett's side', an MP commented; the committee of privileges duly upheld the rival return of Thomas Gorges and the Cromwellian baronet Sir William Wyndham. A by-election at Milborne Port (Hunt, originally returned there, chose to sit for the county) gave Pyne an opportunity. His agents were said to 'offer to the poorer sort very liberally', but it was to no avail.[28]

Parliament's debates soon showed the strength of Country feeling: the gentry's longing for low taxes and legality, their impatience with the army's clichéd puritan reflexes. Old radical stalwarts were turning away. 'It is said, the soldiers have ventured their lives', Sir Thomas Wroth sneered: 'they were well paid for it.' Wroth was still firmly against the Stuarts but others were less rigid. Alexander Popham had been patiently and evasively mending his Country fences ever since 1655. He feared 'the disorders natural to insurrections', would do nothing that put him ahead of moderate, 'presbyterian' opinion. But he was in touch with royalist agents—with Massey, for instance, who had long since gone over to the king and came secretly to England early in 1659. If and when Charles II became the only alternative to anarchy, Popham and many other parliamentarians would be with him.[29]

When in April the officers threw out Richard and recalled the Rump, Popham stayed quietly at Littlecote. Once more there were stirrings of millenarian expectation, talk of abolishing tithes, of putting local government into the hands of the Saints, rumours

even of the appointment of quaker JPs. One Somerset Friend
hopefully sent up a list of suitable men: Thomas Budd and an
array of yeomen, several from the Martock area. Few rumpers
took it seriously, but mere talk was enough to frighten the gentry.
Even more menacing was the reconstruction of the militia. Gorges
lost his command and was temporarily replaced by George Sampson. On 26 July a new ordinance put the county forces back into
the hands of the radicals. Cromwellians like Hunt, Luttrell, and
William Wyndham were left off the commission, and although a
few substantial men were named—Popham and Buckland among
them—there is no sign that they responded. Besides the familiar
Pyne adherents, the commissioners included a large crop of new
men chosen for their revolutionary zeal. The upstart Sutton
Mallet yeoman William Gapper; the Croscombe clothier William
Whiting; the Taunton men Philip Lissante and George Powell:
such people were hardly representative of the county.[30]

The new commissioners went quickly to work, spurred on by
the rumour and reality of an immense presbyterian-royalist conspiracy. Pyne and Edward Ceely again commanded the foot, the
New Model dragoon officer John Okey took charge of the horse;
Bovett, Sampson, Barker, and Pym all held commissions. But the
rebellion—usually known as Booth's rising for its only effective
leader—had already collapsed. The Somerset gentry wisely concluded that this was no time to challenge the still powerful army.
Massey persuaded a few score conspirators to gather on Lansdown
before dawn on 1 August. But Okey's troops were on the way; the
royalists saw that the game was up and went home. Hunstrete was
searched for arms and Popham was fined for not attending parliament, but his contacts with cavalier agents seem to have escaped
detection. The crisis produced the usual indiscretions by lesser
men. A Barwick miller declared that 'he was a cavalier, and he
would be a cavalier, and the devil should take all them that were
not cavaliers'. More practical were the five people who accosted a
Thurloxton man and asked if he was for king or parliament.
Without waiting for a reply they tried to steal his money.[31]

It was not by such means that Charles II would be restored.
The decisive factor was the inexorable tide of moderate opinion,
which saw in the king and the old constitution the only barriers
to anarchy. The changing climate was a compound of many
elements: the collapsing morale and fragmentation of the repub-

licans; the ever-present fear of quakers and other social radicals; the emergence of a new generation, more cynical than ever about the tired quarrels of their elders; the general recognition that neighbourliness and community were preferable to division and conflict. The old men were passing. When Attorney-General Prideaux was buried at Ford abbey in Devon in September, many Somerset gentry came to admire the coffin—'so fine a thing', Amyas Poulett scornfully observed, 'that it might have served more fit for a real person of quality's chamber ornament'. The day after the funeral the mourners went on to Hinton St George 'to be merry'. There was great sport at Hinton in the autumn—a bag of thirty-four bucks in one outing—and Christmas was kept with the old lighthearted frivolity. The season ended, Amyas reported, 'with the usual solemnity of a cushion dance, leaving few beds or tables in the house undanced on'.[32]

Among the yeomen there was widespread disillusion.

> How often promised (but still fooled)
> Were we, the Egyptian taskers should
> be punished for oppression?

Humphrey Willis asked bitterly as he reflected on the decay of honesty and virtue.[33] Even committed radicals were losing faith. Sampson and Bovett agreed to serve as sequestration commissioners, but the system was revived only on paper. Quarrels between Cromwellians and Commonwealthsmen again erupted. When in October the army again expelled the Rump, even Pyne threw up his hands. His soul still panted for 'the true Good Old Cause', but in that gloomy autumn he could see little of it: 'sad are the divisions of Reuben'. As authority weakened, there were recurrent disorders: at Bristol; even at Taunton, where rioters tried to seize the castle in the name of a 'free parliament'. At Christmas there were bells and bonfires there and at Bath when the hopelessly divided army abandoned its committee of safety and allowed the Rump to return. Soon Monck crossed the border from Scotland.[34]

Bovett, Ceely, and Sampson tried vainly to keep their men together. Bovett had raised a new regiment of foot, but the Country had had enough and a taxpayers' strike made it impossible to pay them. Early in January some of them mustered at South Petherton, but only to demand their money. 'Their officers would not come near them', Amyas Poulett gleefully announced, 'so they clapped tail betwixt legs and sneaked every one to his own home.'

The mutinous remainder, scattered between Taunton, Wellington, Bridgwater, and Bruton, was a constant threat to the countryside: it was 1640 in reverse. On 11 February Monck declared that he was standing by the city of London in favour of a free parliament. 'Pull out the Rump', cried rioting Bristol apprentices, and there were open shouts for Charles II; Okey's horse had to be called. On the 21st the assessment commissioners met at Somerton, ostensibly to raise money for Bovett's regiment. Only six turned up and they promptly voted it treasonable to raise taxes on the Rump's authority. Bovett courageously arrested the ringleader, William Strode's son, but confessed that he 'saw never a greater sadness' on the faces of the godly party.[35]

On the same day Monck had taken the next step towards legality by restoring the secluded MPs to their places. Prynne was greeted with applause for his valiant penmanship, but for a time the rising man was Popham, who was elected to the Council of State. A conservative London government quickly stripped Bovett and his friends of what little authority they still possessed. The mutinous regiments were disbanded and the militia restored to the safe hands of the moderate gentry. The names in the new list of commissioners show the continuing process of reunion among the county leaders: old rumpers like Popham and James Ashe; presbyterians like Strode and George Horner; Cromwellians like Hunt and William Wyndham; the royalists Smith, Maurice Berkeley, and Trevelyan. Pyne and the Commonwealth clique were ousted and ignored. When officers were appointed the colonels were Popham, Luttrell, and Strode, and almost all the rest were of gentry rank.[36]

Society had been saved. The Long Parliament at last dissolved itself and new elections were held. George Horner took one of the county seats, Hugh Smyth the other. Technically cavaliers and their sons were ineligible, which raised some doubts about Smyth, but the prohibition was unenforceable. Throughout the country voters equated moderate royalism with support for low taxes and legality; even the inoffensive Buckland was too parliamentarian for 1660. There were the usual complaints of partisanship by the sheriff, but Smyth had the renascent Poulett interest behind him and would have won in any case.[37]

A last fling by the 'fanatic' puritans in April was easily frustrated. A few rebels collected at Yeovil, but went home on the pretext that it was a wet night. The Convention Parliament met and invited Charles II to return. The jubilant celebrations grew in volume. On 3 May Amyas Poulett counted 142 bonfires 'all afire at once' within sight of Hinton; 'such ringing of bells all night, such shouting of the people'. It was, he observed, 'a very busy time in sending out for painters to set up the king's arms again'. Soon a loyal address proclaimed in triumphant terms the rediscovered unity of the Somerset gentry. The signatures were a rollcall of the great families of the county: Pouletts, Phelipses, Stawells, Berkeleys, Wyndhams, Luttrells, Pophams, Horners, Hungerfords. Cavaliers, neutrals, presbyterians, Cromwellians, and plain country gentlemen; Buckland, Hunt, Charles Pym (Alexander's more conservative brother): all were there. Only the Commonwealthsmen were missing.[38]

* * * *

The gentry divided in 1642 and the result was civil war. In 1660 they reunited in the confident, and on the whole justified, expectation that Charles II and his council would leave them to run the county, without the interference to which they had been subjected in the 1630s and even more seriously during the Inter regnum. Their division had undermined the accustomed hierarchy. Men of lower rank had thrust themselves into positions of governance; yeomen and clothworkers, as parliamentarians and clubmen, had shown a dangerous degree of independence; and a radical puritan minority had threatened a more sweeping revolution in the name of godly reformation. The gentry took the lesson to heart: never again would they carry their differences to the battlefield. The days of the 'fanatics' were over. Pyne was several times arrested and in 1662 it was thought that he would 'infallibly be hanged'. But the king and his moderate counsellors averted a white terror. Pyne was not a regicide and he was no longer dangerous.[39]

During the First Civil War Somerset had been a parliamentarian county. The western parts had been less so than the north-east, and most of the leading gentry were royalist; but in so far as the freeholders and townsmen took sides they tended towards parliament. In 1642 two causes—religion, and Country resistance to centralisation and high taxes—had merged under the slogan

'Liberty and Property'. After the war the two causes diverged, and it was clear that militant puritanism had far less appeal than the constitutionalist localism of the gentry. Parliament failed to compose its own divisions and achieve a settlement with the defeated king. The army had to be kept on foot, and with its help Pyne took control of Somerset. But parliament and army replaced the king as the target of Country hostility, being blamed for even more burdensome taxation, more oppressive military rule, more relentless centralisation, than Charles I had ever dreamed of. The turmoil of 1645-8; the Rump; the years of the major-generals: through them all it was clear that parliament and its successor regimes had lost the trust of the Country.

One other lesson seemed plain: that puritanism and social hierarchy were incompatible. Moderate presbyterians, politicians like Horner and Strode, clergy like Fairclough and Newton, were in truth as attached to the old society as the royalists. But memories of Collier's baptists, of wild Ranters, of quakers gathering in Thomas Budd's orchard, swamped the reality, and the presbyterians suffered from guilt by association. Old Bishop Piers came back; but with the ecclesiastical courts deprived of their coercive powers the bishops were no longer dangerous, were indeed to make the church one of the twin pillars of a conservative establishment. But the puritans might be dangerous, might again threaten the gentry's monopoly of leadership. And so those that would not conform were ejected in 1662 and suffered the intermittent rigours of the Clarendon Code.

The 'middling sort' who had been the strength of puritanism during the troubles had also learnt their lesson: that war and revolution bring misery and ruin in their wake, and that the noblest cause can degenerate into anarchic self-seeking. But although most of the commoners accepted the oligarchic status quo after 1660, the revolution had left its mark on Somerset. Even in the worst days of persecution puritanism remained widely diffused throughout the county. Many an ejected minister saw the inside of Ilchester gaol, but nothing could silence them. John Turner, ousted from Cricket Malherbie, used his booming voice to preach through the gaol windows to the faithful outside. Conventicles might be broken up by soldiers or JPs, but the congregations survived. Newton still gave the 11 May thanksgiving sermon at Taunton (the day was observed 'with great solemnity', it was reported in 1671), Richard Allen still preached at Batcombe. There were sermons at Glastonbury 'in a barn ... where a pulpit and seats are built'. Taunton, Wellington, the northern villages, the Chard and Bruton areas: all were hotbeds of nonconformity. Like the ejected royalists before them, many of the clergy were protected by wealthy sympathisers, like William Strode at Barrington. Several established schools and even cavalier gentlemen sometimes sent their sons to them. Would they 'have all their children dunces?' Sir John Helyar asked when there was talk of closing one at Bristol run by Samuel Winney, formerly of Glastonbury.[40]

After 1660 Somerset men were still for 'Liberty and Property', still inclined to suspicion of the Court and popery. A new 'country interest' emerged and attracted many whose family traditions were royalist. But it was the farmers and clothworkers who took up arms with Monmouth in 1685. Without the gentry to lead them, they were smashed at Sedgemoor and suffered the brutal consequences of Kirk's Lambs and the Bloody Assizes. George Speke, the old royalist who was one of the few gentlemen to support Monmouth, lost a son and himself narrowly escaped hanging. But Jeffreys's victims were more often men whose families had formed the radical minority in John Pyne's days. Among several of the name who suffered there was Philip Bovett of Wellington, who had been a lieutenant in the 1659 militia. His fate may remind us that the issues that divided men so passionately for so long did not die in 1660. Somerset long remembered the misery, the exaltation, of 'the late rebellious times'.

Notes to this chapter are on pages 213-15.

List of Abbreviations

A&O   *Acts and Ordinances of the Interregnum,* (ed) Firth, C. H. and Rait, R. S. 1911

BM   British Museum

CAM   *Calendar of the Proceedings of the Committee for Advance of Money,* (ed) Green, M. A. E. 1888

CCC   *Calendar of the Proceedings of the Committee for Compounding,* (ed) Green, M. A. E. 1889-92

CCSP   *Calendar of the Clarendon State Papers,* (ed) Ogle, O., and others. Oxford 1869-1970

CSPD   *Calendar of State Papers, Domestic Series*

DNB   *Dictionary of National Biography*

EHR   *English Historical Review*

HMC   Historical Manuscripts Commission

JHC   *Journals of the House of Commons*

JHL   *Journals of the House of Lords*

PRO   Public Record Office

QSR   *Quarter Sessions Records for the County of Somerset, 3: Commonwealth,* (ed) Bates Harbin, E. H., SRS, 28. 1912

SASP   *Somersetshire Archaeological and Natural History Society Proceedings*

SDNQ   *Somerset and Dorset Notes and Queries*

SP   State Papers

SRO   Somerset Record Office

SRS   Somerset Record Society

VCHS   *Victoria History of the County of Somerset,* (ed) Page, William. 1906-11

§   denotes 'paragraph'

Notes to the Text

Chapter 1. A County Divides
1640-2. Pages 11-30

1 Bates, E. H. (ed). *The Particular Description of the County of Somerset, Drawn up by Thomas Gerard of Trent, 1633*, SRS, 15 (1900), 6, 55, 61
2 Williams, Michael. *The Draining of the Somerset Levels* (Cambridge 1970), 86-108. Barnes, Thomas G. *Somerset 1625-1640* (Cambridge, Mass. 1961), 151-5
3 *Gerard*, 131-2, 172
4 Wickham Legg, L. G. (ed). 'A Relation of a Short Survey of the Western Counties made by a Lieutenant of the Military Company in Norwich in 1635', *Camden Miscellany*, 16 (Camden 3rd series 52, 1936), 80
5 Gough, J. W. (ed). *Mendip Mining Laws and Forest Bounds*, SRS. 45 (1931), intro., 1-11. VCHS 2, 375, 380-2
6 Bowden, Peter J. *The Wool Trade in Tudor and Stuart England* (1962), 33-4, 39-40, 45-8
7 *Gerard*, 123, 232. Williams, *Somerset Levels*, 89-91. Thirsk, Joan. 'The Farming Regions of England', in Finberg, H.P.R. and Thirsk, Joan (eds). *Agrarian History of England and Wales* 4: *1500-1640* (Cambridge 1967), 4, 73-9
8 Fuller, Thomas. *The Worthies of England*, ed by Freeman, John (1952), 490
9 Cockburn, J. S. (ed). *Somerset Assize Orders, 1640-1659*, SRS, 71 (1971), no 12. I am grateful to Dr Cockburn for generously permitting me to use his typescript before publication
10 *Gerard*, 125. On the yeomen, see also Campbell, Mildred. *The English Yeoman under Elizabeth and the early Stuarts* (New Haven, Conn. 1942); and Bridenbaugh, Carl. *Vexed and Troubled Englishmen 1590-1642* (1968), esp. 53-6
11 Jordan, W. K. *The Forming of the Charitable Institutions of the West of England*, American Philosophical Soc. Transactions, new series 50 pt 8 (Philadelphia 1960), 61-5. See also Bridenbaugh, *Vexed and Troubled Englishmen*, 241-51, 318-32; and Barnes, *Somerset*, 154-8, 206, 226, 295
12 Eburne, Richard. *A Plain Pathway to Plantations*, ed by Wright, L. B., Folger Documents of Tudor and Stuart Civilization (Ithaca, N.Y. 1962), 3, 5, 32, 111-13
13 Finberg and Thirsk, *Agrarian History* 4, 80, and table 16. Westcote, Thomas. *A View of Devonshire in MDCXXX*, ed by Oliver, G. and Jones, P. (Exeter 1845), 62. Eburne, *Plain Pathway*, 32, 111-12
14 For Strode, see Serel, Thomas. 'On the Strodes of Somersetshire', SASP 13 pt 2 (1865-6), 6-20; Green, E. 'Col. William Strode', SASP 30 pt 2 (1884),

46-65; and Helyar, H. A. 'The Arrest of Col. William Strode', SASP 37 pt 2 (1891), 15-39. For Ashe, see Keeler, Mary F. *The Long Parliament, 1640-1641*, American Philosophical Soc. Memoirs 36 (Philadelphia 1954), 91-2; and Bates Harbin, S. W. *Members of Parliament for the County of Somerset* (Taunton 1939), 158-9

15 Brown, Frederick. *Abstracts of Somersetshire Wills* (1887-90) 2, 19-20

16 Barnes, *Somerset*. Throughout this chapter my constant debt to this splendid book will be obvious. For comparative purposes I also owe much to Everitt, Alan. *The Community of Kent and the Great Rebellion* (Leicester 1966)

17 Quoted in Zagorin, Perez. *The Court and the Country* (1969), 86. From this point the term 'Country' will be used without the quotation marks. Used with the capital letter, it stands for the general cohesion of county, regional, local, vaguely conservative sentiment, with undertones of a claim to represent the public interest. The Court, on the other hand, stands for centralised (arbitrary?) government; the Court was much more than the elaborate social rigmarole surrounding the king, though the term also implied this. See Zagorin, passim

18 Barnes, *Somerset*, 34, 262-3, 295

19 Barnes, T. G. 'County Politics and a Puritan Cause Célèbre: Somerset Churchales, 1633', *Royal Historical Soc. Transactions* 5th series 9 (1959), 103-22. See also Edgar, F. T. R. *Sir Ralph Hopton* (Oxford 1968), 6-13. For Harington, see Barnes, *Somerset*, 34-5. Stieg, Margaret. 'The parochial clergy in the diocese of Bath and Wells 1625-1685', University of California (Berkeley) PhD thesis (1970), 59-60, notes that the value of livings in these puritan parishes was falling significantly behind those in other parts of the county

20 VCHS 2, 42, 44. Robinson, J. A. (ed). 'Documents of the Laudian Period', in Palmer, T. F. (ed). *Collectanea* 2, SRS, 43 (1928), 208. Stieg, 'Clergy', 181

21 Robinson, 'Laudian Documents', 178, 184-7, 191-217. Barnes, T. G. (ed). *Somerset Assize Orders 1629-1640*, SRS, 65 (1959), 37, 43, 48. Stieg, 'Clergy', 218-22, also notes resistance at Mells

22 Barnes, *Assize Orders 1629-40*, intro., xxiii, and 60-2

23 Barnes, *Somerset*, 286

24 Barnes, *Somerset*, 231-3, 274-6. CSPD, 1640, 436-7

25 Bristol Archives, Ashton Court MSS, AC/C 58/1, 9, 6: Edward Phelips to Thomas Smyth, [Dec 1639?], 29 Jan [1639/40], and 19 Oct [1640]

26 For the elections, see Keeler, *Long Parliament*, 61-2, 343, 349-50. The Phelips-Smyth correspondence (above, n 25) provides some corrections

27 JHC 2, 23, 50, 58, 62-3, 77, 81, 117. JHL 4, 117-18. Rushworth, John. (ed). *Historical Collections*, 2nd ed (1721-3) 4, 21, 61, 134

28 Edgar, *Hopton*, 19-20. Barnes, *Somerset*, 309 and n. Keeler, *Long Parliament*, 242

29 Edgar, *Hopton*, 19. Lists of Somerset subscribers to the Protestation are in House of Lords Record Office, calendared in HMC, *Fifth Report* (House of Lords MSS), 131-2

30 JHL 4, 469. Nalson, John. *An Impartial Collection of the Great Affairs of State* (1682-3) 2, 726

31 BM, Egerton MS 2,711, fol 81: Harington's notes for a charge, 11 Jan 1641/2. HMC, *Wells Dean and Chapter* 2, 426. VCHS 2, 45

32 JHL 4, 237, 262, 312. HMC, *Fourth Report* (House of Lords MSS), 62. CSPD, 1641-3, 298. JHC 2, 491

33 Edgar, *Hopton*, 20-4

34 JHL 4, 385-7, 510. HMC, *Fifth Report*, 5
35 JHC 2, 455, 503. *A Speech Spoken by Sr. Thomas Wroth* (25 Feb 1641/2). See also Green, E. 'On the Civil War in Somerset', SASP 14 pt 2 (1867), 50
36 JHC 2, 426, 495-6, 509-10, 520. JHL 4, 666, 670; 5, 115
37 Hamer, J. H. 'Trading at Saint White Down Fair, 1637-1649', *Somerset Archaeology* 112 (1968), 64
38 JHL 5, 133-4. JHC 2, 625-6. *The Somerset Petition. With an Answer in defence of the Parliament* (June 1642)
39 HMC, *Bath* 4, 217. JHC 2, 684-5. JHL 5, 226. Bristol Archives, Ashton Court MSS, AC/F 6/8: Charles I to Thomas Smyth, 11 July 1642

Chapter 2. Roundhead Somerset
August 1642 - May 1643. Pages 31-48

1 JHL 5, 265
2 Cockburn, *Assize Orders 1640-59*, intro., and nos 21-2. Petitions in PRO, SP 16/49, fols 115-16, 236, calendared in CSPD, 1641-3, 361, 370
3 Clarendon, Edward, Earl of. *History of the Rebellion and Civil Wars in England*, ed by Macray, W. D. (Oxford 1888), bk 6, § 4. CSPD, 1641-3, 376. *A Declaration Made by the Lord Marquesse of Hartford* (Sept 1642). HMC, *Fifth Report* (House of Lords MSS), 44
4 For the events of 28 July-1 August, see: HMC, *Fifth Report*, 44; JHL 5, 265; Clarendon, *History*, bk 6, §§ 3, 6; and Chadwyck Healey, C. E. H. (ed). *Bellum Civile. Hopton's Narrative of his Campaign in the West*, SRS, 18 (1902), 2-5. A useful modern account is Edgar, *Hopton*, 31-5. Green, 'On the Civil War in Somerset', SASP 14 pt 2 (1867), 43-71 is confused and inaccurate, though including some valuable extracts from pamphlet material
5 HMC, *Fifth Report*, 44
6 Clarendon, *History*, bk 6, § 6. *Bellum Civile*, 5 n
7 I remember the late H. E. Balch telling me of a local tradition that bloodshed occurred during the return to Wells; some soldiers were killed and buried at the southern end of Park Fields. The absence of contemporary references to an event which would have had obvious propaganda value makes the story unlikely
8 Events of 3-6 August from: [Ashe, John]. *A Perfect Relation of All the passages and proceedings of the Marquesse Hartford* (12 Aug 1642)—a more complete version of the mutilated letter in JHL 5, 278-9; *A Second Letter Sent from John Ashe Esquire* (16 Aug); *Bellum Civile*, 7-10. See also Edgar, *Hopton*, 36-40
9 *A Declaration Made by the Lord Marquesse of Hartford*. Clarendon, *History*, bk 6, § 6, says that Stawell had less than 100 men; Ashe says 120-40. All accounts agree that the royalists were heavily outnumbered
10 Wells Archives, Acts bk 7 (1635-44), fols 214-15. Edgar, *Hopton*, 39 and n
11 Quoted in Green, SASP 14 pt 2, 63
12 *Bellum Civile*, 10. Presumably Stoberry Warren, but just possibly Milton Hill

13 *Bellum Civile*, 11 n. Some details also from Green, SASP 14 pt 2, 67-70
14 Each side blamed the other for the looting. An untrustworthy parliamentarian source says that the cavaliers did £10,000 worth of damage at Wells: *Exceeding Joyfull Newes From the Earl of Bedford* (23 Aug 1642)
15 *A Memento for Yeomen, Merchants, Citizens, And all the Commons in England* (23 Aug 1642)
16 [Ashe], *Perfect Relation*
17 Clarendon, *History*, bk 6, § 5. Corbet, John. 'A True and Impartial History of the Military Government of the City of Gloucester', in Scott, Sir Walter (ed). *Somers Tracts*, 2nd ed (1809-15) 5, 303-4
18 *A Coppie of a Letter, Read in the House of Commons: Sent from Master Sampford* (26 Aug 1642). The episode of the little boy is from *Exceeding Joyfull Newes from the Earl of Bedford*, which is generally unreliable; but the story is too good to be resisted
19 *Coppie of a Letter . . . from Master Sampford*
20 *Second Letter Sent from John Ashe*, 7-8. JHL 5, 286. *Bellum Civile*, 11. Clarendon, *History*, bk 6, § 7
21 *A Letter written From the Right Honorable the Earle of Bedford* (15 Sept 1642)
22 My account of Babylon Hill attempts to reconcile the conflicting versions in: *A Letter written From the Right Honorable the Earle of Bedford; A Relation of the Actions of the Parliaments Forces Under the command of the Earl of Bedford* (13 Sept 1642); *Propositions Propounded by the Marquesse of Hartford, to the Earle of Bedford* (17 Sept); *A Declaration made by the Lord Marquesse of Hartford* (Sept); Vicars, John. *Jehovah-Jireh. God in the Mount* (1644), 147-8; and *Bellum Civile*, 14-16
23 JHL 5, 367-8
24 *Bellum Civile*, 18
25 JHC 3, 4-18. JHL 5, 656; 6, 30, 48, 118. CCC, 1339
26 VCHS 2, 46-7. SASP 7 pt 1 (1856-7), 11-12. JHL 5, 490. JHC 2, 986. Green, 'Col. William Strode', SASP 30 pt 2 (1884), 54
27 Wells Archives, Acts bk 7, fol 225. HMC, *Wells Dean and Chapter* 2, 427. SRO, Tintinhull churchwardens' accounts, D/P/Tin., 4/1/2, p 162. I am indebted to Dr R. W. Dunning for this reference
28 *The Queenes Resolution Discovered* (1642). JHL 5, 560-670, passim. HMC, *Fifth Report*, 69, 75. JHC 2, 965-6, 1000
29 *A Declaration Made by the Lord Marquesse of Hartford*. HMC, *Portland* 1, 65; *Fifth Report*, 72. JHL 5, 372. JHC 2, 826
30 JHC 2, 872, 890, 925; 3, 38. JHL 5, 469, 511, 543. HMC, *Fifth Report*, 58. Firth, C. H. (ed). *Memoirs of Edmund Ludlow* (Oxford 1894) 1, 441
31 JHL 5, 544-5. CCC, 926, 1311, 1380. There is a great deal of material on local parliamentarian finances in the papers of the Somerset subcommittee of accounts, in PRO, SP 28/175, 28/200, and 28/214. Many of these are falling apart and requests to see them meet the reply, 'unfit for production'. Local historians ought to make fuller use of them before it is too late
32 CSPD, 1645-7, 455. CAM, 653. JHL 5, 658. A&O 1, 67-170, passim. Vicars, *Jehovah-Jireh*, 303-4
33 For the status of the parliamentarian leaders I have relied on such works as: Collinson, John. *History and Antiquities of the County of Somerset* (Bath 1791); Bates Harbin, *Somerset MPs*; Barnes, *Somerset*; and miscellaneous biographical and genealogical articles scattered through the issues of SASP and SDNQ
34 Wells Archives, Acts bk 7, fol 231: Strode and Walker to mayor, 21 Nov

1642. JHC 2, 799, 880, 882. JHL 5, 482. HMC, *Portland* 1, 65, 88-9, 91-2, 102-3

35 JHC 2, 976. JHL 5, 637. Rushworth, *Collections* 5, 153-6. *Ludlow* 1, 50-1, 447. Vicars, *Jehovah-Jireh*, 303-4. CCSP 1, 239. Prynne, William and Walker, Clement. *A True and Full Relation of the Prosecution, Arraignment, Tryall, and Condemnation of Nathaniel Fiennes* (1644), 34

Chapter 3. The Royalists Triumphant
June - July 1643. Pages 49-64

1 His chaplain before the war was the puritan Richard Allen the younger: Matthews, A. G. *Calamy Revised* (Oxford 1934), 6

2 'Vindication of Richard Atkyns', in Young, Peter and Tucker, Norman (eds). *Military Memoirs of the Civil War* (1967), 12. For the events of early June I have relied mainly upon 'Atkyns'; *Bellum Civile*; and Hopton's report in Trevelyan, Sir W. C. and Trevelyan, Sir C. E. (eds). *Trevelyan Papers* 3, Camden series, 105 (1872), 235-8

3 'Atkyns', 25

4 *Bellum Civile*, 47. 'Atkyns', 12. Clarendon, *History*, bk 7, § 98

5 *Trevelyan Papers* 3, 237-8

6 *Bellum Civile*, 48

7 *Trevelyan Papers* 3, 236

8 *Bellum Civile*, 49

9 'Atkyns', 14. Walter Slingsby, in *Bellum Civile*, 91, says that Waller's forces were also aided by a fog in their original check to Carnarvon

10 Clarendon, *History*, bk 7, §§ 99, 103

11 *Trevelyan Papers* 3, 237. *Bellum Civile*, 46 n

12 'Atkyns', 16. Clarendon, *History*, bk 7, § 103

13 *Bellum Civile*, 84-5, 88. Adair, John. *Roundhead General: a military biography of Sir William Waller* (1969), 74

14 Gardiner, S. R. *History of the Great Civil War* (1886-91) 1, 196-7. See also Edgar, *Hopton*, 99; and Adair, *Roundhead General*, 75-6

15 Warburton, Eliot. *Memoirs of Prince Rupert and the Cavaliers* (1849) 2, 232

16 *Bellum Civile*, 51. Vicars, *Jehovah-Jireh*, 376, assigns the incident to Stoke Lane

17 For the events preceding Lansdown, see *Bellum Civile*, 51-3, 91-2; Edgar, *Hopton*, 100-2; and (with caution) Adair, *Roundhead General*, 77-8

18 The best modern account of the battle is in Burne, A. H. and Young, Peter. *The Great Civil War* (1959), 78-83. See also Jex-Blake, T. W. 'The Battle of Lansdown', SASP 41 pt 2 (1895), 38-46; Edgar, *Hopton*, 102-5; and (again with caution) Adair, *Roundhead General*, 80-4

19 'Atkyns', 19

20 *Bellum Civile*, 96

21 'Atkyns', 20

22 Clarendon, *History*, bk 7, § 110. *Bellum Civile*, 55

23 Adair, *Roundhead General*, 86. Clarendon, *History*, bk 7, § 112. Burne and Young, *Civil War*, 84-5

N

24 Adair, *Roundhead General*, 94, 96, 100
25 The best recent accounts of the assault on Bristol are in Burne and Young, *Civil War*, 92-6; and Edgar, *Hopton*, 114-18. See also Clarendon, *History*, bk 7, §§ 123-33; Rupert's Journal, in Warburton, *Rupert* 2, 238-64; and Prynne and Walker, *True and Full Relation of the Prosecution . . . of Nathaniel Fiennes*, esp. 25, 62, 105, and appendix, 7-9, 15-17
26 Burne and Young, *Civil War*, 96
27 'Atkyns', 28. Slingsby was equally appalled by the casualties: *Bellum Civile*, 93
28 Clarendon, *History*, bk 7, § 130. Fiennes's precipitate departure may explain the well-known story that Blake held out at Bristol after the surrender

Chapter 4. Royalist Somerset
July 1643 - March 1645.   Pages 67-85

1 Warburton, *Rupert* 2, 291 n. Edgar, *Hopton*, 145
2 Matthews, *Calamy Revised*, 37, 364, 481. VCHS 2, 47. G[arret], W. *The Life and Death of Mr. Samuel Crook* (1651), 39
3 JHL 6, 240-1, 247. JHC 3, 351-5. The fullest account of the whole affair is in Prynne and Walker, *True and Full relation of the Prosecution . . . of Nathaniel Fiennes*. The controversy provoked numerous other pamphlets
4 Black, William H. (ed). *Docquets of Letters Patent . . . under the Great Seal of King Charles I at Oxford* (1838), 129, 133, 190. CCC, 995. CAM, 1159. Wells Archives, Acts bk 7, fols 247-9
5 Members of the 1643 commission are listed in QSR 3, intro. xx. For changes, see Black, *Docquets*, 10-11, 55, 70. The surviving cases from 1644 are in SRO, Sessions Roll, 1644, CQ3/1/79. Royalist Quarter Sessions were held in Devon in 1643-4: Andriette, Eugene A. *Devon and Exeter in the Civil War* (Newton Abbot 1971), 103-4
6 Black, *Docquets*, 81, 90-1. CSPD, 1644, 107-8. JHL 6, 643. HMC, *Sixth Report* (House of Lords MSS), 19, CCC, 936-7, 1210, 1360-1, 1979-80. There is a list of western gentry indicted for treason, 1644, in BM, Heath-Verney papers, Egerton MS 2,978, fol 152
7 Black, *Docquets*, 55, 70. Edgar, *Hopton*, 144-5
8 Edgar, *Hopton*, 133-4, 143, 145. Black, *Docquets*, 75, 112. CAM, 1039. CCC, 1074, 1271, 1278
9 *Trevelyan Papers* 3, 243. CAM, 980-1. CCC, 926, 1244
10 *Bellum Civile*, 60, 62-3. Edgar, *Hopton*, 142, 146. Black, *Docquets*, 130, 163. *Ludlow* 1, 54, 70-8, 454-5
11 *Trevelyan Papers* 2, 119-21; 3, 238-9, 242-3, 247-8
12 CCC, 1356. See also Green, E. 'On the History of Chard', SASP 28 pt 2 (1882), 57-8
13 *The Association, Agreement, and Protestation of the Counties of Somerset, Dorset, Cornwall and Devon* (Oxford 1644). Black, *Docquets*, 198, 202, 214. Powell, J. R. and Timings, E. K. (eds). *Documents Relating*

NOTES TO THE TEXT 203

to the Civil War, Navy Records Soc., 105 (1963), 156. The association's early efforts are evident in *Trevelyan Papers* 3, 249-50; and in SRO, Phelips MSS, DD/PH/5: E. Hodges to Edward Phelips, 11 June 1644
14 Powell and Timings, *Civil War Documents*, 156-7. CSPD, 1644, 335, 351. JHL 6, 616. Long, C. E. (ed). *Diary of the Marches of the Royal Army during the Great Civil War kept by Richard Symonds*, Camden series, 74 (1859), 98. Whitelock, Bulstrode. *Memorials of the English Affairs* (Oxford 1853), 1, 274, 280. Vicars, John. *Gods Arke Overtopping the Worlds Waves* (1646), 264-5. Walker, Sir Edward. *Historical Discourses* (1705), 41. Snow, Vernon F. *Essex the Rebel* (Lincoln, Nebraska 1970), 432-40
15 A&O 1, 459-61, 489-96
16 Walker, *Historical Discourses*, 27, 41-2. CSPD, 1644, 335
17 For Charles I's movements in Somerset, see *Symonds*, 30-7; and Green, E. 'The King's March through Somerset, 1644', SASP 24 pt 2 (1878), 43-9
18 *Ludlow* 1, 91-3, 459-61. Walker, *Historical Discourses*, 39-40
19 *Ludlow* 1, 95-6. Walker, *Historical Discourses*, 39-40. *Symonds*, 32, 35. Whitelock, *Memorials* 1, 295
20 *Symonds*, 35. Ralph, Philip L. *Sir Humphrey Mildmay: Royalist Gentleman* (New Brunswick, N.J. 1947), 175
21 Walker, *Historical Discourses*, 43-5. Rushworth, *Collections* 5, 688-90
22 Walker, *Historical Discourses*, 45. BM, Add MS 15,750, fol 18: Stawell to J. Ashburnham, 30 July 1644
23 Walker, *Historical Discourses*, 47-8. Wells Archives, Acts bk 7, fols 258-62
24 Wells Archives, Acts bk 7, fols 263-4. There are conflicting accounts of the North Petherton fight in CSPD, 1644, 438; Rushworth, *Collections* 5, 697-8; Walker, *Historical Discourses*, 64-5; and Clarendon, *History*, bk 8, § 114
25 CSPD, 1644, 439-40, 484, 495. *Symonds*, 62, 102. Walker, *Historical Discourses*, 86. HMC, *Portland* 3, 126. *Ludlow* 1, 97-8, 462. Ralph, *Mildmay*, 177
26 Green, 'Chard', SASP 28 pt 2, 58. SRO, Phelips MSS, DD/PH/27, fol 77: warrant of Lord Hopton, 4 October 1644
27 CSPD, 1644, 530, 545. Walker, *Historical Discourses*, 88, 96. *Symonds*, 110
28 *Mercurius Britannicus* 56 (28 Oct-4 Nov 1644). For the proclamation, see Walker, *Historical Discourses*, 96-8; and Rushworth, *Collections* 5, 715-16
29 Walker, *Historical Discourses*, 99-103. Rushworth, *Collections* 5, 717-18. Clarendon, *History*, bk 8, § 255. *Mercurius Aulicus* 42 (12-19 Oct 1644)
30 *A Copie of the Kings Message sent by the Duke of Lenox* (6 Nov 1644). Walker, *Historical Discourses*, 101
31 CSPD, 1644-5, 28. Warburton, *Rupert* 3, 30-1. *Symonds*, 146
32 HMC, *Portland* 1, 197. Mr T. J. Hunt has reminded me that Cooper's observation on the lack of a defence line is curious, given the known survival of the medieval bank and ditch
33 JHL 7, 68-9. CSPD, 1644-5, 124. *Ludlow* 1, 107-8. Bond, John. *Occasus Occidentalis: Or, Job in the West* (20 Jan 1644/5), 76. There is a useful account by Green, E. 'The Siege and Defence of Taunton, 1644-5', SASP 25 pt 2 (1879), 34-8. However, Green is wrong in saying that the town was taken: it is clear from Cooper's letter (HMC, *Portland* 1, 197), that it was not
34 CSPD, 1644-5, 83. Bond, *Occasus Occidentalis*, 12
35 BM, Sir E. Walker's' papers, Harleian MS 6,804, fols 284-7: statement of C. Milton and J. Blythe [Nov 1644]. For the excise commission, see Black, *Docquets*, 210, 263. The episode of the shoes and stockings is from Wells Archives, Acts bk 7, fol 269; and PRO, Chancery (Bridges division),

C5/433/74: Trym v Casbeard, 1649. See also Walker, *Historical Discourses*, 99

36 Clarendon, *History*, bk 8, § 147. Walker, *Historical Discourses*, 88

37 Warburton, *Rupert* 3, 47-8. Clarendon, *History*, bk 9, § 7. CSPD, 1644-5, 230-1, 251-2. Black, *Docquets*, 250

38 Clarendon, *History*, bk 9, § 7 n

Chapter 5. The Battleground
March - July 1645. Pages 86-104

1 Clarendon, *History*, bk 9, §§ 7-10. As Sir Edward Hyde, Clarendon was a member of the prince's council: the *History* is thus an important primary source for the spring of 1645

2 Bulstrode, Sir Richard. *Memoirs and Reflections upon the Reign and Government of King Charles the Ist and K. Charles the IId* (1721), 120. Oldmixon, John. *History of England during the Reigns of the Royal House of Stuart* (1730-5) 1, 278. Burne and Young, *Civil War*, 232, make a rather unconvincing case for Goring

3 Green, 'Taunton 1644-5', SASP 25 pt 2 (1879), 38-9. HMS, *Portland* 1, 217. Clarendon, *History*, bk 9, §§ 11-12. CCSP 1, 261. Adair, *Roundhead General*, 182

4 Bulstrode, *Memoirs*, 120. Clarendon, *History*, bk 9, § 12 and n. CCSP 1, 262. *Ludlow* 1, 471

5 [Davies, Thomas]. 'The Somersetshire Man's Complaint', in Elworthy, F. T. (ed). *Specimens of English Dialects*, English Dialect Soc., 35 (1879), 7-9

6 Ross, D. M. 'Papers of the Former Corporation of Langport', SASP 53 pt 2 (1907), 156. Ralph, *Mildmay*, 180. Clarendon, *History*, bk 9, § 24. Edgar, *Hopton*, 175

7 My account of the events around Brent Knoll is based on the papers printed by Symonds, Henry. 'A By-Path of the Civil War', SASP 65 (1919), 48-75

8 According to his own later statement, Tynte had already resigned his commission: CCC, 1037

9 The official line was that Somerset fomented the riot so that he could escape from returning to the king's army. An order of 13 March had remustered all former officers and soldiers

10 See for example Edward Curll's references to risings by 'the Country': Batten, John. 'Somersetshire Sequestrations, pt 2', SASP 16 pt 2 (1870), 23-4

11 Clarendon, *History*, bk 8, § 256-7; bk 9, § 10

12 Clarendon, *History*, bk 9, §§ 16-17. Warburton, *Rupert* 3, 80

13 *Trevelyan Papers* 3, 317

14 CSPD, 1644-5, 418

15 Newton, George. *Mans Wrath and Gods Praise. Or, A Thanksgiving Sermon, Preached at Taunton* (11 May 1646), 14, 26. For general accounts of the siege and relief, see Green, 'Taunton, 1644-5', SASP 28 pt 2, 39-47; Gardiner, *Civil War* 2, 162-5; and Wedgwood, C. V. *The King's War 1641-1647* (1958), 443-4

16 Lister, Thomas H. *Life and Administration of Edward, first Earl of Clarendon* (1838) 3, 16. CSPD, 1644-5, 479. Clarendon, *History*, bk 9, §§ 18-20

17 CSPD, 1644-5, 499, 506-7. CCSP 1, 265. See also Clarendon, *History*, bk 9, § 45; and Sprigge, Joshua. *Anglia Rediviva* (1647), 22-3

18 CSPD, 1644-5, 581: 'Hampden' [Hopton?] to Charles I, 10 June. See also Ibid, 511; Whitelock, *Memorials* 1, 443-51; and CCSP 1, 268

19 I am indebted to David Jacobson's MA thesis, 'The Clubmen', Brown University (1971), for light on the clubmen in counties other than Somerset

20 *The Desires and Resolutions of the Club-Men of the Counties of Dorset and Wilts.* (12 July 1645). JHL 7, 484. Sprigge, *Anglia Rediviva*, 80

21 CCSP 1, 267. Lister, *Clarendon* 3, 14-18. Clarendon, *History*, bk 9, § 50, gives Marshall's Elm as the site of the meeting

22 JHL 7, 485. There is an annotated list of the Wiltshire and Dorset leaders in *The Kings Answer to the Propositions for Peace* (11 August 1645)

23 Clarendon, *History*, bk 9, §§ 46, 49, 51. CCSP 1, 268-9

24 *Moderate Intelligencer* 19 (3-10 July 1645). See also *True Informer* 12 (5-12 July); and *The Parliaments Post* 2 (8-15 July)

25 My account of the campaign before Langport is based on Sprigge, *Anglia Rediviva*, 60-4; Norris, Hugh. 'The Battle of Langport', SASP 40 pt 2 (1894), 128-33; Gardiner, *Civil War* 2, 234-7; and Burne and Young, *Civil War*, 210-11. The most recent treatment, Wanklyn, M. D. G. 'The Royalist Campaign in Somerset in July 1645', *Journal of Society for Army Historical Research* 46 (1968), 71-5, is unreliable in several important details

26 A countryman who supplied timber for repairing Load Bridge was still unpaid in 1649: QSR 3, 95

27 Warburton, *Rupert* 3, 137. Bulstrode, *Memoirs*, 136-7. Goring's own admission undermines the assertion in Burne and Young, *Civil War*, 211-12, 232, that the Isle Moor thrust was a brilliant strategic move

28 The railway embankment drastically changes the modern appearance of the battlefield

29 Sylvester, Matthew (ed). *Reliquiae Baxterianae* (1696), 1, 54. My account of the battle is based mainly on the works cited in n 25 above

30 Warburton, *Rupert* 3, 137-8

Chapter 6. The War's End
July - September 1645. Pages 105-20

1 *A Letter sent to the Right Honourable William Lenthall . . . Concerning the raising of the Siege of Taunton* (10 July 1645). *A Continuation of the Proceedings of the Army . . . [11-19 July 1645]* (26 July). *Moderate Intelligencer* 19 (3-10 July)

2 *Kingdomes Weekly Intelligencer* 109 (15-23 July 1645). Warburton, *Rupert* 3, 138

3 *A More full Relation of the great Battell . . . on Thursday last* (16 July 1645)

4 *Kingdomes Weekly Intelligencer* 108 (8-15 July 1645)
5 My account of the Willis family is based largely on information generously provided by Conrad Russell, from the Pym MSS in SRO. See also Connor, Arthur B. 'Monumental Brasses in Somerset, Part VI', SASP 82 (1936), 184-6
6 *Continuation of the Proceedings of the Army, 11-19 July*, 12-14. BM, Harleian MS 454, fol 75v: Mildmay's diary, 30 June 1645. See also Ralph, *Mildmay*, 180
7 Willis, Humphrey. *The Power of the Committee of Somerset* (6 July 1646), 1-3. *Continuation of the Proceedings of the Army, 11-19 July*
8 Sprigge, *Anglia Rediviva*, 68. Bell, Robert (ed). *Memorials of the Civil War: comprising the correspondence of the Fairfax family* (1849) 1, 239. *A More full Relation of the great Battell* (16 July 1645). *Moderate Intelligencer* 20 (10-17 July). *True Informer* 14 (19-26 July)
9 There are numerous pamphlet accounts of the siege and storm. My account also draws heavily on Oldmixon, *History of England* 1, 283-8. Oldmixon's value as a local man helps to counterbalance his obvious partisanship. For a later treatment, see Green, E. 'The Siege of Bridgwater, July, 1645', SASP 23 pt 2 (1877), 12-25
10 Warburton, *Rupert* 3, 147
11 Sprigge, *Anglia Rediviva*, 75
12 *True Informer* 14 (19-26 July 1645). *Symonds*, 210. Wedgwood, *King's War*, 467. CAM, 1419-20
13 *Kingdomes Weekly Intelligencer* 110 (22-9 July 1645). Warburton, *Rupert* 3, 153. Wedgwood, *King's War*, 467
14 *A Full Relation of the Taking of Bath by Sir Thomas Fairfaxes Forces* (2 Aug 1645). *Kingdomes Weekly Intelligencer* 111 (29 July-5 Aug). *Proceedings of the Army* (24-31 July)
15 Bell, *Memorials* 1, 244
16 *Two Letters: the one, Sent to . . . Lord Fairfax, from Sir Tho: Fairfax . . . The other sent to Sir Tho: Fairfax, from Lieutenant Generall Cromwell* (9 Aug 1645)
17 Sprigge, *Anglia Rediviva*, 82-6. Bond, John. *Ortus Occidentalis: or, a Dawning in the West* (22 Aug 1645), 46
18 Green, E. 'On the Parish and Castle of Nunney', SASP 22 pt 2 (1876), 94-5
19 For the operations leading to the fall of Bristol, see Sprigge, *Anglia Rediviva*, 89-118; Warburton, *Rupert* 3, 156-82; Gardiner, *Civil War* 2, 281, 287-91; and Wedgwood, *King's War*, 484-8
20 *Mercurius Civicus* 119 (28 Aug-4 Sept 1645). *Kingdomes Weekly Intelligencer* 115 (26 Aug-2 Sept). Sprigge, *Anglia Rediviva*, 91, 99. CSPD, 1645-7, 128. *Moderate Intelligencer* 28 (4-11 Sept)
21 Gardiner, *Civil War* 2, 288
22 Sprigge, *Anglia Rediviva*, 111-12
23 CSPD, 1645-7, 200-1. Whitelock, *Memorials* 1, 520. Gardiner, *Civil War* 2, 341 n, 466. Beadon, Roger. *Robert Blake* (1935), 53-6. VCHS 2, 217. There are many references to 'club money' in PRO, Committee of Accounts, SP 28/175, 28-214
24 *A Copy of a Petition, commended to the Peace-making Association in the West, by Colonell Blake, and Colonell Pyne* (30 July 1645)
25 Humphreys, Arthur L. *Materials for the History of the Town of Wellington* (1889), 101
26 Wells Archives, Acts bk 7, fols 238-9. On the general outlook of the corporation, see Underdown, David. 'A Case Concerning Bishops' Lands: Cornelius Burges and the Corporation of Wells', EHR 78 (1963), 21-4

27 W[illis], H. *England's Changeling: Or, the Time Servers Laid open in their Colours* (25 June 1659?). Willis, *Power of the Committee of Somerset,* 1

28 HMC, *Portland* 1, 237, 310

Chapter 7. The Committee and the County
1645-6. Pages 121-37

1 *Articles of Treason* . . . *committed by John Pine of Curry-Mallet* (2 March 1648/9), 3. *Mercurius Aulicus,* 23 Feb-2 March 1644/5. See also JHC 4, 97; Warburton, *Rupert* 3, 62; and Clarendon, *History,* bk 8, §§ 240-1

2 HMC, *Ninth Report* 2 (Pyne MSS), 494. HMC, *Leybourne-Popham,* 51. BM, Sloane MS 1,519, fol 188 : Pyne to Rushworth, 16 Dec 1648

3 Cockburn, *Assize Orders 1640-59,* no 28. QSR 3, 2, 12-13, 17, 36, 90-1

4 HMC, *Portland* 1, 237, 283. Harington, H. (ed). *Nugae Antiquae* (1769-75) 2, 230-2. King, A. J. and Watts, B. H. *Cavaliers and Roundheads: a Chapter in the History of Bath* (1887), 28

5 Bell, *Memorials* 1, 250. HMC, *Sixth Report* (Acland-Hood MSS), 347. JHL 7, 554

6 CCC, passim

7 For the original committee, see above, 46-7. The changes in 1644 are listed in A&O 1, 460. Biographical information from the same sources as in ch 2 above, n 33

8 HMC, *Bath* 4, 279

9 *Perfect Weekly Account* 9 (3-10 May 1648)

10 *Articles of Treason,* 4. SRO, Hippisley MSS, DD/HI/8, 10: Preston to John Hippisley, 30 April 1647; Preston's receipts, March-Nov 1647. Somerset possesses nothing like the volume of committee records that survive for Kent, Staffordshire, and a few other counties. But the committee's work can be reconstructed in part from documents in PRO, Committee for Advance of Money, SP 19; Committee for Compounding, SP 23; and Committee of Accounts, SP 28

11 For Barker, see Bates Harbin, *Somerset MPs,* 163; for Blackbourne, QSR 3, 203-25; for Barrett, Underdown, 'Burges and Wells', EHR 78, 31-2

12 Curll's accounts are in SRO, Coker Court MSS, 136. Extracts are printed in Batten, John. 'Somersetshire Sequestrations during the Civil War', SASP 4 pt 2 (1853), 60-77; 16 pt 2 (1870), 13-34. For an example of Curll's methods, see Ralph, *Mildmay,* 190

13 CCC, passim

14 SRO, Hippisley MSS, DD/HI/10: Walrond to Preston, 20 June 1647. For the Stawell case see CCC, 1425-30; 'The Humble Petition of Sir John Stawell', *Somers Tracts* 6, 32-6; and DNB

15 PRO, Committee of Accounts, SP 28/214: sequestration accounts, Hundred of Hartcliffe and Bedminster. SDNQ 1 (1888-90), 48-9. Cockburn, *Assize Orders 1640-59,* nos 28-9. For the committee's ecclesiastical activities, see below, 143-5

16 Walker, Clement. *The History of Independency* 1 (1648), 91. HMC, *Portland* 1, 307. On the by-elections, see Underdown, David. 'Party management in the recruiter elections, 1645-1648', EHR 83 (1968), 235-64. There is a large and wearisome literature on the confusion of religious and

political party names: see, for example, the exchanges in *Past and Present* 47 (May 1970), and references there cited

17 The following account of the county election is based on: *Scottish Dove* 119 (21-9 Jan 1645/6); JHC 4, 565-6; and HMC, *Portland* 1, 318-9. For Horner's earlier experience, see Farnham, Edith. 'The Somerset Election of 1614', EHR 46 (1931), 579-99

18 The unprinted signatures and postscript to the protest are in Bodleian, Nalson Papers 5, MS Dep C 156, fol 101v

19 The voting at Bath was 18 (Ashe) to 3 (Popham): King and Watts, *Cavaliers and Roundheads*, 26-7. The Milborne Port election is noted in *Scottish Dove* 115 (24 Dec 1645-1 Jan 1645/6)

20 The committee intervention at Wells is apparent in PRO, Committee for Compounding, SP 23/166, 12: mayor, etc, to County Committee, 20 Dec 1645. For Ilchester, see Underdown, David. 'The Ilchester Election, February 1646', SASP 110 (1966), 40-51

21 Bodleian, Tanner MS 59, fol 353: County Committee to Lenthall, 20 June 1646. JHC 4, 369, 394, 401, 405, 565-8, 662

22 BM, Add MS 10, 114, fols 13v-16: Harington's diary, 24 April-13 July 1646. Willis, *Power of the Committee of Somerset*, 1-7

23 *Scottish Dove* 144 (22-31 July 1646). SRO, Hippisley MSS, DD/HI/10: Preston to Henley, 21 July 1646

24 Willis, Hum. *Times Whirligig, or, The Blew-new-made-Gentleman mounted* (9 Feb 1646/7). Willis, *England's Changeling*

25 Bodleian, Tanner MS 60, fols 545-7: constables of Frome to Skippon, 10 March 1645/6

26 HMC, *Egmont* 1, 318. JHC 4, 638, 640. *Moderate Intelligencer* 75 (6-13 Aug 1646). BM, Add MS 10,114, fol 17: Harington's diary, 6-7 Aug. Bodleian, Nalson Papers 14, MS Dep C 167, fol 309: orders of councils of war, 23 and 30 July

27 *Mercurius Aulicus*, 23 Feb-2 March 1644/5. Bodleian, Tanner MS 59, fol 353: County Committee to Lenthall, 20 June 1646. Willis, *Power of the Committee of Somerset*, 6. Cockburn, *Assize Orders 1640-59*, nos 24, 41, 46-7, 55, 62-6

28 Willis, *Power of the Committee of Somerset*, 6. *Articles of Treason*, 5. Walker, *Independency* 1, 91

29 HMC, *Portland* 1, 283, 309. PRO, Committee of Accounts, SP 28/175: Combe Hay accounts, 2 June 1646. CCC, 1277-8, 1495-7

30 For the various versions, see Underdown, 'Burges and Wells', EHR 78, 32 n

31 HMC, *Tenth Report* 6 (Pym MSS), 95. Willis, *Times Whirligig*. Walker, Clement. 'Mystery of the Two Juntoes', in Maseres, Francis (ed). *Select Tracts Relating to the Civil Wars* (1815) 1, 338. JHC 4, 644. JHL 8, 684. *Scottish Dove* 160 (11-18 Nov 1646). Cockburn, *Assize Orders 1640-59*, nos 45, 49, 67

32 Willis, *Power of the Committee of Somerset*, 3. Underdown, David. *Pride's Purge: Politics in the Puritan Revolution* (Oxford 1971), 38-9

Chapter 8. Conflict and Revolution
1646-9. Pages 138-54

1 HMC, *Portland* 1, 447-8

2 JHL 9, 172. JHC 5, 318. *Perfect Occurrences* 15 (9-16 April 1647). *Moderate Intelligencer* 129 (2-9 Sept 1647). *Trevelyan Papers* 3, 257. HMC, *Egmont* 1, 403, 407-8. BM, Add MS 10,114, fol 25: Harrington's diary, 4 June 1647. QSR 3, intro, xxix, and 45

3 SRO, Hippisley MSS, DD/HI/10: [Hill] to [Pyne], 23 Feb [1646/7]. JHC 5, 103. CSPD, 1645-7, 535

4 Cockburn, *Assize Orders 1640-59*, no 28. I know of no copy of the original postwar commission, but the names of active JPs can be retrieved from QSR 3, and from the Sessions Rolls in SRO. For additions to and withdrawals from the commission I have relied on the card-file of JPs at the History of Parliament Trust

5 Cockburn, *Assize Orders 1640-59*, nos 23-33. QSR 3, 1-2

6 The surviving records of the Somerset subcommittee are in PRO, Committee of Accounts, SP 28/175; 200; 214; and 242. For the general subject, see Pennington, D. H. 'The Accounts of the Kingdom 1642-1649', in Fisher, F. J. (ed). *Essays in the Economic and Social History of Tudor and Stuart England* (Cambridge 1961), 182-203

7 PRO, Committee of Accounts, SP 28/253A, fols 8v, 10, 49-50: London committee to Somerset subcommittee, 14 and 17 July 1646, 15 April 1647; SP 28/256: Strode to London committee, 27 Oct 1646; SP 28/257: Pyne to London committee, 30 April 1647

8 A&O 1, 974. Biographical information from sources indicated above, ch 2, n 33

9 HMC, *Portland* 1, 274. BM, Add MS 10,114, fol 23: Harington's diary, 24 April 1647. Shaw, William A. *History of the English Church during the Civil Wars . . . 1640-1660* (1900) 2, 413-21. Shaw suggests that the classical organisation may date from late 1645 or early 1646, but the Harington entry makes this unlikely

10 Walker, John. *An Attempt towards recovering an Account of the . . . Sufferings of the Clergy* (1714). But I have followed the more reliable entries in Matthews, A. G. *Walker Revised* (Oxford 1948). Stieg, 'Clergy', 158-69, gives many examples of the inadequacies of the prewar clergy

11 VCHS 2, 48, suggests 110 ejections, which is roughly confirmed by Matthews, *Walker Revised*. However, quantification is hazardous because of the number of later ejections, and the difficulty of identifying pluralists and men who moved to other parishes

12 *Trevelyan Papers* 3, 260. *Scottish Dove* 144 (22-31 July 1646). Biographical information from DNB

13 Newton, *Mans Wrath and Gods Praise*, 7-8. B[att], T. *The Waters of Marah Sweetned. A Thanksgiving Sermon. Preached at Taunton* (11 May 1647). VCHS 2, 50

14 HMC, *Fourth Report* (Denbigh MSS), 273. Bodleian, Rawlinson MS D 945, fol 34: C. Paman to W. Sancroft, 29 Sept 1646. VCHS 2, 50. Edwards, Thomas. *Gangraena* pt 3 (Dec 1646), 41, 53, 107

15 *Perfect Weekly Account* 9 (3-10 May 1648)

16 HMC, *Portland* 1, 457. *Mercurius Pragmaticus* 2 (4-11 April 1648). Abbott, Wilbur C. (ed). *Writings and Speeches of Oliver Cromwell* (Cambridge, Mass. 1937-47) 1, 606. Washington, DC, Folger Library, Bennet Papers, MS Add 494: Derby House Committee to Sir H. Waller, 15 Aug 1648. Powell, J. R. (ed). *Letters of Robert Blake*, Navy Records Soc, 76 (1937), 5. CSPD, 1648-9, 251, 258-9

17 Powell, *Letters of Robert Blake*, 4-7. Powell and Timings, *Documents Relating to the Civil War*, 390

18 JHC 5, 569-70, 656; 6, 59. CSPD, 1648-9, 159, 210, 297. *Perfect Occur-*

rences 82 (21-8 July 1648). *Mercurius Pragmaticus* 19 (1-8 Aug). HMC, *Portland* 1, 499. Bodleian, Nalson Papers 15, MS Dep C 168, fols 245, 251: statements by County Committee and MPs, [Oct 1648]

19 *Perfect Weekly Account* 9 (3-10 May 1648). Prynne, William. *Irenarchus Redivivus* (13 July 1648), 43-4. A&O 1, 1091, 1113

20 Willis, *Times Whirligig*. Underdown, David (ed). 'Parliamentary Diary of John Boys, 1647-8', *Bulletin of the Institute of Historical Research* 39 (1966), 155. *Mercurius Elencticus* 11 (2-9 Feb 1647/8)

21 Underdown, *Pride's Purge*, 93

22 JHC 5, 460, 534. *The Humble Petition and Grateful Acknowledgement of the Town of Taunton* (9 Feb 1647/8). Walker, *Independency* 1, 91-2. HMC, *Portland* 1, 448

23 SRO, Hippisley MSS, DD/HI/9: Preston's shrievalty papers. The signatures to the grand jury presentment are in Bodleian, Nalson Papers 15, MS Dep C 168, fol 122v; and printed in *Perfect Diurnal* 247 (17-24 April 1648). The elder George Smith had tried to deliver the borough for Pyne's candidates in 1646: Underdown, 'Ilchester election', SASP 110, 46-8

24 Mells Manor House, MSS E3 (Sundries): 'An Account for Sutch Provision as was sent to Crikett house before the assiies', [Sept 1648]. I am indebted to Mr I. P. Collis for drawing my attention to this document, and to the Earl of Oxford for permitting me to examine it. JHC 6, 49. *The Parliamentary or Constitutional History of England*, 2nd ed (1761-3) 18, 31-2. The evidence for packing is presented in Underdown, *Pride's Purge*, 110 n

25 QSR 3, 59-61, 83. *Mercurius Elencticus* 49 (24-31 Oct 1648). *Perfect Occurrences* 105 (29 Dec 1648-5 Jan 1648/9). *The Moderate* 29 (23-30 Jan 1648/9). Bristol Archives, Ashton Court MSS, AC/WO/12 (36): lease at Shirehampton, Glos, 24 Dec [1648]. *Trevelyan Papers* 3, 269-70

26 A&O 1, 1243

27 *Mercurius Militaris* 3 (24-31 Oct 1648). *The Moderate* 21 (28 Nov-5 Dec). Whitelock, *Memorials* 2, 475. Underdown, *Pride's Purge*, chs 5, 6

28 BM, Sloane MS 1,519, fol 188: Pyne to Rushworth, 16 Dec 1648

29 *The Humble Petition of divers Gentlemen, Ministers, and well-affected Inhabitants in the County of Somerset* (21 Dec 1648). JHC 6, 102. HMC, *Seventh Report* (House of Lords MSS), 113. PRO, State Papers Charles II, SP 29/1, fol 94: information of Joshua Garment, 1660. For Blinman, see QSR 3, 205-35, 314. Gapper is described as a yeoman in Preston's freeholders' book, and in 1651 was signing militia papers with a mark: PRO, SP 28/242. Talk of a second petition to bring further charges against Prynne and Strode does not seem to have been followed up: *Kingdomes Weekly Intelligencer* 291 (19-26 Dec 1648)

30 *Articles of Treason*, 7. Underdown, *Pride's Purge*, 186 and n, 216

Chapter 9. The County and the Commonwealth 1649-53. Pages 155-74

1 Cranston, Maurice. *John Locke* (1957), 20. SRO, Tintinhull churchwardens' accounts, D/P/Tin., 4/1/2. p 173. *The Moderate* 26 (2-9 Jan 1648/9). JHC 6, 104. SDNQ 19 (1929), 168. *A Declaration of the Cornishmen Concerning the Prince of Wales* (9 Feb). The Agreement of the People was the radical constitutional programme proposed by the Levellers

2 Cockburn, *Assize Orders 1640-59*, no 89. QSR 3, 85
3 Prynne, William. *A Legall Vindication of the Liberties of England against Illegall Taxes and pretended Acts of Parliament* (1649), 36-40
4 *The Moderate* 29 (23-30 Jan 1648/9). Collier, Thomas. *A Looking-Glasse for the Quakers* (1656), 16. Whitelock, *Memorials* 3, 234. Hill, Christopher. *Puritanism and Revolution* (1958), 141, 316
5 *Perfect Occurrences* 127 (1-8 June 1649); I am indebted to Blair Worden for this reference. JHC 6, 221. HMC, *Leybourne-Popham*, 51
6 Cary, Henry (ed). *Memorials of the Great Civil War* (1842) 2, 113-14. SRO, Hippisley MSS, DD/HI/9: Buckland to Preston, 18 Dec 1648; DD/HI/10: Pyne to Preston, 16 April 1649. JHC 6, 134. For changes in the Commission of the Peace I have used the sources described above, in ch 8, n 4, supplemented by the lists for January 1650 in the 'Liber Pacis' in PRO, C 193/13/3; and for Michaelmas term 1650 in *The Names of the Justices of Peace, in England and Wales* (27 Nov 1650). For Swanton's royalist past, see JHC 4, 323, 500. Pyne's son was bound with him at Middle Temple in 1651, suggesting that he was now under Pyne's protection: Hopwood, C. H. and others (eds). *Middle Temple Records* (1904-5) 3, 1029
7 HMC, *Leybourne-Popham*, 51. HMC, *Portland* 1, 523. JHC 6, 407. SRO, Hippisley MSS, DD/HI/10: engagement certificate, 15 Jan 1650/1; and Swanton to Preston, 27 March 1652
8 Whitelock, *Memorials* 3, 288, 294. *Perfect Diurnal* 61 (Feb 1651). Matthews, *Calamy Revised*, 47, 318, 331, 367
9 CSPD, 1654, 282. CCC, 623. See also Hardacre, Paul H. *The Royalists during the Puritan Revolution* (The Hague 1956), 65
10 PRO, Committee for Advance of Money, SP 19/124, fol 181: deposition of Robert Hole. For the matters discussed in this and the following paragraphs, see CCC, passim
11 CCC, 1360-1
12 'The Humble Petition of Sir John Stawell', *Somers Tracts* 6, 32-6. CCC, 1256-7, 1425-30. On the early recovery of lands by royalists, see Thirsk, Joan. 'The Sales of Royalist Lands during the Interregnum', *Economic History Review* 2nd series 5 (1952-3), 188-207
13 An incident at Wells in November 1649, for example: QSR 3, intro, xxxii. For the lawyers, see Cockburn, *Assize Orders 1640-59*, no 89
14 Wyndham, H. A. *A Family History 1410-1688: the Wyndhams of Norfolk and Somerset* (1939), 248-51. Edgar, *Hopton*, 191-2, 196-8. Coate, Mary. *Cornwall in the Great Civil War and Interregnum* (Oxford 1933), 251, 257
15 CSPD, 1649-50, 354-5. Wyndham, *Family History*, 189
16 Underdown, David. *Royalist Conspiracy in England, 1649-1660* (New Haven, Conn. 1960), 29-34
17 CSPD, 1650, 294, 338, 364, 371-2. *Perfect Diurnal* 64 (March 1650/1). Cockburn, *Assize Orders 1640-59*, no 103. Underdown, *Royalist Conspiracy*, 32-3, 47-9
18 HMC, *Leybourne-Popham*, 51 (my italics). Whitelock, *Memorials* 3, 159, 241, 247, 276, 362. *Weekly Intelligencer* 5 (22-9 Oct 1650); again I am indebted to Blair Worden
19 DNB ('Walker, Clement'). Green, 'Col. William Strode', SASP 30 pt 2, 61. Maxwell Lyte, Sir H. C. *History of Dunster* (1909) 1, 197-8. CSPD, 1651, 263
20 Matthews, William (ed). *Charles II's Escape from Worcester* (Berkeley, Cal. 1966), 60-1
21 'Coll. Phillipp's Notes', in Matthews, *Charles II's Escape*, 139-42

22 HMC, *Leybourne-Popham*, 51. BM, Film 331, Letter-book of John Fitz-james (Northumberland MSS) 3, fol 5v: Fitzjames to Edward Ceely, 30 Nov 1649. For the reorganisation of the sequestration system, see Underdown, *Pride's Purge*, 301-2

23 My account of the Pyne-Ashe conflict is based on CCC, 173-358, passim, with some recourse to the originals in PRO, SP 23; and CSPD, 1650, 126, 206, 379, 410, 442, 614, 621

24 CCC, 222, 226-7

25 Contrary to the printed version in CCC, 221, Mason did not directly accuse Pyne of attempted bribery. The passage printed as 'get me some money' actually reads 'show me some mercy': PRO, SP 23/118, 892

26 CSPD, 1649-50, 256. Washington, DC, Folger Library, Bennet Papers, MS Add 494: Disbrowe to R. Bennet, 9 Feb 1649/50. See also Underdown, *Pride's Purge*, 302-3

27 The names of the commissioners have been extracted from militia documents in PRO, Committee of Accounts, SP 28/242. A commission was sent to Horner (Mells Manor House, MS 247), but there is no evidence that he ever acted on it. The elder Sampson is noted as 'Null. freehold' in Preston's freeholders' book: SRO, Hippisley MSS, DD/HI/9. His son was Popham's biggest tenant at Middle Lambrook (SRO, Popham MSS, DD/Po/32; DD/Pot/137: Popham accounts), but was obviously transferring his loyalties to Pyne, in whose regiment he was major. For John Gorges, see Bates Harbin, *Somerset MPs*, 165-6

28 CSPD, 1649-50, 521. PRO, Committee of Accounts, SP 28/242. SRO, Pyne MSS, DD/CM: commission to T. Collins, 26 March 1650

29 CSPD, 1650, 144-9, 175, 281, 294, 338, 364; 1651, 59-60, 65, 109, 148, 304, 335, 359-63, 384, 394, 434, 532-3, 577. Whitelock, *Memorials* 3, 247, 288. Bodleian, Tanner MS 55, fol 10: Somerset militia cmrs. to Council of State, 29 Aug 1651. Matthews, *Charles II's Escape*, 52

30 BM, Locke MSS, Add MS 28,273, fol 120: assessments made at Somerton, 6 July 1649. Assessment commissioners from A&O 2, 42, 120, 307-8, 476, 674. JPs from QSR 3; and card-file at History of Parliament Trust

31 JHC 7, 17, 24-6. CSPD, 1651, 474, 505-6; 1651-2, 17; 1652-3, 290, 301. Chard, Minehead, and Wells were among other towns submitting their charters. See also Underdown, *Pride's Purge*, 305-6

32 QSR 3, 102. Whitelock, *Memorials* 3, 220. For a local witchcraft case, see Cockburn, *Assize Orders 1640-59*, no 79

33 'John Taylor's Wandering to see the Wonders of the West' (1649), in Ashbee, E. W. (ed). *Occasional Facsimile Reprints* 8 (1869). SRO, Sessions Rolls, CQ3/1/82 (2), nos 64-6: depositions of J. Balch, H. Marsh, and R. Atwell, Feb 1650. Lambeth Palace, MS Comm. XIIa/15, fol 350: inquisition taken by commissioners to survey church livings, 13 Nov 1650. For Burges's purchase, see Underdown, 'Burges and Wells', EHR 78, 18-20, 279

34 Shaw, *Church during the Civil Wars* 2, 421-2. Jeanes, Henry. *The Want of Church-Government No warrant for a total omission of the Lord's Supper* (Oxford 1653). CSPD, 1648-9, 30-1. Cockburn, *Assize Orders 1640-59*, no 92. Lambeth Palace: MS Comm. XIIa/15, fols 348-451, passim: returns by commissioners to survey church livings, 1650

35 SRO, Way MSS, DD/X/WA, 2-4: documents concerning purchase of manor and castle of Taunton, 1648-50. Grey, Zachary. *An Impartial Examination of the Fourth Volume of Mr. Daniel Neal's History of the Puritans* (1739), Appendix, 18-21. Underdown, 'Burges and Wells'. EHR 78, 24

36 *Collectanea Topographica et Genealogica* 1 (1834), 122. Underdown, 'Burges and Wells', EHR 78, 24-43
37 Fullwood, Francis. *The Churches and Ministery of England* (1652), preface
38 *Moderate Publisher*, 25 March-1 April 1653; again I am indebted to Blair Worden. Underdown, 'Burges and Wells', EHR 78, 33. Nuttall, G. F. 'The Baptist Western Association', *Journal of Ecclesiastical History* 11 (1960), 213-14. There is a copy of the March 1653 petition in SRO, Hippisley MSS, DD/HI/10
39 BM, Add MS 10, 114, fol 34: Harington's diary, 24 Aug 1653. Bodleian, Clarendon MS 46, fols 182-3: Phelips, 'Passages of my Examination before Cromwell'. Underdown, *Royalist Conspiracy*, 67-70
40 CCC, 595-663, passim, esp 625, 629

Chapter 10. A County Reunites
1654-60. Pages 175-95

1 HMC, *Ninth Report* 2 (Pyne MSS), 493. 'Memorandum Book of Robert Hunt', in Cockburn, *Assize Orders 1640-59*, appendix 2, no 160; I am most grateful to Dr Cockburn for letting me use his transcript of this document. The general dislike of Gorges can be inferred from CCC, 672-90
2 HMC, *Buccleuch and Queensberry* 1, 311. For the MPs, see Bates Harbin, *Somerset MPs*, 158-63
3 A&O 2, 974, 982. Nuttall, 'Baptist Association', *Journal of Ecclesiastical History* 11, 214. CSPD, 1655, 30-1, 61, 68
4 CSPD, 1654, 75, 326, 409-10; 1655, 69, 131, 162-3, 301-3; 1655-6, 337-8; 1656, 94. Williams, *Somerset Levels*, 101
5 Birch, Thomas (ed). *Collection of the State Papers of John Thurloe* (1742) 3, 172-3, 181-2, 191. There are recent accounts of Penruddock's rising in Underdown, *Royalist Conspiracy*, ch 7; and Woolrych, A. H. *Penruddock's Rising, 1655* (1955)
6 *Thurloe Papers* 3, 237-8, 246, 306-8. 'Hunt Memorandum Book', in Cockburn, *Assize Orders 1640-59*, app 2, no 177. CSPD, 1655, 84, 99
7 Woolrych, *Penruddock's Rising*, 21-2. Hunt's account (Cockburn, *Assize Orders 1640-59*, app 2, nos 177-82), provides some new information. For Swanton's role, see *Thurloe Papers* 3, 330-1, 376-8
8 SRO, Phelips MSS, DD/PH/2, fols 208, 211: R. P[helips Jr] to Hillard, 5 April 1655. 'Hunt Memorandum Book', in Cockburn, *Assize Orders 1640-59*, app 2, nos 179, 182. The grandfather referred to in Phelips's letter is Edward Phelips's father-in-law, Sir Robert Pye
9 CSPD, 1655, 93-4
10 BM, Harington MSS, Add MS 46,373, fol 40: commission to John Harington, 28 May 1655. Harington, *Nugae Antiquae* 1, 204-5. The militia establishment is recorded in PRO, State Papers Interregnum, SP 25/77, 868. The most complete account of the major-generals is still that by Rannie, D. W. 'Cromwell's Major-Generals', EHR 10 (1895), 471-506
11 HMC, *Bath* 4, 281. PRO, State Papers Interregnum, SP 18/126, fols 3, 5: certificates of Somerset commissioners, 1 April 1656
12 *Perfect Diurnal* 290 (25 June-2 July 1655). CSPD, 1656-7, 255. The move-

ments of numerous Somerset royalists are recorded in the registers of the London major-generals' office: BM, Add MSS 19,516; 34,014

13 *Thurloe Papers* 4, 325, 353, 520. Abbott, *Cromwell* 4, 87-8. Cockburn, *Assize Orders 1640-59*, nos 138-40. QSR 3, 298-9, 347

14 QSR 3, 285, 302, 347

15 QSR 3, 302. CSPD, 1656-7, 219

16 *Thurloe Papers* 5, 303. 'Hunt Memorandum Book', in Cockburn, *Assize Orders 1640-59*, app 2, no 189

17 For the election, see 'Hunt Memorandum Book', in Cockburn, *Assize Orders 1640-59*, app 2, nos 189-91. For the MPs, see Bates Harbin, *Somerset MPs*, 164-70

18 Rutt, J. T. (ed). *Diary of Thomas Burton* (1828) 1, 362-3. Abbott, *Cromwell* 4, 417

19 Information on JPs from History of Parliament Trust. For the Assessment Commission, see A&O 2, 1079, 1247

20 QSR 3, 291, 338

21 [Besse, Joseph]. *An Abstract of the Sufferings of the People call'd Quakers* 1 (1733), 210-16, 220-6. QSR 3, intro, xli

22 Collier, *A Looking-Glasse for the Quakers*, 16. *Burton's Diary* 1, 153, 169

23 Wastfield, Robert. *A True Testimony of Faithfull Witnesses recorded* (1657), 28. Penney, Norman (ed). *Extracts from State Papers Relating to Friends*, Journal of Friends Hist Soc, Supplements 8-11 (1910-13), 107-8

24 [Besse], *Abstract of the Quakers' Sufferings*, 216-22. Wastfield, *True Testimony*, 8-10, 27, 40-1. QSR 3, 339-40. Cockburn, *Assize Orders 1640-59*, no 139

25 BM, Film 331, Letter-book of John Fitzjames 6, fol 15v: Fitzjames to Peregrine Palmer, 19 May 1658. Bristol Archives, Ashton Court MSS, AC/C64/35: A. P[oulett] to [Hugh Smyth], 17 April 1658

26 Shaw, *Church during the Civil Wars* 2, 422-3. Peck, Francis (ed). *Desiderata Curiosa* (1779), 497. For augmentations paid to Somerset clergy, see CSPD, 1655-8, passim, and Shaw, *Church during the Civil Wars* 2, 511, 594

27 Prynne, William. *A True and Perfect Narrative of what was done . . . the 7. and 9. of this instant May* (1659), 54-5

28 *Burton's Diary* 4, 276, 299, 333-4. BM, Film 331, Letter-book of John Fitzjames 6, fol 71: Fitzjames to Robert Hunt. For the MPs see Bates Harbin, *Somerset MPs*, 171; and Willis, Browne. *Notitia Parliamentaria* (1715-30) 3, 292

29 *Burton's Diary* 3, 414; 4, 17. Underdown, *Royalist Conspiracy*, 117, 192, 218, 224, 242, 261

30 Penney, *Extracts from State Papers*, 107. CSPD, 1658-9, 365-6; 1659-60, 24. A&O 2, 1332. Luttrell was originally named to the militia commission. but rejected by the Commons: JHC 7, 720. For officers, see Bodleian, Clarendon MS 63, fols 185-8: Somerset militia cmrs. to Council of State, 11 August 1659

31 CSPD, 1659-60, 50, 53, 68. CCSP 4, 323, 330. QSR 3, 370-1. Underdown, *Royalist Conspiracy*, 263-4

32 Bristol Archives, Ashton Court MSS, AC/C64/21; 34: A. P[oulett] to H. Smyth, 11 Sept [1659]; and 7 Jan [1659/60]

33 Willis, *England's Changeling*

34 CCC, 752, 754 (there was no further correspondence). CSPD, 1659-60, 238-9. HMC, *Ninth Report* 2 (Pyne MSS), 493-4. Whitelock, *Memorials* 4, 380. *Mercurius Politicus* 599 (15-22 Dec 1659). HMC, *Portland* 1, 690

35 Bristol Archives, Ashton Court MSS, AC/C64/34: A. P[oulett] to H.

Smyth, 7 Jan [1659/60]. CSPD, 1659-60, 319-20, 330, 351-2. HMC, *Ley-bourne-Popham*, 158. Davies, Godfrey. *The Restoration of Charles II* (San Marino, Cal. 1955), 283. CCSP 4, 564

36 CSPD, 1659-60, 379, 381. HMC, *Leybourne-Popham*, 157-8. A&O 2, 1442. Davies, *Restoration*, 288-98. A list of officers is printed in *Mercurius Publicus* 17 (19-26 April 1660)

37 Bristol Archives, Ashton Court MSS, AC/C74/11: John Ashburnham to Smyth, 24 March 1659/60. HMC, *Leybourne-Popham*, 173. The sheriff was William Lacey

38 Bristol Archives, Ashton Court MSS, AC/C64/71; 72: A. Poulett to Smyth, 30 April; and 5 May 1660. PRO, State Papers Charles II, SP 29/1, fol 74: Somerset Loyal Address to Charles II, 1660

39 Bristol Archives, Ashton Court MSS, AC/C74/19: Ashburnham to Smyth, 17 July 1662. Pyne took the oath of allegiance to Charles II in June 1660: HMC, *Ninth Report* 2, 494

40 Stieg, 'Clergy', 225. Matthews, *Calamy Revised*, 4, 539, and passim

Bibliography

Primary Sources

1. Unpublished Manuscripts

Bodleian Library. Clarendon MSS
—. Nalson Papers ('MSS Dep C')
—. Tanner MSS
Bristol Archives. Ashton Court MSS
British Museum. Additional MSS 10,114 (Diary of John Harington), 28,273 (Locke MSS)
—. Film 331, Northumberland MSS (Letter-book of John Fitzjames)
Lambeth Palace. Commonwealth Church Survey, 1650
Mells Manor House. Horner MSS
Public Record Office. Committee for Advance of Money papers
—. Committee for Compounding papers
—. Committee of Accounts papers
—. State Papers Domestic, Interregnum
—. State Papers Domestic, Charles II, vol 1
Somerset Record Office. Coker Court MSS (Edward Curll's accounts)
—. Hippisley MSS (John Preston's papers)
—. Phelips MSS
—. Popham MSS
—. Pyne MSS
—. Sessions Rolls, 1644, 1646-60
Wells Archives. Corporation Acts Book

2. Printed Sources

Abbott, Wilbur C. (ed). *Writings and Speeches of Oliver Cromwell* (Cambridge, Mass. 1937-47)

Barnes, Thomas G. (ed). *Somerset Assize Orders 1629-1640*. SRS, 65 (1959)

Bates, E. H. (ed). *The Particular Description of the County of Somerset, Drawn up by Thomas Gerard of Trent*. SRS, 15 (1900)

Bates Harbin, E. H. (ed). *Quarter Sessions Records for the County of Somerset*, 3: *Commonwealth*. SRS, 28 (1912)

Batten, John. 'Somersetshire Sequestrations during the Civil War', SASP 4 pt 2 (1853), 60-77; 16 pt 2 (1870), 13-34

Bell, Robert (ed). *Memorials of the Civil War: comprising the correspondence of the Fairfax family* (1849)

Birch, Thomas (ed). *Collection of the State Papers of John Thurloe* (1742)

Black, William H. (ed). *Docquets of Letters Patent . . . under the Great Seal of King Charles I at Oxford* (1838)

Brown, Frederick. *Abstracts of Somersetshire Wills* (1887-90)

Bulstrode, Sir Richard. *Memoirs and Reflections upon the Reign and Government of King Charles the Ist and K. Charles the IId.* (1721)

Chadwyck Healey, C. E. H. (ed). *Bellum Civile. Hopton's Narrative of his Campaign in the West*. SRS, 18 (1902)

Clarendon, Edward, Earl of. *History of the Rebellion and Civil Wars in England*. (ed) Macray, W. D. (Oxford 1888)

Cockburn, J. S. (ed). *Somerset Assize Orders 1640-1659*. SRS, 71 (1971)

Colby, Frederic T. (ed). *Visitation of the County of Somerset in the Year 1623*. Harleian Society Publications, 11 (1876)

Firth, Charles H. (ed). *Memoirs of Edmund Ludlow* (Oxford 1894)

—, and Rair, R. S. (eds). *Acts and Ordinances of the Interregnum* (1911)

Green, Mary A. E. (ed). *Calendar of State Papers, Domestic Series, 1649-1660* (1875-86)

—. *Calendar of the Proceedings of the Committee for Advance of Money* (1888)

—. *Calendar of the Proceedings of the Committee for Compounding* (1889-92)

Hamilton, William D. (ed). *Calendar of State Papers, Domestic Series, 1640-1649* (1880-93)

Harington, H. (ed). *Nugae Antiquae* (1769-75)

Historical Manuscripts Commission Reports. See references in notes above

Journals of the House of Commons, 1640-1660

Journals of the House of Lords, 1640-1649

Lister, Thomas H. *Life and Administration of Edward, first Earl of Clarendon* (1838) vol 3; correspondence

Long, C. E. (ed). *Diary of the Marches of the Royal Army during the Great Civil War kept by Richard Symonds*. Camden series, 74 (1859)

Ogle, O., Bliss, W. H., Macray, W. D., and Routledge, F. J. (eds). *Calendar of the Clarendon State Papers* (Oxford 1869-1970)

Penney, Norman (ed). *Extracts from State Papers Relating to Friends*. Journal of Friends Historical Society, Supplements 8-11 (1910-13)

Powell, J. R. (ed). *Letters of Robert Blake*. Navy Records Society, 76 (1937)

—, and Timings, E. K. (eds). *Documents Relating to the Civil War*. Navy Records Society, 105 (1963)

Rushworth, John (ed). *Historical Collections*. 2nd ed (1721-2)

Rutt, J. T. (ed). *Diary of Thomas Burton* (1828)

Scott, Sir Walter (ed). *Collection of scarce and valuable Tracts . . . Selected from . . . libraries, particularly that of the late Lord Somers*. 2nd ed (1809-15)

Sprigge, Joshua. *Anglia Rediviva: England's Recovery* (1647)

Symonds, Henry. 'A By-Path of the Civil War', SASP 65 (1919), 48-75; papers concerning the Brent Knoll riots, 1645

Trevelyan, Sir Walter C. and Sir Charles E. (eds). *Trevelyan Papers 3*. Camden series, 105 (1872)

Vicars, John. *Gods Arke Overtopping the Worlds Waves* (1646)

—. *Jehovah-Jireh. God in the Mount* (1644)

'Vindication of Richard Atkyns', in Young, Peter and Tucker, Norman (eds). *Military Memoirs of the Civil War* (1967)

Walker, Clement. *The History of Independency* 1 (1648)

Walker, Sir Edward. *Historical Discourses* (1705)

Warburton, Eliot. *Memoirs of Prince Rupert and the Cavaliers* (1849)

Whitelock, Bulstrode. *Memorials of the English Affairs* (Oxford 1853)

3. Newsbooks, Pamphlets, etc

See references in the notes, above. Almost all the newsbooks, pamphlets, printed sermons, and other contemporary works used in this book are in the Thomason Collection in the British Museum, though in some cases

P

copies in American libraries had to be consulted. The dating adopted is normally that given by Thomason in the case of pamphlets; for newsbooks it is the inclusive dates of the issue. See [Fortescue, G. K.] *Catalogue of the Pamphlets . . . collected by George Thomason, 1640-1661* (1908)

Secondary Works

Adair, John. *Roundhead General: a military biography of Sir William Waller* (1969)

Barnes, Thomas G. *Somerset 1625-1640* (Cambridge, Mass. 1961)

Bates Harbin, S. W. *Members of Parliament for the County of Somerset* (Taunton 1939)

Beadon, Roger. *Robert Blake* (1935)

[Besse, Joseph]. *An Abstract of the Sufferings of the People call'd Quakers* 1 (1733)

Burne, A. H. and Young, Peter. *The Great Civil War* (1959)

Collinson, John. *History and Antiquities of the County of Somerset* (Bath 1791)

Edgar, F. T. R. *Sir Ralph Hopton: The King's Man in the West* (Oxford 1968)

Gardiner, Samuel R. *History of the Great Civil War* (1886-91)

Green, Emanuel. *Bibliotheca Somersetensis* (Taunton 1902)

—. 'Col. William Strode', SASP 30 pt 2 (1884), 46-65

—. 'On the Civil War in Somerset', SASP 14 pt 2 (1867), 43-71

—. 'On the History of Chard', SASP 28 pt 2 (1882), 28-78

—. 'On the Parish and Castle of Nunney', SASP 22 pt 2 (1876), 71-105

—. 'The King's' March through Somerset, 1644', SASP 24 pt 2 (1878), 43-9

—. 'The Siege and Defence of Taunton, 1644-5', SASP 25 pt 2 (1879), 33-48

—. 'The Siege of Bridgwater, July, 1645', SASP 23 pt 2 (1877), 12-25

Humphreys, Arthur L. *Materials for the History of the Town of Wellington* (1889)

Jex-Blake, T. W. 'The Battle of Lansdown', SASP 41 pt 2 (1895), 38-46

Keeler, Mary F. *The Long Parliament, 1640-1641*, American Philosophical Society, Memoirs, 36 (Philadelphia 1954)

King, A. J. and Watts, B. H. *Cavaliers and Roundheads: a Chapter in the History of Bath* (1887)

Matthews, A. G. *Calamy Revised* (Oxford 1934)

—. *Walker Revised* (Oxford 1948)

Maxwell Lyte, Sir H. C. *History of Dunster* (1909)

Norris, Hugh. 'The Battle of Langport', SASP 40 pt 2 (1894), 123-40

Oldmixon, John. *History of England During the Reigns of the Royal House of Stuart* (1730-5)

Page, William (ed). *Victoria History of the County of Somerset* (1906-11)

Ralph, Philip L. *Sir Humphrey Mildmay: Royalist Gentleman* (New Brunswick, New Jersey 1947)

Shaw, William A. *History of the English Church during the Civil Wars . . . 1640-1660* (1900)

Stieg, Margaret. 'The parochial clergy in the diocese of Bath and Wells 1625-1685'. University of California (Berkeley) PhD thesis (1970)

Underdown, David. 'A Case Concerning Bishops' Lands: Cornelius Burges and the Corporation of Wells', EHR 78 (1963), 18-48

—. *Pride's Purge: Politics in the Puritan Revolution* (Oxford 1971)

—. *Royalist Conspiracy in England, 1649-1660* (New Haven, Conn. 1960)

—. 'The Ilchester Election, February 1646', SASP 110 (1966), 40-51

Wedgwood, C. V. *The King's War, 1641-1647* (1958)

Williams, Michael. *The Draining of the Somerset Levels* (Cambridge 1970)

Wyndham, H. A. *A Family History 1410-1688: the Wyndhams of Norfolk and Somerset* (1939)

Acknowledgements

Many of the obligations I have incurred in writing this book date back to days long before I knew much about my county's history or had any idea that I should ever write about it. Some are intangible, the outcome of birth and upbringing. Who can say that the subtle influences of soil and climate—of Atlantic westerlies on the mudflats of Bridgwater Bay, the bleak austerity of the Mendips, the wide skies of the Somerset moors—have done more or less for this book than the typewriter and the card index? Easier to estimate are the debts I still owe to those who awakened my interest in history in general and Somerset history in particular: my parents; Mr E. A. Harrison, my history master at Wells Blue School; the late H. E. Balch, my first guide in the intricacies of local records; and Dr R. D. Reid among them.

The early stages of research for this book were aided by grants from the John Simon Guggenheim Memorial Foundation, the American Philosophical Society, and Brown University. I am as always grateful for the patience and courtesy shown by the staffs of the British Museum, the Public Record Office, the Bodleian Library, the Bristol City Archives, and the Somerset Record Office, where Mr I. P. Collis was an invaluable source of friendly advice and assistance. Through the kindness of Mr H. Bottomley I was also able to use the Wells Museum Library. Dr T. G. Barnes's earlier work on Somerset was a constant stimulus; Dr J. S. Cockburn generously made available his work on the Assize Orders while it was still in typescript; Mr Conrad Russell and Mr Ivor Popham were most helpful on Humphrey Willis and the Popham family respectively; Dr R. W. Dunning and Dr Blair Worden supplied many useful references. For help in selecting illustrations I am grateful above all to Mrs S. W. Bates Harbin; also to Mrs Caroline Pilkington, of the Courtauld Institute of Art; the staff of the National Portrait Gallery; the vicar of Brent Knoll, Prebendary B. J. W. Tarnock; and the Earl of Oxford and

Asquith, who also kindly permitted me to consult documents at Mells.

Mr T. J. Hunt read the pages dealing with Taunton and made helpful comments. My brother, Dr P. T. Underdown, patiently read the entire typescript and saved me from many stylistic, topographical, and historical errors. Some parts of chapters 7-10 have appeared in different form in my *Pride's Purge: Politics in the Puritan Revolution,* and are here printed with the permission of the Delegates of the Clarendon Press.

Whatever value this book may possess can be attributed to all these and others unmentioned who have given so freely of their time and expertise. The defects that remain are my own. To my wife the book owes the special debt due to one who has so often uncomplainingly supervised transatlantic family migrations to Somerset, and has in so many other ways made possible its completion.

Index

References to illustrations are printed in italic

References to forces in the civil war are indexed under the names of their commanders

Accounts, subcommittee of, 141-2
Allen, Richard, of Batcombe, 27, 117, 143, 171, 177, 195, 201 n1
Allen, Richard, of Ditcheat, 27, 117, 143, 177
Ancketyll, Henry, 144
Ashe, James, 131, 133, 149, 185, 192
Ashe, John, 18, 40; chairman, Goldsmiths' Hall Committee, 128, 159, 164, 167; in civil war, 29-30, 35-7, 41, 43, 46-7, 113; MP, 68, 125, 129, 153, 176, 185; religion, 23, 143
Ashley Cooper, Sir Anthony, 80-1, 173
Assessments: commissions of, 142, 149, 169, 178, 186, 192; parliamentarian, 46, 123, 128, 167-8; royalist, 71, 90
Assizes, 31, 70, 139, 140, 150-1, 158, 179, 181, 188
Associations: parliamentarian, 45, 50, 74, 97, 155; royalist, 72-3, 76, 82, 92, 96, 161
Aston, Sir Thomas, 111
Atkyns, Richard, 51, 53-4, 60-1, 63-4
Axbridge, 70, 90, 126

Baber, John, 70
Babylon Hill, 42, 178
Bagenall, Robert, 62-3
Baker, John, 122, 143, 153
Bampfield, Thomas, 142
Baptists, 146, 172-3, 177
Barker, John, 126, 160, 173, 176, 189-90
Barnard, Nathaniel, 126
Barrett, David, 126, 136, 172-3
Basset, William, 25, 39, 69, 117-18, 124, 127, 159
Batcombe, 22, 44, 117
Bath, 13; assizes, 23, 31; in civil war, 40, 50, 56-7, 60-2, 74, 77, 80, 111,

123, *58*; politics, 25, 29, 131, 147, 156, 169, 177, 191; religion, 143, 146, 186
Batt, Jasper, 186
Batt, Timothy, 68, 145-6
Baxter, Richard, 104
Baynard, Thomas, 126-7, 180
Beauchamp, Lord, *see* Seymour, Henry
Beckington, 23, 25
Bedford, Earl of, *see* Russell, William
Bedminster, 113
Berkeley family, 19, 29, 32, 44, 69, 116, 178, 186, 193
Berkeley, Sir Charles, 44-5, 75, 128
Berkeley, Edward, 128
Berkeley, Sir Edward, 44-5, 70, 158, 161
Berkeley, Sir Henry, 21, 24, 70
Berkeley, Sir John, 41, 73, 93
Berkeley, Maurice, 192
Berrow, 90-1
Blackbourne, Thomas, 126, 151
Blake, Humphrey, 22, 167
Blake, Robert, *84*; admiral, 168-9, 182; in civil war, 62, 68, 74, 78, 80, 87, 89, 93-5, 115-16, 202 n28; and County Committee, 47, 125; MP, 131, 172; religion, 146
Bond, John, 81, 112
Bonner, Henry, 124-5, 140, 152, 187
Booth's Rising, 190
Bourne, John, 69, 81
Bovett, Philip, 195
Bovett, Richard, 151, 159, 164-8, 171, 173, 176, 182, 187, 189-92
Boyle, Roger, Lord Broghil, 177
Brent Knoll, *see* South Brent
Bridges, Sir Thomas, 46, 69, 111, 128
Bridgwater, 13-14, 126, 139-40, 169;

in civil war, 51, 74, 76-7, 92, 104-5, 108-10; politics, 24, 131, 137, 158; religion, 22

Bristol, 14; in civil war, 37, 45, 48, 62-4, 110, 113-14; politics, 152, 178, 191-2; religion, 119, 146

Broghil, Lord, see Boyle, Roger

Brooke, Thomas, 145

Bruton, 24, 44, 75, 89, 135

Buckland, John, 140, 142, 157, 164, 171, 173, 176-7, 182-5, 189-90, 192-3

Budd, Thomas, 187, 190

Bull, John, 124

Bull, William, 34, 39, 47, 69, 124

Burges, Cornelius, 170-3

Burnham-on-Sea, 91

Burrowbridge, 104, 107-8

Byam, Henry, 144

Capell, William, 140

Carent, William, 131, 133, 157, 168, 185

Carnarvon, Earl of, see Dormer, Robert

Cary, John, 180, 187

Casbeard, John, 171-2

Casbeard, Richard, 81

Castle Cary, 99, 112, 133, 162

Catholics, 28, 112, 159

Ceely, Edward, 125-6, 142, 149-50, 152, 168, 171, 182, 190-1

Ceely, William, 149, 152, 164-8

Chaplain, Jasper, 47

Chapman, Henry, 147

Chard, 13-14, 177, 212 n31; assizes, 150, 158, 179, 181, 188; in civil war, 49, 69, 72-4, 76, 78, 82, 89, 95, 114

Charles I, 29, 50, 82, 92, 94, 97, 114, 147, 149, 151-2; government, see Court; in Somerset, 74-6, 78-80; trial and execution, 153-5

Charles, Prince of Wales, 82, 86, 91-2, 99; Council, 82, 87, 92-3, 97, 100, 106; King Charles II, 161-3, 169; restoration, 193

Chewton Mendip, 35, 36-7, 52-3, 113, 33

Clarendon, Earl of, see Hyde, Sir Edward

Clement, Robert, 144

Clergy: Independent, 177, 188; Laudian, 25, 45, 144-5; presbyterian, 143, 146, 158, 161-2, 171-2, 177,

188; puritan, 22, 68, 145

Clift, Matthew, 125-6, 150

Cloth industry, 14, 17-18, 22, 27, 39-40, 43, 152

Clubmen, 86, 98, 105, 112, 115, 130, 152; central Somerset, 99-100, 104-8, 112, 132-3; north Somerset, 111, 113, 139; south-east Somerset, 99, 105-6, 132, 135; west Somerset, 116, 119, 123

Cole, Richard, 37, 47, 69, 139, 142

Collier, Richard, 126

Collier, Thomas, 146, 153, 156, 172-3, 187

Collier, William, 126, 151

Collins, Hugh, 44, 144

Commission of Array, 29-32, 38

Commonwealthsmen, see Radical parliamentarians

Compounding, 127-8, 159; Committee for, 127, 163-4

Cooth, John, 34

Cottington, James, 169

Country, 20, 198 n17; in civil war, 39, 51, 54-5, 61, 75, 79, 91-2, 98, 113; and Parliament, 118, 137, 194; see also Clubmen; Gentry; Yeomen

County Commissioners, royalist, 70, 72, 76-7, 81, 87, 91-2, 96

County Committee, parliamentarian; in civil war, 32-4, 37-8, 41, 44-5, 47; conflict in, 125-6, 130-1, 133, 138; dissolution, 163; membership, 47, 124-5; postwar, 126-9, 131-2, 135-7, 140-3, 147-8

Court, 15, 20-1, 23, 198 n17

Courtenay, Sir William, 96-7

Coventry, John, 24-5, 28-9, 36, 162

Cradock, Walter, 100

Crewkerne, 100-2

Cromwell, Oliver, 89, 109, 112-13, 148, 172-3; Lord Protector, 174, 177, 179-80, 185, 188-9

Cromwell, Richard, 189

Crooke, Samuel, 22, 68, 143

Cucklington, 89

Curll, Edward, 127, 159

Davies, Edward, 99

Devenish, John, of Bridgwater, 22

Devenish, John, of Weston Zoyland, 188

Devereux, Robert, Earl of Essex, 73-4, 78, 121
Digby, (Sir) John, 25, 32, 36, 89
Disbrowe, John, 104, 167-8, 176, 179-82
Dodington family, 29, 186
Dodington, Christopher, 132, 160
Dodington, Sir Francis; atrocities, 75, 128; in civil war, 32, 36, 39, 45, 71, 75, 77, 82; estates, 128, 159
Dormer, Robert, Earl of Carnarvon, 49, 53, 57, 59
Dugdale, James, 45
Dunster, 13, 43, 51, 104, 115, 162, 169
Dyer, Sir Edward, 124
Dyve, Sir Lewis, 110, 112

Eburne, Richard, 17-18
Elford, Thomas, 162, 177
Enclosure riots, 27, 43-4, 177
Engagement to the Commonwealth, 158
England, John, 145
English, Thomas, 125-6, 169, 185
Essex, Charles, 41
Essex, Earl of, see Devereux, Robert
Essex, Thomas, 45, 48
Excise: parliamentarian, 135, 152, 156, 169; royalist, 81

Fairclough, Richard, 145, 177
Fairfax, Sir Thomas, 93-4, 98, 100, 102-5, 108-15, 127, 135; army, see New Model army
Farleigh Castle, 115, 148
Fiennes, Nathaniel, 48, 55, 62-4, 68
Fleetwood, Charles, 102, 112
Foster, Sir Robert, 31-2
Fraunceis, John, 35, 47, 124
Fraunceis, Thomas, 124
Frome, 56, 122, 156
Fullwood, Francis, 172

Gapper, William, 153, 168, 190, 210, n29
Gauler, Thomas, 144
Gay, John, 141, 151, 169, 185
Gentry, 18-20, 23, 39, 47, 74, 117, 185-6, 193
Gerard, Thomas, 11-12, 14-16
Glastonbury, 52, 54, 89, 187
Glyn, John, 179
Goldsmiths' Hall, Committee at, see

Compounding; Committee for
Gorges, Sir Edward, 111
Gorges, Sir Ferdinando, 34, 90
Gorges, John, 167-8, 173, 176, 178, 180, 182, 188, 190
Gorges, Thomas, 168-9, 172-3, 176, 189
Goring, George, Lord, 43, 85-90, 92-4, 96-7, 99-106, 115
Greenfield, Joseph, 144
Grenville, Sir Bevil, 49, 60
Grenville, Sir Richard, 87, 89-90, 93
Grey, Henry, Earl of Stamford, 45, 47-9
Grove, Thomas, 131, 142
Gutch, John, 153, 169

Hamilton, Sir James, 54, 56
Harbin, Robert, 37, 47, 69, 124, 142, 159
Harington, John (d1654): and County Committee, 30, 47, 124; politics, 123, 125, 130-3, 139, 141, 153, 157, 169; religion, 22, 27, 143, 171
Harington, John (d1700), 123, 176-7, 180, 185
Harrison, Thomas, 104, 132, 156, 167
Haselrig, Sir Arthur, 50, 55, 60, 78, 81
Hawley, Sir Francis, Lord, 32, 36, 67, 188
Helyar, William, 127, 181
Henley, Henry, 47, 125, 130-3, 140, 142-3, 157-8, 172
Hertford, Marquis of, see Seymour, William
Hill, Roger, of Poundisford, 25, 124-5, 129, 139, 171, 180
Hill, Roger, of Taunton, 46-7, 126
Hill, William, 126
Hinton St George, 41, 43, 191, 193
Hippisley family, 46
Hippisley, John, 37, 47
Hippisley, Richard, 63
Hippisley, Thomas, 177
Hodges, Henry, 78
Hodges, Thomas, 132
Holborne, James, 81-2, 87-9, 108, 135
Hollis, Thomas, 99, 105
Hollister, Denis, 172
Holt, Thomas, 45
Hopton family, 19
Hopton, Sir Ralph, Lord of, 65; in

civil war (1642), 11, 32-5, 39, 41-3;
composition, 128, 159; and Cornish
army, 48-9, 51-2, 54-62; exile, 124,
160; Field Marshal of the West, 82,
91, 94-5, 97, 115; Governor of Bristol, 67, 69-71, 75, 80; MP, 25-8;
religion, 22, 201 n1
Horner family, 19, 39, 68, 116, 125,
142-3, 193
Horner, George, 127, 129-33, 142,
192
Horner, Sir John, *166*; in civil war,
11, 29-30, 35-8, 62-3, 71, 74; and
County Committee, 47, 125; high
sheriff, 113, 129-33; politics, 118-19,
157, 168, 177; religion, 143, 145
Horner, Samuel, 124
Hungerford, Sir Edward, 37, 45,
124-5, 148
Hunt family, 118
Hunt, John, 47, 124
Hunt, Robert, 24, 176, 179-80, 182,
186-90, 192-3
Hyde, Sir Edward, afterwards Earl of
Clarendon, 82, 204 n1; quoted, 32,
40, 51, 54, 61, 64, 82, 92

Ilchester, 13, 126; in civil war, 42, 44,
75-7, 102; politics, 24, 130, 132,
189; religion, 143
Ilminster, 82, 97, 126
Independent party, *see* Radical parliamentarians
Independents, *see* Clergy: Independent
Isle Moor, 102, 106, *101*

JPs, 21; Commonwealth, 155, 157-8,
169-70, 173; postwar, 140-1, 149,
152; Protectorate, 176, 185, 187;
royalist, 69-70
Jeanes, Henry, 145
Jervis, Thomas, 99
Jett, Alexander, 70
Jones, Richard, 140, 164, 173, 177

Kemp, William, 144
Keynes, Alexander, 161
Keynsham, 55, 62, 186
King's Moor, 75-6, 96, *101*
Kirton, Edward, 25, 81, 162
Knowles, John, 177

Lacey, William, 186, 215 n37

Lands, confiscated: church, 171; roy-
alist, 159-60
Langport, 13, 16, 82, 89-90, 100, 126;
battle, 103-4, *101*
Langrish, Hercules, 63
Lansdown, 111, 190; battle, 57, 59-61,
58
Law, Matthew, 144
Leigh-on-Mendip, 56
Levellers, 152, 155, 157, 178
Levels, drainage of, 12, 177
Ley, James, Earl of Marlborough, 19,
180
Lilburne, John, 106, 157
Locke, Edward, 181
Locke, John (d1661), 46
Locke, John (d1704), 46, 155
Lockyer, John, 132
Long, Lislebone, 124, 132, 185
Long, Richard, 144-5
Long, William, 14, 34, 47
Long Ashton, 90
Long Load, 102
Ludlow, Edmund, 72, 75, 77, 81
Lunsford, Henry, 32, 36, 63
Luttrell family, 19, 131, 193
Luttrell, Francis, 185-6, 190, 192,
214 n30
Luttrell, George, 140, 142, 162
Luttrell, Thomas, 43, 51
Lye, Thomas, 158
Lympsham, 90-1

Mackworth, Sir Francis, 82, 87, 89-90,
99-100, 104
Major-generals, Cromwellian, 180-2,
185
Marlborough, Earl of, *see* Ley, James
Marshall's Elm, 36, 45, 205 n21, *33*
Martock, 15-16, 96, 102, 110, 117,
187, 190
Mason, Benjamin, 164, 167
Massey, Edward, 77, 97, 100, 102-3,
105, 110, 135, 189-90
Maurice, Prince, 49-54, 57, 59, 63,
71-3, 78, 80
Mead, Thomas, 151, 169, 172
Mells, 25, 74
Mendips, 12, 37, 52-3; miners, 14, 42,
71, 112
Middleton, John, 77-8
Milborne Port, 25, 131, 189
Mildmay, Sir Humphrey, 78, 90, 107
Militia, 24; Commonwealth, 167-8; in

1659-60, 190-2; ordinances, 29-30, 152-3; parliamentarians and, 37, 41, 47-8, 50, 52; Protectorate, 180; royalists and, 34-5, 37, 71-2
Milward, George, 34, 46
Minehead, 13, 28, 43, 77, 100, 115, 131, 135, 182, 212 n31
Minterne, Henry, 125-6, 137, 150
Moderate parliamentarians, 118-19, 121-2, 125, 129, 138-40, 142, 152-3, 162
Mogg, Richard, 159
Monkton Farleigh, 57
Morgan, Robert, 117-18, 125-6, 157
Morgan, William, 46
Morley, John, 46
Mountagu, Edward, 102-3, 114

Naylor, James, 187
Neutrals, 39, 69, 86, 117, 124; see also Clubmen
New Model army, 93-4, 98, 100-6, 108-15, 119, 123, 138-9, 146, 152-3
Newton, George, 68, 95, 119, 143, 145, 177, 194
Norman, John, 158
North Petherton, 77
Norton, George, 162, 185
Norton St Philip, 169
Nunney, 112

Okey, John, 108, 113, 182, 190, 192
Orange, William, 142
Othery, 122

Palmer, John, 125, 131, 157, 185, 189
Parliament: 1640 (Short), 24; 1640-60 (Long), 25-30, 137-9, 147, 149, 152-3; dissolution, 192; elections, 24-5, 129-33; Rump, 155, 163, 172, 189, 191-2; 1653, 172; 1654, 176-7 1656, 182-5, 187; 1659, 189; 1660, 192
Peace party, see Moderate parliamentarians
Penruddock's rising, 178-80
Pensford, 114, 181
Perry, Samuel, 176
Peryam, Samuel, 144
Peter, Hugh, 109, 113, 131
Petherton Bridge, 96-7, 102
Phelips family, 19, 29, 193
Phelips, Edward, 24, 69-70, 179

Phelips, Robert (d1707), 71, 160-3, 173, 178
Phelips, Sir Robert, 19-20, 22-3, 173
Piers, William, Bishop, 22-3, 25, 194
Pilton, 135
Pitt, Jonathan, 125
Pittard, Christopher, 125, 150, 186
Plague, 16, 110, 114, 122
Plundering, 86, 98; parliamentarian, 44, 48, 72, 89, 93, 135; royalist, 51, 54, 64, 72, 87, 89-91, 99-100, 111
Popham family, 19, 40, 47, 72, 74-5, 93, 107, 125, 143, 193
Popham, Alexander: in civil war, 11, 35-7, 41, 44, 46-8, 50, 55-6, 61-2, 68, 113, 115; MP, 25, 129, 177, 185, 190, 192; politics, 29, 132, 164, 189; 190, 192; politics, 29, 132, 164, 189; religion, 145
Popham, Edward, 50-2, 68, 93, 121-2, 131, 168, 66
Popham, Sir Francis, 25, 124
Popham, Hugh, 48
Porter, Charles, 102, 106
Portishead, 111, 113
Portman, Sir William, 19, 21, 25, 41, 124, 127
Poulett family, 29, 35, 69, 186, 192-3
Poulett, Amyas, 82, 188, 191, 193
Poulett, John, first Baron (d1649), 11, 19, 32, 39, 41, 43, 46, 70, 76, 79, 127
Poulett, Sir John, second Baron (d1665), 24, 36, 45, 71, 127, 144, 180-1, 188
Prater, Richard, 112, 159
Presbyterian party, see Moderate parliamentarians
Presbyterians, see Clergy: presbyterian
Preston, John, 128; in civil war, 35-6, 39, 45; and County Committee, 47, 126; high sheriff, 150-1; politics, 133, 142, 157-8, 177
Pride, Thomas, 153, 164, 169
Prideaux, Edmund, 129, 131-2, 180, 191
Propositions of 10 June 1642, 30, 46
Prynne, William, 183; and County Committee, 124, 126, 128, 141; JP, 140, 147, 149; politics, 68, 153, 156 162, 173, 188-9, 192; religion, 21 143
Puritans: in civil war, 37, 40, 44, 81,

117; postwar, 119, 145-6, 170; pre-
war, 21-3, 26-7; Protectorate, 181;
Restoration, 194-5; and social
order, 27, 194; *see also* Baptists;
Clergy
Pye, Sir Robert, 74, 110
Pym, Alexander, 38, 124, 132, 137,
142, 149, 168, 182, 185, 190
Pym, Charles, 193
Pym, John, 24-5, 27, 29, 68, 107
Pyne, Hugh, 20
Pyne, John, 121, *134*; in civil war,
35-6, 41, 47, 50, 116; and County
Committee, 47, 124-6, 135-6, 138,
142, 163; elections, 131-3, 182, 189;
MP, 25, 154, 172; militia, 29-30,
148, 152, 167-9, 190; politics, 121-2,
129, 157-8, 176, 191, 193, 215 n35;
religion, 122, 143, 162, 187; revolution, 149-51, 153-4; sequestrations,
126, 145, 164, 167, 173

Quakers, 186-8, 190
Quarter Sessions, 69, 140, 154
Quartering, 51, 78, 123, 135, 139,
152, 156

Radical parliamentarians, 119-20,
138, 152; Commonwealth, 155-7,
167, 169; in 1659-60, 190-2; Pro-
tectorate, 176, 182, 185; Pyne fac-
tion, 121-2, 125, 129, 140, 142,
149-51, 154, 173, 191
Rainsborough, Thomas, 112, **114**
Ralegh, Walter, 136
Ranters, 156, 186
Rich, Nathaniel, 111
Rich, Robert, Earl of Warwick, 73
Richardson, Anthony, 144
Robins, John, 156
Rodney, Sir Edward: in civil war,
32, 34, 36-7, 41, 44, 76, 78; compo-
sition, 128; conspiracy, 161, 178;
MP, 25
Rogers, Henry, 185
Rogers, Hugh, 35, 47
Rolle, Francis, 185
Rolle, Henry, 176
Royalists: conspiracies, 148, 160-1,
173, 178, 189-90; exiled, 124, 160;
financial burdens, 127-8, 159-60,
180; imprisoned, 123-4, 180-1, 188;
leadership, 29, 32, 39, 67; war ad-

ministration, 70-1; *see also* Associations; County Commissioners
Rump, *see* Parliament
Rupert, Prince, 45, 48, 62-4, 80, 110-
11, 113-14
Russell, William, Earl of Bedford,
29, 41-3

Salthouse, Thomas, 187-8
Samborne, William, 47
Sampson, George, of Kingsbury, 151,
164, 167-8, 173, 190-1, 212 n27
Sampson, George, of Lopen, 168, 212
n27
Sampson, Latimer, 63, 164, 167
Sandys, Nicholas, 125
Sanford, Henry, 34, 47, 69
Sanford, Martin, 28, 31
Sedgemoor, 12, 107-8, 177
Selwood Forest, 13, 43, 135, 177
Sequestration: parliamentarian, 46,
126-7, 136, 159, 163-4, 167, 173,
176, 191; royalist, 70-1
Serle, George, 25, 47, 129, 157, 172,
185
Seymour, Henry, Lord Beauchamp,
148, 161
Seymour, William, Marquis of Hert-
ford, 19, 26-7, 29, 148, 180; in civil
war, 11, 31-3, 41-3, 48-9, 52, 54,
56, 69, 72, 118
Shepton Mallet, 32, 34-5, 50, 112,
140, *33*
Sherborne, 38, 41-3, 48, 92, 110, 112
Ship money, 21, 24-5
Shute, Thomas, 164, 167
Slanning, Sir Nicholas, **49, 59, 63**
Slingsby, Walter, 60, 148
Smith, George, sr, 151, 210 n23
Smith, George, jr, 69
Smyth, Hugh, 178, 185-6, 192
Smyth, Thomas, 24, 34, 39, 43
Somerset, John, 91, 117, 159, 204
n9, *165*
Somerton, 13, 14, 35-6, 38, 42, 52,
126, 135
South Brent, 90-1
South Petherton, 78, 102
Speke, George, 127, 181, 195
Stamford, Earl of, *see* Grey, Henry
Stawell family, 19, 35, 116, 193
Stawell, (Sir) Edward, 42, 71
Stawell, Sir John, 19, 118; in civil
war, 11, 32, 35-6, 39-40, 67, 70, 76,

106, 109; imprisoned, 128, 159-60, 178; MP, 24, 28; peace campaign, 79-80, 91-2, 99
Steynings, Charles, 72, 140, 152, 158, 160, 177
Stocker, Anthony, 39
Stocker, John, 124
Strangways, Giles, 140
Strode, James, 142
Strode, William, 18, 21, 40, *83*; in civil war, 29-30, 32-5, 41, 44, 46-8, 50-2, 61-3, 68, 74; and County Committee, 47, 125, 141-2; JP, 140; politics, 119, 130, 132-3, 138, 149, 153, 162, 192; religion, 143, 195
Swanton, Francis, 158, 160, 179
Syderfin, Thomas, 173
Symes, John, 69, 90, 117-18
Symonds, Richard, 75, 78

Taunton, 12, 14, 16, 122, 126, 139-40, 169, 172; assizes, 139-40, 151; in civil war (1642-4), 40-1, 48, 50-2, 54, 67, 74; defence and sieges, 78, 80-2, 87, 89, 93-5, 97, 100, 160; politics, 25, 131, 135, 150, 178, 189, 191; religion, 22, 80-1, 143, 145-6, 171, 194-5
Taunton Dene: manor, 171; Vale, 15, 51, 116
Thomas, William, 22, 68, 143, 146, 177
Timsbury, 181
Tintinhull, 44, 155
Trained Bands, *see* Militia
Trent, 160, 162-3
Trevelyan, George, sr, 70, 72, 81, 93, 127
Trevelyan, George, jr, 185-6, 192
Trevillian family, 19, 124
Trevillian, Richard, 125-6, 142, 149, 152, 158
Turberville, John, **139, 155, 158, 169,** 173
Tuthill, Francis, 126, 151, 158
Tynte, Henry, 91
Tynte, John, of Chelvey, 90-1, 204 n8
Tynte, John, of Halswell, 181

Uphill, 100

Walker, Clement, 47, 62, 68, 120, 129, 132, 136-7, 149-50, 153, 162

Walker, Sir Edward, 74-6
Waller, Sir Hardress, 152, 154
Waller, Sir William, 45, 50, 53-62, 78-81, 89, 93
Walrond, Humphrey, 124, 128
War party, *see* Radical parliamentarians
Warre, Thomas, 46, 69, 124
Warwick, Earl of, *see* Rich, Robert
Wastfield, Robert, 186, 188
Watchet, 13, 100
Wedmore, 177
Weldon, Ralph, 94-7, 108, 114
Wellington, 14, 22, 24, 54, 81, 93, 117
Wells, 13, 25, 122, 126, 131-2, 182, 212 n31; assizes, 70; Cathedral, 23, 27, 38, 44, 67, 170, 173; in civil war, 11, 32, 34-8, 44, 50, 52, 69, 77, 79, 81, 110, 117-18, 199 n7, 200 n14, *33*; corporation, 32, 36, 71, 172; puritanism, 143, 156, 170-3
Western Association, *see* Associations
Weston-super-Mare, 111
Whetcombe, Samuel, 126, 151, 167, 172
Whichcott, Benjamin, 145
Willis, Humphrey, 107-8, 118, 133, 136-7, 149, 191, *134*
Wincanton, 32, 80
Witham, 75, 77
Wiveliscombe, 122, 172
Woodhouse, 75, 128
Worle, 111
Wrentmore, Thomas, 169
Wroth, Sir Thomas, 28, 157, 168; in civil war, 30, 47-8, 50; and County Committee, 47, 125, 142; MP, 131, 149, 187, 189; religion, 143
Wylde, John, 150-1
Wyndham family, 69, 96, 193
Wyndham, Edmund: in civil war, 36, 78, 80, 82; exile, 160; governor of Bridgwater, 67, 87, 91, 108-10; high sheriff, 69-70; MP, 24
Wyndham, Francis, 51, 70, 78, 115, 160-2, 178, 181, *184*
Wyndham, Sir Hugh, 181
Wyndham, (Sir) William, 185-6, 189-90, 192

Yeomen, 16-17, 39-40, 86, 115, 193
Yeovil, 13, 42, 102, 122, 192